Pot-Pourri
from a
Surrey Garden

BY
MRS. C. W. EARLE

WITH AN APPENDIX
BY
LADY CONSTANCE LYTTON

THOMAS NELSON & SONS
LONDON, EDINBURGH, DUBLIN
AND NEW YORK
(*By arrangement with Messrs. Smith, Elder, & Co.*)

British Library Cataloguing-in-Publication Data
A catalogue record for this book is available from the
British Library

A Short History of Gardening

Gardening is the practice of growing and cultivating plants as part of horticulture more broadly. In most domestic gardens, there are two main sets of plants; 'ornamental plants', grown for their flowers, foliage or overall appearance – and 'useful plants' such as root vegetables, leaf vegetables, fruits and herbs, grown for consumption or other uses. For many people, gardening is an incredibly relaxing and rewarding pastime, ranging from caring for large fruit orchards to residential yards including lawns, foundation plantings or flora in simple containers. Gardening is separated from farming or forestry more broadly in that it tends to be much more labour-intensive; involving *active participation* in the growing of plants.

Home-gardening has an incredibly long history, rooted in the 'forest gardening' practices of prehistoric times. In the gradual process of families improving their immediate environment, useful tree and vine species were identified, protected and improved whilst undesirable species were eliminated. Eventually foreign species were also selected and incorporated into the 'gardens.' It was only after the emergence of the first civilisations that wealthy individuals began to create gardens for aesthetic purposes. Egyptian tomb paintings from around 1500 BC provide some of the earliest physical evidence of ornamental horticulture and landscape design; depicting lotus ponds surrounded by symmetrical rows of acacias and palms. A notable example of an ancient ornamental garden was the 'Hanging Gardens of Babylon' – one of the Seven Wonders of the Ancient World. Ancient Rome had dozens of great gardens, and Roman estates tended to be laid out with hedges and vines and contained a wide variety of flowers – acanthus, cornflowers, crocus, cyclamen, hyacinth, iris, ivy, lavender, lilies, myrtle, narcissus, poppy, rosemary and violets as well as statues and sculptures. Flower beds were also popular in the courtyards of rich Romans. The Middle Ages represented a period of decline for gardens with aesthetic purposes however. After the fall of Rome gardening was done with the purpose of growing **medicinal herbs** and/or decorating church **altars**. It was mostly monasteries that carried on the tradition of garden design and horticultural techniques during the medieval period in Europe. By the late thirteenth century, rich Europeans began to grow gardens for leisure as well as for medicinal herbs and vegetables. They generally surrounded them with walls – hence, the 'walled garden.'

These gardens advanced by the sixteenth and seventeenth centuries into symmetrical, proportioned and balanced designs with a more classical appearance. Gardens in the renaissance were adorned with sculptures (in a nod to Roman heritage), topiary and fountains. These fountains often contained 'water jokes' – hidden cascades which suddenly soaked visitors. The most famous fountains of this kind were found in the Villa d'Este (1550-1572) at Tivoli near Rome. By the late seventeenth century, European gardeners had started planting new flowers such as tulips, marigolds and sunflowers.

These highly complex designs, largely created by the aristocracy slowly gave way to the individual gardener however – and this is where this book comes in! Cottage Gardens first emerged during the Elizabethan times, originally created by poorer workers to provide themselves with food and herbs, with flowers planted amongst them for decoration. Farm workers were generally provided with cottages set in a small garden—about an acre—where they could grow food, keep pigs, chickens and often bees; the latter necessitating the planting of decorative pollen flora. By Elizabethan times there was more prosperity, and thus more room to grow flowers. Most of the early cottage garden flowers would have had practical uses though —violets were spread on the floor (for their pleasant scent and keeping out vermin); **calendulas** and **primroses** were both attractive and used in cooking. Others, such as **sweet william** and **hollyhocks** were grown entirely for their beauty.

Here lies the roots of today's home-gardener; further influenced by the 'new style' in eighteenth century England which replaced the more formal, symmetrical '**Garden à la française**'. Such gardens, close to works of art, were often inspired by paintings in the classical style of landscapes by Claude Lorraine and Nicolas Poussin. The work of **Lancelot 'Capability' Brown**, described as 'England's greatest gardener' was particularly influential. We hope that the reader is inspired by this book, and the long and varied history of gardening itself, to experiment with some home-gardening of their own. Enjoy.

UNIFORM WITH THIS VOLUME.

Others to follow.

'Often times he would make it his prayer that he should not be accounted as an hypocrite by reason that his life sorted not with his teaching ; insisting there is a duality in unity in most of us, and that to a writer it hath still been permitted (not for his own behoof, since what true profit is there to a man in seeming that he is not ?) to put his better mind in his books.'

TO MY SISTER
THE COUNTESS OF LYTTON

PREFACE

THESE 'Notes' would never have been extracted from me without the encouragement I have received from all my dear nieces, real and adopted, and the very practical assistance of one of them. Now that the book is written, I can only hope that it will not prove too great a disappointment to them all.

CONTENTS

CONTENTS—*Continued.*

CONTENTS—Continued.

CONTENTS—*Continued.*

CONTENTS—Continued.

CONTENTS—Continued.

POT-POURRI FROM A
SURREY GARDEN

JANUARY

Introductory—Indispensable books—An old Hertfordshire garden—
Reminiscences—My present garden plants in a London room—
Japanese floral arrangement—Cooking vegetables and fruit—
Making coffee—Early blossoms—Winter gardening—Frost pic-
tures on window-panes.

January 2nd.—I am not going to write a gardening
book, or a cookery book, or a book on furnishing or
education. Plenty of these have been published lately.
I merely wish to talk to you on paper about several subjects as they occur to me throughout one year ; and if
such desultory notes prove to be of any use to you or
others, so much the better. One can only teach from
personal knowledge ; yet how exceedingly limited that is !
The fact that I shall mention gardening every month
will give this subject preponderance throughout the book.
At the same time I shall in no way attempt to super-
sede books on gardening, that are much fuller and more
complete than anything I could write. For those who
care to learn gardening in the way I have learnt, I may
mention, before I go further, three books which seem to
me absolutely essential—' The English Flower Garden,'
by W. Robinson ; ' The Vegetable Garden,' translated
from the French, edited by W. Robinson ; and John-

son's 'Gardener's Dictionary,' by C. H. Wright and D. Dewar. This last supplies any deficiencies in the other two, and it teaches the cultivation of plants under glass.

The cookery book to which I shall refer is 'Dainty Dishes,' by Lady Harriet Sinclair. It is an old one, and has often been reprinted. I have known it all my married life, and have found no other book on cooking so useful, so clear, or in such good taste. It is the only English cookery book I know that has been translated into German.

I have given you the names of these books, as it is through them I have learnt most of what I know, both in gardening and cooking. It is, however, undeniable that, as the old proverb says, you may drag a horse to the water, but you can't make him drink; and unless, when I name plants or vegetables for the table, you look them up in the books, you will derive very little benefit from these notes.

Just now it seems as if everybody wrote books which nobody reads. This is probably what I am doing myself; but, so far as gardening is concerned, at any rate, I have read and studied very hard, as I began to learn quite late in life. I never buy a plant, or have one given me, without looking it up in the books and providing it with the best treatment in my power. If a plant fails, I always blame myself, and feel sure I have cultivated it wrongly. No day goes by without my studying some of my books or reading one or more of the very excellent gardening newspapers that are published weekly. This is how I also learnt cooking when I was younger, always going to the book when a dish was wrong. In this way one becomes independent of cooks and gardeners, because, if they leave, one can always teach another. Nothing is more unjust than the way a great many people find fault with their gardeners, and, like the Egyptians of old, demand bricks

without straw. How can a man who has had little
education and no experience be expected to know
about plants that come from all parts of the world,
and require individual treatment and understanding
to make them grow here at all ? Or how can a cook be
expected to dress vegetables when she has never been
taught how to do it ? In England her one instruction
has usually been to throw a large handful of coarse soda
into the water, with a view to making it soft and keeping the colour of the vegetables, whereas, in fact, she
by so doing destroys their health-giving properties ; and
every housekeeper should see that it is not done. Her
next idea is to hand over the cooking of the vegetables
to a raw girl of a kitchen-maid, if she has one.

I am most anxious that anybody who does not care
for old Herbals should pass over those catalogued in
March; but, on the other hand, that those who are
interested in gardening should look through the November list of books, as they will find many modern ones
mentioned there which may be useful to them for
practical purposes.

My hope and wish is that my reader will take me
by the hand ; for I do not reap, and I do not sow. I
am merely, like so many other women of the past and
present, a patient gleaner in the fields of knowledge, and
absolutely dependent on human sympathy in order to
do anything at all. I cannot explain too much that
the object of my book is to try to make everyone think
for him or herself, and at the same time to profit by the
instruction which in these days is so easy to get, and
is all around us. Women are still behind the other sex
in the power of thinking at all, much more so in the
power of thinking of several things at once. I hope
the coming women may see the great advantage of
training their minds early in life to be a practical denial
of Swift's cynical assertion that ' mankind are as unfit
for flying as for thinking.' Nothing can be done well

without thought—certainly not gardening, nor house-keeping, nor managing children. A curious example of this is given in a recently published account of the most famous of modern jugglers. He says that he trained his brain in youth to exert itself in three different ways at the same time. This no doubt is the reason that he is now pre-eminent in his own line.

January 3rd.—I will begin by telling you that I was brought up for the most part in the country, in a beautiful, wild, old-fashioned garden. This garden, through circumstances, had remained in the hands of an old gardener for more than thirty years, which carries us back nearly a century. Like so many young people I see about me now, I cared only for the flowers growing, that I might have the pleasure of picking them. Mr. Ruskin says that it is luxurious and pleasure-loving people who like them gathered. Gardening is, I think, essentially the amusement of the middle-aged and old. The lives of the young, as a rule, are too full to give the time and attention required.

Almost all that has remained in my mind of my young days in this garden is how wonderfully the old man kept the place. He succeeded in flowering many things year after year with no one to help him, and with the frost in the valley to contend against in spring. It was difficult, too, for him to get seeds or plants, since the place was held by joint owners, whom he did not like to ask for them. The spot was very sheltered, and that is one of the greatest of all secrets for plant cultivation. An ever-flowing mill-stream ran all round the garden ; and the hedges of China-roses, Sweetbriar, Honeysuckle, and white Hawthorn tucked their toes into the soft mud, and throve year after year. The old man was a philosopher in his way, and when on a cold March morning my sisters and I used to rush out after lessons and ask him what the weather was going to be, he would stop his digging, look up at the sky, and say :

' Well, miss, it may be fine and it may be wet ; and if the sun comes out, it will be warmer.' After this solemn announcement he would wipe his brow and resume his work, and we went off, quite satisfied, to our well-known haunts in the Hertfordshire woods, to gather Violets and Primroses for our mother, who loved them. All this, you will see, laid a very small foundation for any knowledge of gardening ; and yet, owing to the vivid character of the impressions of youth, it left a memory that was very useful to me when I took up gardening later in life. To this day I can smell the tall white double Rockets that throve so well in the damp garden, and scented the evening air. They grew by the side of glorious bunches of Oriental Poppies and the on-coming spikes of the feathery *Spiræa aruncus*. This garden had peculiar charms for us, because, though we hardly realised it, such gardens were already beginning to grow out of fashion, sacrificed to the new bedding-out system, which altered the whole gardening of Europe. I shall allude to this again. I can never think of this old home without my thoughts recurring to Hood's poem ' I remember ! I remember ! ' too well known perhaps, even by the young, to justify my quoting it here. Equally graven on my memory is a much less familiar little poem my widowed mother used to say to me as we walked together up and down the gravel paths, with the primrose sky behind the tall Beeches of the neighbouring park. For years I never knew where it came from, nor where she learnt it in her own sentimental youth. Not long ago I found it in a book of selections. It was written by John Hamilton Reynolds, that warm friend of poor Keats, who, as Mr. Sidney Colvin tells us in his charming Life of the poet, never rose to any great eminence in either litera-ture or law, and died in 1852, as clerk of the county, at Newport, Isle of Wight. As Mr. Colvin remarks, it is only in his association with Keats that his name will

live.   Yet my mother loved the poem, which is full of
the sentiment of our little home :—

> Go where the water glideth gently ever,
>   Glideth through meadows that the greenest be ;
> Go, listen to our own belovèd river,
>   And think of me.
>
> Wander in forests where the small flower layeth
>   Its fairy gem beneath the giant tree ;
> Listen to the dim brook pining while it playeth,
>   And think of me.
>
> Watch when the sky is silver pale at even,
>   And the wind grieveth in the lonely tree ;
> Go out beneath the solitary heaven,
>   And think of me.
>
> And when the moon riseth as she were dreaming,
>   And treadeth with white feet the lullèd sea,
> Go, silent as a star beneath her beaming,
>   And think of me.

But enough of these old woman's recollections, and back
to the present, for the sentiment of one generation is very
apt to appear as worthless sentimentality to the next.
The garden I have now is a small piece of flat ground
surrounding an ordinary suburban house.   Kitchen-
garden, flower-garden, house and drive can scarcely
cover more than two acres.   The garden is surrounded
by large forest trees, Spanish Chestnuts and Oaks, whose
wicked roots walk into all the beds almost as fast as we
cut them off.   The soil is dry, light and sandy, and
ill-adapted to garden purposes.   We are only sixteen
miles from London, and on unfavourable days, when
the wind is in the blighting south-east, the afternoons
are darkened by the smoke of the huge city.   This is
an immense disadvantage to all plant life and very
injurious to Roses and many other things.   For five or
six months in the winter I live away in London.   People
often envy me this, and say : ' What could you do in
the garden in the winter ? '   But no true gardener would

make this remark, as there is much to be done at all
times and seasons. Half the interest of a garden is the
constant exercise of the imagination. You are always
living three, or indeed six, months hence. I believe
that people entirely devoid of imagination never can be
really good gardeners. To be content with the present,
and not striving about the future, is fatal.

Living in London in the winter necessitates crowding
the little greenhouse to overflowing with plants and
flowers adapted for sending to London—chosen because
they will bear the journey well, and live some time in
water on their arrival.

January 16th.—I can hardly do better to-day than
tell you about my dark London room, and what I have
in it as regards plant life in this the worst month of the
year. I will begin with the dead and dried things that
only bear the memory of the summer which is gone. At
the door stand two bright-green olive-jars that came
from Spain, into which are stuck large bunches of the
white seed-vessels of Honesty and some flowers of Everlastings (*Helichrysum bracteatum*). These last are tied
in bunches on to Bamboo sticks, to make them stand
out. Inside the room, on the end of the piano, is a
large dish of yellow, green, and white Gourds. I grow
them because they have that peculiar quality, in common
with Oranges and autumn leaves, of appearing to give
out in the winter the sunlight they have absorbed in
the summer. Their cultivation does not always succeed
with me, as they want a better, sunnier place than I
can sometimes afford to give them. In a very wet
summer they fail altogether. The seeds are sold in
mixed packets; we sow them at the end of April,
grow them on in heat, and plant them out at quite the
end of May. In fact, we treat them exactly as you
would Vegetable-marrows, only we train them over a
fence.

On the backs of my armchairs are thin Liberty silk

oblong bags, like miniature saddle-bags, filled with dried Lavender, Sweet Verbena, and Sweet Geranium leaves. This mixture is much more fragrant than the Lavender alone. The visitor who leans back in his chair wonders from where the sweet scent comes.

On the side ledge of two large windows I have pots of the common Ivy of our hedges. We dig it up any time in the spring, and put it into the pots, which are then sunk into the ground under the shade of some wall, and kept well watered. Before bringing it into the room in winter, it is trained up on an iron stake or Bamboo-cane, singly or in bunches, to give variety to its shapes. If kept tolerably clean and watered, this Ivy is practically unkillable, even in London.

Then there are some pots of the long-suffering *Aspidistras*, the two kinds—variegated and dark green. These also want nothing but plenty of water, and sponging the dust off the leaves twice a week. They make pretty pot-plants if attended to during the summer in the country. They should be well thinned out and every injured leaf cut off, tied together towards the middle, kept growing all the summer in the greenhouse, and encouraged to grow tall ; they are then more graceful and satisfactory. They seldom want dividing or re-potting. I have two sorts of India-rubber plants—the large-leaved, straight-growing common *Ficus elastica*, and the *Ficus elastica indica*, which is a little more delicate, and the better for more heat in summer ; but it has a smaller leaf, and grows in a much more charming way than the other. Keeping the leaves very clean is of paramount importance with both these plants. During the winter they want very little watering, yet should never be allowed to get quite dry, as this would make the leaves droop. If, on the other hand, you see a single yellow spot on the leaves, you may be sure that they are too damp ; and, if watering is continued, the leaves will turn yellow, and eventually fall one by one.

JANUARY. 25

When they are growing in heat during the summer, they must be watered freely and the leaves well syringed. Both kinds propagate very easily. The top shoots strike in sand and heat ; and so do single leaves, if cut out with the eye and stuck round the edge of the pot. Another plant on the window-sill, *Phalangium liliago variegatum,* is of the same family as St. Bruno's Lily, that lovely early June flower in our gardens. It makes a most excellent pot-plant, young or old, for a room at all times of the year. It has a charming growth, and throws out branches on which young plants grow ; these can be left alone, or cut off and potted up in small pots, in which case they root easily in summer, or in a little heat at other times of the year. The flower which comes on the plant in summer is quite insignificant. It is very easy of cultivation, though not quite hardy ; and yet, when grown in a little heat, has all the appearance of the foliage of a delicate stove-plant.

In the middle of the room is a *Pandanus veitchii.* This must be sparingly watered. It is a delightful winter pot-plant in all its sizes. The offsets that come round the stems of the old plant root very easily in heat. It does not mind the heat of the fire, but resents frost on the window-pane. *Cocos weddeliana* and its varieties are most useful and well-known drawing-room plants, from South America. To save time, it is best to buy small plants from a nurseryman, and grow them on. They can, however, be grown from seed in a hot-bed in spring, but they are not very quick growers.

I have, wedged in Japanese vases in the Japanese way, which is so highly decorative,* two branches of *Physalis*

* For a description of what this means I must refer you to Mr. J. Conder's interesting book (*The Flowers of Japan and the Art of Floral Arrangement*), and to a review of it reprinted at the end of this volume, by kind permission of Mr. W. Robinson, from *The Garden* (37 Southampton Street, Strand) of October 6th, 1894. My allusions to cut-flower decorations all the year round will not be understood without a careful reading of this article.

Alkekengi (Winter Cherry) grown from seed. They last much longer in a room, I find, if cut, stuck into clean water, and held up by the wedge, than they do when growing in a pot ; cutting the plants well back makes them a better shape, and they flower and fruit more freely the following year.

In a brass Indian vase on a corner of the chimney-piece there are some long branches of the Double Plum (*Prunus spinosa flore pleno*). These branches, with their bright green, bring spring into the room more effectively than anything I know. The little shrub is easy of cultivation, and more than most things repays potting-up and forcing. We plant them out in spring in a half-shady reserve border, and in August we cut with a spade round the roots of those plants which we intend to pot up in October. They do best if allowed to rest alternate years. The charming single *Deutzia gracilis* is treated in exactly the same way.

Never forget, in the arranging of cut flowers, that all shrubby plants and many perennials last much longer in water if the stalks are peeled. The reason is obvious : the thick bark prevents the absorption of enough water. In the case of succulent plants, splitting up the ends of the stalks is often sufficient.

On a table below the chimney-piece is a small flower-glass filled with a pretty early greenhouse flower, orange and red, called *Chorozemia,* which does well in water. I have made a considerable study of the things that last well in water, as my greenhouse room is very limited, and it has to hold all the plants that are planted out next summer. The usual *Primula sinensis,* Cinerarias, and many other things die before they get up to London at all. In summer the study is for the sake of my friends, as I send away flowers in large quantities, and I know nothing so disappointing as to receive in London a box of flowers, none of which are capable of reviving when put into water. On the table, by the side of the glass mentioned above, stands a little saucer with precious, sweet-smelling Geranium leaves. These float on the water, patterning the white surface of the saucer, and supporting the delicious scented flowers, so valuable in January, of the *Chimonanthus fragrans,* with its pretty brown and yellow petals growing, as they do, on the bare branches of the shrub. My plant of *Chimonanthus* is against a wall. It flowers every year with a little care, for it is not very old, but it does not grow in our light soil with the strength and luxuriance it acquires in clay or loam. In Hertfordshire, for instance, quite long branches can be cut from it, which look very beautiful in the Japanese wedges. Our plant gets sufficiently pruned by cutting back the flowering branches. We water it thoroughly with liquid manure when the leaves are forming in May, and mulch it with rotten manure in October. *Jasminum nudiflorum,* which also flowers well in the winter with us, we treat in the same way, only pruning out whole branches when it has done flowering in spring. No general cutting-back is desirable, as that spoils the growth of the plant for picking next year. In separate different-sized glasses round the saucer I have a bunch of Neapolitan Violets, some Roman Hyacinths, Ivy-leaved sweet Geraniums, and an excessively pretty light-red *Amaryllis,* from bulbs sent to me this autumn straight from Mauritius, which flower well in the little stove. All these come from a small greenhouse, part of which is divided off so as to allow of its being kept at stove heat. A fortnight ago we had large bunches of *Echeveria retusa,* a most useful, easily managed, winter-flowering plant. It looks very well on the dinner-table, and lasts a long time in water. Dividing and re-potting in April, and keeping it on a sunny shelf through the summer, is almost all the care it requires. Freesias, too, are well worth growing. The success of all Cape flowering bulbs seems to depend on the attention paid to the plant while the leaves are still growing. Many gardeners, when they have cut the flowers, neglect the plants. When the leaves die down, the bulbs want well baking and drying up in full sun, laying the pots on their sides, shaking out the bulbs in June or July, sorting them, taking off the young ones, re-potting, and growing on for early forcing.

On a flower-table by the window are glasses with evergreens. I always cut with discretion my *Magnolia grandiflora;* not a very large plant either, yet I think it does it nothing but good. The clean, shiny, dark-green leaves, with their beautiful rust-red lining, are so effective in a room ; and if the stalks are peeled, they last quite a month in water without deterioration. You know, I daresay, the old nursery secret of growing either wheat or canary-seed on wet moss. You fill some shallow pan or small basin with moss, and keep it quite wet. Sow your seed thickly on the moss, and put the pan away in a dark cupboard for nine or ten days. When about two inches high, bring it out and put it in a sunny window, turning it round, so as to make it grow straight. Wheat is white at the base with brave little sword-blades of green, on which often hangs a drop of clear water. Canary-seed is red, like Rhubarb, at the bottom and green at the top. I know nothing more charming to grow in dull town rooms or sick rooms than these two seeds. They come to perfection in about three weeks, and last for another five or six. Grown in small saucers, they make a pretty dinner-table winter decoration. Another rather effective change for a dinner-table is the leaves of Bamboos, put all day into water to prevent them curling up. They are then laid on the table-cloth in a Japanese pattern, according to the taste of the decorator, with an occasional flower to give point to the design. Double red Geraniums, late-flowering Chrysanthemums, Primulas, even clumps of Holly or red berries, all do equally well for this purpose.

Growing acorns, either suspended by a thin wire in a

bottle, or planted in wet moss—five or six of them together—in flat pans, are pretty. If put into heat in October, they are in full leaf in the middle of January; but if grown in a cool room, the leaves only expand later.

I think it may be desirable for me to say something each month about cooking. Many people neglect to use things which are now so easily got with or without a garden. This foreign way of cooking Potatoes makes a nice variety :—After partially boiling them, cut the Potatoes into slices when cold, and put them into a saucepan. Cover them with milk to finish cooking them, and add fresh butter, Parsley, pepper, and salt.

Salsifys are quite easily grown, and are very good if thrown into vinegar and water, well boiled, cut into small slices, and warmed up with a white sauce in shells, like scalloped oysters. Add a little cheese and breadcrumbs, and brown in the oven.

No one who cares for vegetables and has a garden should fail to refer constantly to ' The Vegetable Garden,' already mentioned. It is an invaluable book, and the number and variety of the vegetables it describes is a revelation to those who have only the ordinary English idea of the vegetables that are worth growing.

Celeriac is an excellent vegetable, not very common in England, and when carefully cooked, with a good brown sauce, forms a valuable contribution to the winter supply. One of the constant difficulties in the management of a house, whether large or small, where the vegetables are grown and not bought, is that the gardener brings them in, and the cook throws them away into a corner of the scullery or into the pig-tub. Only last summer a gardener from a large place in the neighbourhood said to me while walking round my small garden : ' What ! you grow Cardoons ? I took in beautiful ones last year, but they were never used ; the cook said she didn't know how to cook them.' The following is a good receipt :—

The length of time Cardoons require in cooking depends on age and size, and varies from half an hour to three or four hours. Scrape the stalks, and pull off all that is thready outside. Cut them into bits about four or five inches long, or longer if served in a long narrow dish with marrow on toast at each end. As you cut them, throw them into a basin full of water, into which you put a little flour to keep them a good colour. When all are prepared, have ready a large crockery stewpan with boiling water, herbs, a little salt and pepper, and a good-sized piece of raw bacon. The rind of the bacon should be cut in little bits, but not so small as to get mixed with the Cardoons. Boil the whole slowly, and prepare a brown sauce apart with well-flavoured stock. Thicken this with flour (burnt to a light-coffee colour), butter, and a little sherry. Let it simmer for two hours, skimming it well. Strain it half an hour before serving.

The American Cranberries, so generally and so cheaply sold in London, are very pretty and very nice if well stewed in a crockery saucepan with water and sugar ; a small pinch of powdered ginger brings out their flavour. They are always eaten in America with turkeys, as we eat apple-sauce with goose. Many people do not know that turkeys are natives of America, and that the French word *dinde* is merely a shortening of *coq d'Inde* (India being the name given to America for some time after its discovery). It is curious to think that these birds, now so common an article of food at this time of year, were totally unknown to the luxurious Romans. The Cranberries should not be mashed up, but should look like stoned cherries in syrup. They can be eaten with chicken or game, or with roast mutton instead of red-currant jelly. In Norway the small native Cranberry is eaten with any stew, especially with hares and ptarmigan. The custom of eating sweets with meat seems to come to us from Germany and the North ; the French hate it.

One of the eternal trials to every housekeeper is the making of coffee. I always use half Mocha and half Plantation. When in the country, I roast the beans at home ; and the two kinds must be done separately, as they are not the same size. For breakfast coffee a small quantity of ground Chicory—the best French—is a great improvement, and increases the health-giving properties of coffee and milk ; but it should never be used for black coffee. The beans should in damp weather be warmed and dried a little before grinding ; it freshens them up, as it does biscuits. One of the mysterious reasons for the flat tastelessness of coffee one day and not another is the coffee-grinder not being cleaned out ; a tablespoonful of stale ground coffee will spoil the whole. Other reasons are—either the water not boiling, or the water having boiled a long time, or water that has boiled and cooled being warmed up again ; this is fatal, as it is with tea. I find the modern crockery percolators a great improvement on the old tin ones, which make very good coffee for a short time ; but the lining rubs off, and the tin gets black inside, which will destroy the colour of the best coffee. At Goode's, in Audley Street, or at the Atmospheric Churn Company, in Bond Street, they will sell you any portion of these percolators apart ; and the most terrible of breakers can hardly smash everything at once. Many cooks refuse to use Goode's excellent crockery fireproof stewpans, on the plea that they break. But new ones cost no more than the re-tinning of copper stewpans, which has to be done every year. For all stews, and for the cooking of vegetables and fruit, they are invaluable—and, in the case of fruit, indispensable.

January 18th.—One excellent way of arranging flowers in most rooms is to have a table, a kind of altar, especially dedicated to them. This does the flowers or plants much more justice than dotting them about the room. If, however, flowers or branches are arranged in vases in the Japanese style, the more they are isolated in prominent places that show them off, the better.

I am now staying with a friend who has no stove, only one greenhouse ; and her flower-table, standing in the window, looks charming. At the back are two tall glass vases with Pampas grass in them, feathery and white, as we never can keep it in London ; a small Eucalyptus-tree in a pot, cut back in summer and well shaped ; a fine pot of Arums, just coming into flower ; a small fern in front, and a bunch of paper-white Narcissus. These last, I fear, must have been grown elsewhere, as they could not be so early here without heat and very careful growing-on.

January 20th.—I came from London, to pass two or three days in the country and look after my garden, as usual. I make lists and decide on the seeds for the year, and look to the mulching of certain plants. Hardly anything grows here to perfection when left alone. Most plants require either chalk, peat, leaf-mould or cow-manure, and half-tender things are now the better for covering up with matting or Bracken-fern. It is seldom of any use to come so early as this ; but there has been no cold this year, though one feels it must come. Oh ! such days and days of gloom and darkness ; but to-day the wind freshened from the north-east, and I could breathe once more. How delightful it is to be out of London again ! There is always plenty to do and to enjoy. How the birds sing, as if it were spring ! I love the country in winter ; one expects nothing, and everything is a joy and a surprise. The Freesias are flowering well ; they improve each year as the bulbs get larger. Cyclamens are in the greenhouse, and a large, never-failing, old white Azalea, which forces faithfully and uncomplainingly every year, and from which we cut so many blooms.

The first Aconite ! Does any flower in summer give

the same pleasure ? The blue-green blades of the Daffodils and Jonquils are firmly and strongly pushing through
the cold brown earth ; nothing in all the year gives such
a sense of power and joy. One is grateful, too, for our
Surrey soil and climate—to live where it never can rain
too much, and where it never accords with Shelley's
wonderful description of damp :—

> And hour by hour, when the air was still,
> The vapours arose which have strength to kill.
> At morn they were seen, at noon they were felt,
> At night they were darkness no star could melt.

These mild winters have a wonderful effect on plant
life. The *Solanum jasminoides* looks as fresh as in
November, and as if he meant to stand it out ; we shall
see. In front of my window, on the ground floor, I have
been rigging up a delightful arrangement for feeding Tom-
tits. I hang half a pound of suet and a cocoanut on
either end of a piece of thick string. This should be long
enough to reach the lower window when suspended from
a small iron rod by a ring hanging at the end of it, the
rod being nailed to the window-sill above. The string is
passed through the top of the cocoanut, of which the
bottom is cut off, making a hole large enough for a bird
to get in. It greatly adds to the artistic effect to hang
the cocoanut about a foot lower than the suet, or *vice
versa*. The small birds cling to the string while they
peck their food, and so make a continual and beautiful
design. To help them to cling, a few little crossbars of
wood are knotted into the string and form a sort of rough
ladder. In really cold weather, or with snow on the
ground, they become wonderfully tame. Another way
is to plant a post in the ground with one or two crossbars nailed to the top, on which are hung similar arrangements to those just described of cocoanut and suet, or
an old bone.

This warm winter has suited the Christmas Roses,

which are uncommonly good. The great secret in light
soils is to mulch them well while they are making their
leaves. Water them with liquid manure when their
flower-buds are forming, and protect them with lights
in the flowering season, especially keeping them from
heavy rains or snow. For these reasons grow them in a
bed by themselves. In the greenhouse I found a *Choisya
ternata*, which I had cut back hard last May, covered all
over with its beautiful white flowers. It had been forced
in the stove for about ten days. This is a most delightful plant in every way, easy to strike and to layer,
quite hardy ; though, when growing outside, the flowers
are sometimes a little injured by hard late frosts. It is
invaluable for cutting to send to London at all times of
year, as it lasts for a long time in water, and the shiny
dark-green leaves look especially well with any white
flowers. The more it is cut, the better the plant flourishes. Every spare piece of wall should have a plant of
Choisya against it. It is restrained and yet free in its
growth, and is therefore even more useful in small gardens than in large ones. It does very well in light soil,
but responds to a little feeding. I have some giant
Violets which I got from the South of France ; here, I
believe, they are called ' Princess Beatrice.' They are
twice the size of Czars, and very sweet. They are doing
well in the frame, but look rather draggled and miserable outside ; after all, it is only the end of January.

In mid-winter my heart warms to the common Laurels.
In wet winters, especially, they look so flourishing and
happy, and they will grow in such bad places. I am
sure I shall abuse them so often that I must say, however much they are reduced in a garden, keep some
plants in places where few other things would flourish.
They will always remain a typical example of Mme. de
Stael's good description of evergreens :—' Le deuil de
l'été et l'ornement de l'hiver.' All hardy fruit-trees, as
well as *Jasminum nudiflorum* and *Chimonanthus fragrans*

are better pruned in January than in February, if the weather make it possible.

January 22nd.—I take back to London with me to-day, amongst other things, some *Lachenalia aurea.* All Lachenalias are worth growing. They are little Cape bulbs, which have to be treated like the Freezias, watered as long as the leaves are green, and then dried. They all force well, and *L. aurea* flowers earlier than the other Lachenalias, and is very pretty and effective. This variety has the great merit of being a true yellow by candle-light.

Walking along the streets to-day, I stopped to look at a really beautiful large cross, entirely composed of moss dotted all over with the lovely little early single Snow-drops. Although I have the strongest objection to the modern use of flowers for the dead, natural and lovable as was the original idea, I had to admire this specimen. Could a more beautiful winter memorial for a young girl be seen, or one which better carries out in these cold days the idea of the French poet Malherbe ?

> Elle était du monde où les plus belles choses
> Ont le pire destin ;
> Et rose, elle a vécu ce que vivent les roses—
> L'espace d'un matin.

The French have carried the abuse of this fashion of funeral wreaths and crosses to an even greater extent than we have here. I shall never forget once in Paris going up to the Père-Lachaise cemetery on a fine morning to visit the grave of a young and much-lamented woman. The wreaths were so numerous that they had to be taken up in a cart the day before. The night had been wet, and the surroundings of the grave were a mass of un-approachable corruption and decay.

Last April, when I was at Kew, the gardener there shook into my pocket-handkerchief a little seed of *Cineraria cruenta,* the type-plant from the Cape, and the origin of all the Cinerarias of our greenhouses. It has a very different and much taller growth than the cultivated ones, and I am most anxious to see if it will live in water, which the ordinary ones do not. It varies in shade from pale to deep lilac, rather like a Michaelmas Daisy. Getting seeds from abroad of type-plants is very interesting gardening. Pelargoniums of all kinds are weeds at the Cape, and, in order to be able to resist the long droughts, they have, in South Africa, tuberous roots like Dahlias. This is well seen in Andrews' ' Botanist's Repository,' which I shall mention among the March books. Pelargoniums, under cultivation and with much watering, no longer require these tubers, and they disappear. Seed was sent to me from some of the wild plants at the Cape, and even the first year, as the plants grew, there were the little tubers, quite marked and distinct.

January 31*st.*—With the high temperature we have had this year, one is apt to forget the horrors of a severe winter, till reminded just lately by two very cold nights. The frosted windows of my bedroom made me think of a charming little poem which appeared last year in the *Pall Mall Gazette* at the time of the very cold weather :—

JOHN FROST

The door was shut, as doors should be,
  Before you went to bed last night,
Yet John Frost has got in, you see,
  And left your windows silver white.

He must have waited till you slept,
  And not a single word he spoke,
But pencill'd o'er the panes and crept
  Away again before you woke.

And now you cannot see the trees
  Nor fields that stretch beyond the lane ;
But there are fairer things than these
  His fingers traced on every pane.

JANUARY.

Rocks and castles towering high,
Hills and dales, and streams and fields,
And knights in armour riding by
With plumes and spears and shining shields.

And here are little boats, and there
Big ships with sails spread to the breeze,
And yonder palm-trees, waving fair
On islands set in silver seas.

And butterflies with gauzy wings,
And birds and bees, and cows and sheep,
And fruit and flowers, and all the things
You see when you are sound asleep.

For, creeping softly underneath
The door when all the lights are out,
John Frost takes every breath you breathe,
And knows the things you think about.

He paints them on the window-pane,
In fairy lines, with frozen steam ;
And when you wake, you see again
The wondrous things you saw in dream.

Londoners have the great advantage, in hard frosts,
of being able to enjoy these frozen pictures, for nowhere
can they be seen to such perfection as on the large window-panes of cold empty shops. Many people must
have remarked this last winter.

FEBRUARY

February 8th.—This is essentially the month of forced
bulbs—Hyacinths, Tulips, Jonquils, Narcissuses—charming things in themselves, and within easy reach of everyone who can afford to buy them either as bulbs in the
autumn or as cut flowers from the shops in spring.
Bulbs do not even require a greenhouse, as they can be
grown in a cellar and then in a frame, or, with care,
quite as successfully in a room with a south window.
They depend on attention, and the result is so certain
that they are not very interesting to the gardener, nor
do they represent any variety of greenhouse culture.
All the spring bulbs are cultivated in much the same
way. Any of the old garden books published between
1840 and 1850, especially Mrs. Loudon's ' Gardening for
Ladies,' give detailed instructions on the growing of
bulbs in pots and glasses, and in all other ways.

One of my great pleasures in London in the early
spring is going to the exhibition of the Royal Horticultural Society, at the Drill Hall, Westminster. I think
all amateurs who are keen gardeners ought to belong to
this society—partly as an encouragement to it, and also
because the subscriber of even one guinea a year gets a
great many advantages. He can go to these fortnightly
exhibitions, as well as to the great show at the Temple
Gardens in May, free, before the public is admitted. He

has the run of the society's library in Victoria Street ;
he receives free the yearly publications, which are a
series of most interesting lectures (I will give some
account of them at the end of the year) ; and he is
annually presented with a certain number of plants.
These fortnightly meetings at the Drill Hall are instructive and varied, though they might be much more so.
Nevertheless, I think an amateur cannot go to them
without learning something, and I am surprised to find
how few people take advantage of them. The entrance
fee is only a shilling. I went to one of these exhibitions
the other day. The great mass of blooms shown con-
sisted of beautifully grown potfuls of Cyclamens in great
variety of colour, and of Chinese Primulas ; these last,
to my mind, are rather uninteresting plants, but they
show great improvement in colour as now cultivated.
What pleased me most were miniature Irises, grown in
flat pans, and some charming spring Snowflakes (*Leu-
cojum vernum*) grown in pots. These are far more
satisfactory grown in this way than are the finest
Snowdrops in pots, their foliage being so much prettier.
The little blue Scillas are extremely effective grown
in pans through a carpet of the ordinary mossy Saxifrage.

February 14th.—Salads are rather a difficulty during
the early spring in English gardens. In seasonless London everything is always to be bought. I wonder why
Mâche (Corn Salad, or Lamb's Lettuce), so much grown
in France, is so little cultivated here ? People fairly well
up in gardening come back from France in the winter,
thinking they have discovered something new. *Mâche*
is a little difficult to grow in very light soils, and the
safest plan is to make several sowings in July and
August. We find it most useful, but, without constant
reminding, no English gardener thinks of it at all, though
it is in all the seed catalogues. As it is an annual, without sowing you naturally don't get it ; and if sown too

late, it is bound to fail. In very dry weather we have
to water it at first.

If Beetroot is carelessly dug up and the roots broken,
they bleed, which causes them to come to the table pale
and tasteless. This is the fault of the gardener, not of
the cook. Some English cooks boil them in vinegar ;
this hardens them, and makes them unwholesome. They
are much better slowly baked in an oven, and not boiled
at all. The poor Beetroot is often considered unwholesome, but if it is served with a little of the water it is
boiled in, or if baked with a little warm water poured
over it, a squeeze of lemon instead of vinegar, and a
little oil added, I think the accusation is unjust. Beetroot served hot and cut in slices, with a white Béchamel
sauce (see ' Dainty Dishes '), makes a very good winter
vegetable. The Old English dish of Beetroot sliced and
laid round a soup-plate with pulled Celery, mixed with
a Mayonnaise sauce, built up in the middle, is excellent
with all roast meats. At all the best Italian grocers in
London they sell a dried Green Pea from Italy, which
makes a pretty purée both as a vegetable and as a soup
in winter, especially if coloured with a very little fresh
Spinach, not the colouring sold by grocers. The Peas
must be soaked all night, then well boiled, rubbed smooth
through a sieve, and a little cream and butter added.
A nicer winter vegetable cannot be. It is really made
exactly like the old pease-pudding served with pork,
only not nearly so dry.

Imantophilums are one of the most effective and beautiful of our greenhouse plants at this time of the year,
and last very well in water. We kept ours out of doors
in an open pit all through last summer. As they threw
up several flower-spikes, which we picked off, we feared
that they might not do so well this spring ; instead of
which, I think they have never done better or flowered
more freely. A little liquid manure helps them when
in flower. Though a Cape plant, the leaves do not die

down ; and so it must be kept growing, or the foliage is injured.

February 27th.—I have lately evolved a good spring vegetable dish. The common green Turnip-tops, which are wholesome, but not palatable if plainly boiled, are delicious when treated like the French purée of Spinach (*see* 'Dainty Dishes'), rubbed through a sieve, and mixed with butter and cream. They are a beautiful bright green. In the country young Nettles done in the same way are very good, but they must be fresh—a state in which they are not to be had in large towns. I have been told how curious it is that nettles never grow in absolutely wild places, but are only to be found in localities more or less haunted by man.

I think Rhubarb, which is so largely grown and eaten in England, both forced and out of doors, is never used on the Continent. I wonder if this is because it does not stand the severe frosts of the mid-Europe winters. We dig up plants and put them into boxes, and force them under the frames of our greenhouse. For later eating, we also cover it in the garden, as everybody does, with pots surrounded by leaves. I do not think that the ordinary English tart is the best way of cooking Rhubarb, unless done in the following manner :—When young and tender, cut it up into pieces the length of a finger, and throw them into cold water, to prevent the ends drying, while a syrup is prepared in an earthenware saucepan with sugar, a few of the rough pieces of the Rhubarb, and a small pinch of ginger. Throw the cold water away from the Rhubarb, strain the syrup, boil it up, and pour it over the pieces. Stew it for a very short time till tender without mashing it up. It looks better if the pieces are slightly arranged in the dish. If anything iron touches the Rhubarb or the syrup, they turn purple and look horrid. Properly cooked, Rhubarb should be of a pretty pink or green colour. Many doctors forbid it. I think it probably may be unwholesome for meat-eating people; this is the case with so many fruits and vegetables.

All my tarts throughout the year are made with the crust baked apart, and the fruit, stewed previously, juicy and cold. Shortly before dinner make the paste called in 'Dainty Dishes' 'crisp paste' for tarts; crumple up kitchen paper into a mound the height you wish your crust to be, place it in the pie-dish—the round-shaped dishes are the prettiest—cover this with a clean sheet of buttered paper, lay your paste over this, bake in the usual way. When done, lift off the crust, take out the paper, pour in the fruit (which can be iced, if desired), put a little raw white of egg round the rim of the pie-dish, and replace the crust. In this way an orange or a strawberry tart can be made without cooking the fruit at all, except in the usual compote way of pouring boiling syrup over it.

Towards the end of February is the best time for making Orange Marmalade (see 'Dainty Dishes'), as the Seville oranges in London are then at their best. In all cases when old jam pots, glasses, &c., are used for preserving, it is very desirable to wash them thoroughly in clean water, avoiding all soda or soap, and, when dry, powder them with a little sulphur and wipe clean. If soda is used in anything connected with fruit, it has an injurious chemical action.

The following are the translations of a few careful receipts which were written out by a very excellent French *chef*. They belong to so entirely different a *cuisine* from our ordinary modest and economical receipts, that I think they may be not without interest to some people. It is worth noting how, when a really good French cook wishes to instruct, he is careful to go into the minutest details.

Pot au feu Soup.—Proportions: 15 lbs. of beef, 5½ lbs. of veal, 1 chicken, 2½ gallons of water, 3 fine carrots, 1 big turnip, 1 large onion, a bunch of parsley, half a head of celery, a parsnip, 2 cloves, and some salt.

Remove the fat and tie up the beef and the veal, putting them in a large saucepan ; fill the saucepan with cold water to within a little more than an inch from the brim, place the saucepan on the fire with the lid off, add some salt, and let it boil till the scum shows on the surface ; remove it with a skimmer. As soon as it seems inclined to boil over, add a few spoonfuls of cold water, so as to make the scum accumulate as much as possible. When at last it boils violently, drop in the vegetables ; remove the saucepan to one side of the fire, so that it shall boil only on one side ; put on the lid, and let it boil undisturbed, evenly and regularly. After two hours remove the veal. An hour later add the chicken, and, three hours after, strain the soup, without stirring it up, through a strainer on to a napkin stretched over a receptacle large enough to contain the soup. The soup may be skimmed before or after straining.

This stock does for making any kind of soup, Julienne, Brunoise, Croûte au pot, and for all purées of vegetables.

Consommé.—Consommé means the foundation of the soup ; this foundation ought always to be clear, lightly coloured, and, above all, strong.

Take about 2 lbs. of beef and veal, without fat, chop them up together, and put into a basin. Add half of the white of an egg, work the meats with a wooden spoon and a glass of water, continue to mix with about 1¼ gallon of good strong stock ; put the whole into a small saucepan with some carcases of birds (raw or cooked), a branch of celery, and put it to boil on the fire ; stir it when there with a wooden spoon, so that the meat shall not stick to the bottom. As soon as it bubbles, remove the saucepan to a very slow, very moderate, well-regulated fire for two hours. The stock, made in this way, ought to become a fine colour, and above all be very clear. Strain it through a napkin that has been previously rinsed in hot water.

Julienne Soup.—Ingredients : 3 fine carrots, 2 turnips, 2 small pieces of celery, 2 sprigs of parsley, 1 onion, the quarter of a large Savoy cabbage, the hearts of 2 lettuces, a bunch of sorrel, and a sprig of chervil.

Scrape each of the vegetables according to its requirements. The carrots are cut, in the thickest parts of them, in transverse sections, about two-thirds of an inch thick ; shape these into thin, even ribbons by turning the piece round and round till you reach the centre of the carrot, which is not used ; then cut these ribbons again into very fine shreds. Cut the turnips into squares ; divide them into oblong squares about two-thirds of an inch thick ; cut and make them into shreds like the carrots. Cut and shape the celery in the same way. Remove the hard sides of the cabbage, and slice it as fine as possible. Slice in the same way the lettuces, parsley, and onions. The similarity of the vegetables, as much with regard to their thickness as to their length, must be strictly preserved ; it is one of the distinguishing characteristics of this soup. Now put a lump of butter into a good saucepan, rather a large one and very thick at the bottom. Add the vegetables, all except the cabbage and the sorrel ; these must be scalded in boiling water apart. Place the other vegetables on a slow fire till they turn a fine yellow colour without being burnt ; that is the chief characteristic of the soup. As soon as they are done to a turn, add about 2 quarts of good stock or consommé, and a pinch of sugar. When it bubbles, remove to side of fire ; add the sorrel and cabbage, after drying them, through a strainer or sieve. The bubbles should only appear on one side. Skim, and, while on the fire, remove the grease as it forms. Let it boil for an hour, if the vegetables are tender ; if not, for longer.

Consommé aux Ailerons (*Wing-bone Soup*).—Cut up

FEBRUARY. 45

the whole of 3 or 4 carrots and 2 turnips into slices of about the thickness of a shilling. Cut in rounds of the same thickness, and shaped in the same column-shape, some cabbage-leaves—very white ones. This done, wet the carrots first with about 2 pints of stock (consommé). After it has boiled for an hour, add the turnips and cabbage. Let it boil quite gently by the side of the fire for a good hour, till the vegetables are quite cooked.

Separately take 12 or 15 wing-bones of chickens, basted and well trimmed ; let them soak during 1 or 2 hours in tepid water, drain and put them into a small saucepan, cover them with stock, and boil up. One hour is enough to cook them. Drain the wings, trim them very neatly, bone them, put them in the soup-tureen, add some fried crusts of bread of the same thickness as the vegetables, also a bunch of chervil and a pinch of sugar, and put all together into the soup-tureen. The boiling of all these vegetables must be done quite slowly, so as to prevent the stock being disturbed.

Gnocchi à la Creme.—Make a paste (pâte à choux) as follows :—Ingredients : 4½ oz. of flour, 4½ oz. of butter, 1½ pint of water, 3 whole eggs (4 if small), a pinch of salt and of sugar. Put the water, salt, and sugar in a small saucepan on the fire ; when it begins to boil, add the flour all at once. Stir quickly with a wooden spoon, and, when well mixed, put the saucepan on a slower fire ; let it dry for a few minutes, and when smooth mix in the eggs, one by one, till smooth and thick, sticking to the saucepan. If the paste seems a little too dry, add a little cream—2 or 3 spoonfuls. Add by degrees 3 or 4 spoonfuls of grated Parmesan cheese. Take a smaller saucepan of water with some salt in it. When the water is boiling, remove it to the edge of the fire. Then take two tablespoons, and fill one with the paste, flattening it with a knife warmed in warm water so as to form the paste into an oval shape ; warm the other spoon, and push it under the quenelle to remove it from the first spoon; then drop it into the boiling water. When all the quenelles are shaped in this way and thrown into the saucepan, put it on to the open fire, and let the quenelles poach for some minutes. As soon as they feel firm to the touch, remove the Gnocchi one by one with a strainer, and place them on a cloth till wanted. Make a Béchamel white sauce. Butter a soufflé-dish, place the quenelles round the bottom, in a single row one beside the other, sprinkle this first row with a little grated Parmesan, and add on the top another layer of Gnocchis, laid on alternately to the others. Hide the Gnocchis entirely with the sauce Béchamel, dust them over with a little grated Gruyère, sprinkle them lightly with some melted butter, and put them to bake in a slow oven till well browned without being burnt. Given about forty to forty-five minutes of baking, the Gnocchi should swell to twice their original size. Serve at once.

Béchamel Sauce.—Cut into little squares the half of a carrot and a small onion; take a small saucepan, put in a good bit of butter, add the vegetables, fry them lightly without letting them brown. This done, add a good tablespoonful of flour, and let the flour cook quite gently for several minutes on a moderate fire; be especially careful that it does not stick or get coloured, which would quite spoil its quality. This done, let it cool for a moment, then add little by little one pint and a half of boiling milk; work and stir the sauce without ceasing until it boils, remove to side of a slow fire, and let it cook for an hour. Strain the sauce through a flannel or muslin into a bain-marie, with a pinch of salt, and of grated nutmeg very little. Add a good bit of butter while working it with a small egg-whisk. The sauce should be very smooth, creamy, and of a good flavour; if by chance it is too thick, this can be remedied by adding a few spoonfuls of good, thick, and sweet cream.

Pâte à Ravioli.—Ingredients for the paste: 9 oz. of

flour, the yelks of 4 eggs, a pinch of salt, a little tepid water.

Put the flour on a marble slab, make a hole in the centre, add the yelks of the eggs and the salt, make a paste, not too solid ; when it is quite even, let it rest for an hour or two, and cover it with a cloth to prevent it from getting dry.

Preparation for Ravioli.—Forcemeat of chicken, or, failing this, one can use veal, if nice and white and tender. Ingredients : 4½ oz. of meat, 2¼ oz. of panade, ¼ oz. of fresh butter, 2 yelks of eggs, salt, and nutmeg.

Remove the sinews and fat carefully from the 4½ oz. of meat. Cut it into little squares, and pound well in a mortar. Add the panade little by little ; when mixed, add (only a little at a time) the butter when quite cooled and solid, salt, and nutmeg ; mix these ingredients thoroughly, giving to them as much consistency as possible. Now take some boiling salted water in a little saucepan, and test in it a little bit of the forcemeat the size of a walnut ; let it poach while well on the fire. If it is rather too firm, one can always add a spoonful of Béchamel or a little thick cream to moisten it.

Parboil in water 1 lb. of spinach, strain it on to a moistened sieve—the sieve must have been well wiped to ensure no water remaining in it. Pass the spinach through a fine wire sieve. This done, add to the forcemeat two or three dessertspoonfuls of spinach, as much grated Parmesan cheese, some salt, pepper, and nutmeg, and a pinch of sugar. Mix all these well together.

Now divide the paste into two equal parts ; roll one part out as thin as possible with a roller, keeping it square in shape ; slightly moisten the surface with a brush, put some of the forcemeat in a linen jelly-bag with a narrow tin socket at the bottom, and drop little balls of the forcemeat all over the surface, in straight lines about 2 in. to 2½ in. apart from each other. When the whole is covered, roll out the remainder of the paste to exactly the same size and shape, and place it carefully on the top of the other so as to fit exactly; press down round each Ravioli with a small shaping-tin, so as to stick the two layers of paste together; cut each Ravioli into rounds, and arrange them on a small lid of a saucepan floured over so that the paste should not stick to it.

Have ready a sauté-pan with some boiling water and salt in it. Five minutes before serving, drop the Ravioli into the water. As soon as they bubble up, remove to side of fire to finish cooking, strain them on to a sieve, from there into a sauté-pan (fairly large), powder them over with a little grated Parmesan, throw on the Béchamel sauce, which should be very smooth and not too thick; finally, add a good-sized piece of fresh butter and a chip of Paplika. Stir quite gently, so as not to spoil the Ravioli, and serve them in a casserole or in a crust of pastry.

Panade for the Forcemeat.—Put about a gill of water in a saucepan, with a bit of butter the size of a walnut. Put the saucepan on the fire; as soon as it boils up, add one tablespoonful and a half of flour; work the mixture at the side of the fire. This paste should be of a good, rather firm, consistency. Put it on to a rather flat dish. Butter the surface lightly, to keep it from drying, and put it to cool.

Mousse de Volaille.—Take off the fillets, &c., of three chickens, cut them up into little dice, pound them into a mortar, and reduce them to a paste; this done, pass them first through a wire sieve, and afterwards through a hair sieve or a quenelle sieve. Put this meat into a moderate-sized basin, and stand it in a cool place till wanted. Remove the legs from the carcases of the chickens (these may be used for something else), wash the carcases in cold water, and let them soak for an hour.

Now take 1½ lb. of lean veal, mince it up rather fine, put it in a saucepan which will hold about three quarts of liquid, add the half of one white of egg; mix all to-

gether, add two pints of water and nearly a quart of
stock, one chopped onion, one carrot, a little celery, and
the carcases ; boil up on a quick fire, stirring from time
to time with a wooden spoon. As soon as it boils,
remove to side of fire, so that it should only boil on one
side, and quite slowly, removing the grease from time to
time. Let it boil for three hours. Strain the foundation through a well-rinsed cloth. The above is the foundation for the Sauce Suprême.

   Sauce Supreme.—This sauce requires great care in
making. Put in a saucepan 4½ oz. of butter and 3½ oz.
of flour. Put the saucepan on a slow fire, and let the
flour cook lightly without getting coloured. As soon as
the flour is cooked, dilute it with the foundation of
chicken, little by little, stirring all the time with a wooden
spoon. So as to be able to spread it out without lumps,
keep it much lighter than ordinary sauces. Stir it all
the time till it boils ; when remove it to side of fire,
so that it should but just boil, and that only on one side.
Add two or three raw chopped mushrooms ; as the
butter and steam rise gently to the surface, remove
them, and let it cook for a good hour. Afterwards strain
your sauce through a fine cullender into a frying-pan,
more wide than deep. Put it on a hot fire, and stir
without stopping with a wooden spoon to prevent it
sticking ; this is an important point. Add one or two
gills of good sweet cream. As soon as the sauce sticks
to the spoon, that means it is ready. Strain it through
a muslin in a little bain-marie ; stand the sauce to heat
in a saucepan with hot water in it.

   Now put the half of a white of raw egg with the chicken,
mix them well together, add little by little some good
thick fresh cream, and make it blend as much as possible ;
add three or four spoonfuls of cold Sauce Suprême, and
about three gills of thick cream. Test it by dropping
a little of the mixture into water. It should be soft,
not too solid, and well-flavoured. Always try it before

putting in all the cream, or it might become too limp, which would spoil its quality.

Butter the inside of a round cylinder-shaped mould with a hole in the centre of it. Put the mould on the ice for a moment to harden the butter. Fill the mould with the mixture up to about an inch from the rim. Tap the mould gently on a napkin folded several times to equalise the mixture and to heap it together, to prevent the holes which might form themselves inside the sponge.

Put a little boiling water in a saucepan large enough to contain your mould, cover it with a lid, put it in a very slow oven, and let it poach for twenty-five to thirty minutes. See that the water in the saucepan does not boil, for which it is necessary from time to time to add a drop of cold water. Turn out the mould on to an entrée-dish ; trim with one or two truffles cooked in Madeira. Cover the mould lightly with a little of the Sauce Suprême, and put the rest of the sauce in a sauce-boat.

Mousse de Foies Gras à la Gelée.—Take a cylinder-shaped mould with an opening in the centre, put the mould for a second or two on to the ice. This done, pour into it a glassful of meat jelly, cold without being frozen. Turn your mould on the ice so as to line it— that is to say, to make the jelly adhere to the inside of the mould in a thin layer. Replace the mould on to the ice till wanted.

Put into a saucepan or a bain-marie well cleaned out about three gills of good cream, thick and sweet, stand it on the ice for several hours ; when about to use it, beat it up with an egg-whisk for seven or eight minutes, without taking it off the ice. It should rise and become firm, like the white of an egg. Put it to strain through a fine strainer.

Pound in a mortar a cooked foie-gras of from 1 lb. 3 oz. to 1 lb. 5 oz. in weight. Pass the foie-gras through a fine hair-sieve. Pound with the foie-gras $4\frac{3}{4}$ oz. of fresh butter, put it into a basin, and work it with an egg-whisk or wooden spoon, and absorb into it gradually three or four spoonfuls of Sauce Suprême, add a wineglassful of rather firm meat jelly. The jelly should be tepid and added quite gradually, working it in all the time, so as to make it quite smooth and soft. Season with salt, pepper, and nutmeg. If it is winter, work it in a warm place to prevent its turning, add the whipped cream quickly, and fill up the mould to the rim. Put the mould into a good-sized jar, and cover it well with pounded ice, and surround the mould with it. Leave it in the ice for two hours or more, according to the season, and especially in summer. When ready to serve, have a basin filled with hot water, dip the mould into it so as to be entirely covered, that it may come away clearly from the mould. Trim with pieces of jelly.

Nouilles Fraiches (*Fresh Nouille Paste*).—The paste for Nouille is made in exactly the same way as for Ravioli, only it must be kept much firmer. Roll it out very thin with a roller, and flour it well, so as not to stick. Cut some strips about 3 in. wide, put several of them one on the top of the other, and slice them with a knife into very narrow strips, $\frac{1}{10}$th of an inch wide or less. Spread them out on to a floured plate and cover them with a cloth. When ready to use them, throw them into a saucepan of boiling water with salt in it ; after boiling for two or three moments put the saucepan on the side of the fire, stirring a little. Let the paste cook for some minutes, then strain them well, put them back in the same saucepan, add a good bit of fresh butter (about 4½ oz. to 5 oz.), three or four spoonfuls of grated Parmesan, salt, nutmeg, a pinch of sugar, and one of Paplika, a little veal-stock or meat gravy, mix all well together, and serve in a casserole.

Céleris en branches, demi-glacés.—Pick and peel very carefully six or eight heads of celery, according to their size. Bleach them for fifteen or twenty minutes in boiling water, dip them in cold water to cool them strain them on to a cloth, cut them in two if they are large, fasten them—that is, re-form the Celery by tying it together with a little string at each end. Put them into a saucepan with an onion, one carrot, and a little bunch of herbs—parsley, thyme, bay. Fill up to the brim with half stock and half fat—dripping. Boil it up, then let it cook quite gently by the side of a slow fire or in the oven. They ought to be just done to a turn after three or four hours. Strain them on to a cloth, cut them to equal sizes, remove the outside leaves, if they are hard, serve in a silver casserole, and sauce them over with a good half-glaze or a good veal gravy a little thickened.

Lettuce can be treated in the same way.

MARCH

March 2nd.—Of all the low-growing quite hardy shrubs, especially in small gardens, nothing is more useful for picking and arranging with all kinds of flowers than the common Box. The kinds vary a little, some being larger-leaved than others, and the growth of some plants a little more graceful and branching. The most desirable kinds can quite easily be propagated by cuttings stuck into the ground in a shady place in spring. Its depressing characteristic for beginners is that Box is very slow-growing. Next to this in utility comes the common Barberry, or *Berberis vulgaris*, as we ought to call it, which is so well known to everybody now, as it is sold in the streets of London all through the winter months with its leaves dyed a dull-red colour. How this is managed I do not know ; I think it spoils the beautiful foliage by making it all of one tone. With us it turns brown in severe winters, with an occasional red leaf, but in damp soils it gets much redder. Berberis is one of those things much sown about by the birds, for they eat its pretty purple berries in quantities. The young seedlings which come up with us in the beds and shrubberies are easily moved when quite young, and can be put where they are wanted to grow. The best time to move them is wet weather in July or August. They are plants with a perfect growth and exceedingly well adapted to waste places in gardens and the fronts of shrubberies. Spring bulbs will grow through them, and their yellow flowers and dark leaves arrange admirably with the common Daffodil in glass vases. They can also take the place of the picked Arum leaves, which always droop before the flowers when put into water. Out of the little stove, all the winter through, I have long branches of the *Asparagus plumosa*. When cut, it is much more effective if trained up a light branching stick or feathery bamboo. This gives it support, and it is astonishing how long it lasts in water. It is extremely decorative, and will produce a most excellent effect if arranged in the above manner with only one bright flower added at its base.

March 8th.—To-day there has come up from the country one of the spring gems of the year, a large bunch of the lilac Daphne, the old *Mezereum*. It is a small shrub, not a quick grower, and most people, especially gardeners, are afraid to cut it. But if this is done bravely at the time of flowering, I think it only grows stronger and flowers better the following year, and you get the benefit of the exceedingly fragrant blossoms. For a few hours the whole of a London house smells sweeter for its presence. Its perfume is peculiar and not quite like anything else I know. The common lilac sort alone seems easy to grow—at least, the white one I have tried has died ; but then one must always say in gardening, ' That is probably my fault ; I must try again.' No garden, however small, ought to be without this plant. It likes peat and moisture, but is not particular.

Yesterday I paid a visit to the Horticultural College at Swanley, with its branch for women students. It immediately struck me as quite possible that a new employment may be developed for women of small means out of the modern increased taste for gardening. In many of the suburban districts the dulness of the small plots of ground in front of the houses is entirely owing to the want of education in the neighbouring nurserymen, whose first idea is always to plant Laurels or other coarse shrubs. The owners of such villas have little time to attend to the garden themselves. A lady gardener might easily undertake to lay out these plots in endless variety, supplying them throughout the year with flowers and plants suited to the aspect of each garden. The smaller the space, the more necessary the knowledge of what is likely to succeed. Another opening may be found in cases of larger villas, where single ladies might prefer a woman head-gardener with a man under her to do the rougher and heavier work. The maintaining of a garden and the tending of a greenhouse is work particularly suited to women of a certain age. A small greenhouse never can be productive of flowers for picking through the dull months without a great deal of thought, care, and knowledge. It seemed to me that the lady pupils at Swanley were too young to profit by the instruction. The parents who sent them there evidently looked upon it as an ordinary school. Surely eighteen or twenty is a better age than sixteen for a woman to know whether she really wishes to learn gardening professionally or not. The employment of women as gardeners is still very much in embryo, although two of the Swanley pupils have been accepted at Kew.

March 10th.—The Aucubas fruit well with us, and a branch of their bright shining green leaves and coral berries looks exceedingly well in a Japanese wedge and lasts a long time. We plant the male and female plants close together, but I am not sure that that is necessary.

March 12th.—Asparagus should be planted now, and, to save time, it is best to get two-year-old plants from France. I recommend Godfroy le Bœuf, Horticulteur, Argenteuil, près Paris. Dig the ground three spits deep —that is, the depth of three spades—and put in everything you can that is good : well-rotted farm-manure, the emptying of cesspools, butcher's offal, dead animals, anything to enrich the soil for a long time. Cover up, cut out one spit deep in trenches, and plant the Asparagus a good way apart in single crowns. They do best planted in single rows with other crops in between. The goodness of Asparagus depends on the summer top-growth, so, if the weather is dry, they must be watered or liquid-manured, and should never be cut down till late in the autumn.

It is a great mistake, when marking the nurseryman's seed list, to order the vegetable described as 'giant,' 'large,' 'perfection,' etc. Unless your soil is very strong such vegetables do not grow large, and they do grow tough and tasteless. This 'giant' cultivation has been brought about to win prizes at shows. Amongst the delicious vegetables that have been ruined by growing them too large are Brussels Sprouts. I consider those sold in the London shops are not worth eating, they are so coarse ; but one can get the seeds of old-fashioned small kinds. These are far sweeter, nicer, and prettier, either for putting into soup, for boiling and frying afterwards in butter, or for boiling quite plainly in the ordinary English way. They are also far more delicate for a purée, which is an excellent way of dressing them. If fried and put on buttered toast, they make a very nice second-course vegetable in winter.

Do other housekeepers ever wonder why we are condemned invariably to eat Whitings with their tails in their mouths and always skinned ? One of the reasons is that small Haddocks are constantly sold by fishmongers for the rarer Whiting ; and if skinned, they are not so easy to recognise. Try Whitings sometimes as they are eaten in Paris—lay them flat, not curled nor skinned, and cook them in a deep dish with butter or parsley. Squeeze lemon into them, and serve with brown bread and butter. They can also be fried in the usual way, only not curled. I think your male kind will approve of the change.

March 15th.—I find that this is the best time for sowing annuals that have to be sown in place. If sown later, they never do so well. Poppies, Love-in-the-Mist, Mignonette, Sweet Sultans, *Bartonia aurea*, etc. This latter is a very effective annual. It must be sown in a large clump and well thinned out, which is the secret of most annuals. Twice a year, about March 15th and September 15th, I sow together broadcast Love-in-the-Mist and *Gypsophila gracilis*. They seem to support each other, and fixing a day for the sowing prevents one from forgetting.

In the old convent gardens Calvary Clover was supposed not to grow unless sown on Good Friday. It is a curious little annual, with a blood-red spot on each leaf, and the seed-pod is surrounded by a case which pulls out, or rather unwinds, into a miniature crown of thorns. A friend has asked me what she should plant on the front of a lovely old house facing south. It now has on it at one end Ivy and on the other an old Wistaria. My first advice is take away the Ivy ; the place is too good for it, and it hides the beautiful old brickwork. An old Wistaria is quite lovely if part or all of it is dragged away from the house and trained over wooden posts, either in front of a window or a door, so as to form a kind of pergola. Until this is done, or it is grown as they do it in Japan—namely, as a standard, with its branches spread and supported all around, and you stand beneath it—you have no idea of the joy that is to be got out of a Wistaria, with its beautiful lilac blooms hanging from the bare and twisted branches above your head and the blue sky behind them. The whole effect is indeed different and very superior to that of seeing the blooms hanging straight and flat from branches nailed close to the wall. Unless it is protected from the north and east, it is of course more liable, in unfavourable springs, to have its blooms injured by late frosts. The plant itself, I believe, is absolutely hardy.

The creepers I recommended to plant on a south front are as follows :—

Magnolia grandiflora—the roots must be pulled about, not cut, and manured in the autumn for the first few years after planting, to make it grow quickly ; a Yellow Banksia, single if possible, but they are not easy to get ; an early yellow Dutch Honeysuckle ; a *Pyrus japonica ;* *Chimonanthus fragrans*, now called *Calycanthus præcox ;* a *Rêve d'Or* Rose ; a *La Marque* Rose (no house is perfect without one) ; a few Clematises, which in non-chalky soils must have chalk and lime or brick-rubbish put to their roots, not manure ; *Choisya ternata*, a low-growing shrub, wherever there is room between the other plants ; a *Maréchal Niel* Rose. *Forsythia suspensa*, *Jasminum nudiflorum, Clematis montana*, and late Dutch Honeysuckle will all do on the east and west sides of a house as well as on the south. Two other things that would grow on the south wall are *Bignonia radicans* and *Garrya elliptica*, a charming evergreen with fascinating catkins, which form in January. The male or pollen-bearing plant is the handsomest.

This list I actually made in the autumn, which is really the best time for planting ; but there is often so much to do then that planting is apt to get postponed, and rather than lose a whole year, spring planting is quite worth trying. In damp soils I really believe it answers best. In dry soils, or where a plant is likely to be robbed by the roots of neighbouring shrubs, or by old-established climbers, it is not a bad plan to sink in the ground an old tub or half-cask, or even an old tin footbath with the bottom knocked out. Then fill it with the best soil, and put in your plant ; it will benefit more in this way from watering in dry weather. There is nothing so disappointing as to lose a plant in spring, as that means the loss of a whole year.

Having given the above list, which is pretty well as large as any moderate-sized house would hold, I may as

well add some further names to choose from, all of which
are worth growing. *Magnolia purpurea, M. stellata*, and
M. conspicua may all be grown against walls, or planted
in sheltered situations as shrubs. Yellow Jasmine (not
nudiflorum) in favourable situations does well. *Cratægus
pyracantha lælandi* is the best of the Pyracanthuses—I
believe, an invaluable shrub. If well pruned, it berries
so brilliantly that where people only inhabit their houses
in late autumn it is perhaps one of the most satisfactory
plants that can be planted. I know one large red house
which is covered all round up to a certain height with
this plant, and the effect is very decorative, though to
have a house entirely covered with only one species of
plant is very dull from a gardener's point of view. Unless carefully cut back and pruned early in the winter,
it never flowers and berries well, but forms a dense mass
of dark-green leaves.

Cotoneasters, various, are useful much in the same
way, and, I think, endure better very dry situations.
Forsythia fortunei and other varieties. *Pyrus japonica*,
now called *Cydonia*, various shades (this is one of
the most precious and invaluable of the early flowering shrubs, and deserves the best places to be
found on warm walls). *Ceanothus grandiflorus (Gloire
de Versailles)* is the largest flowering variety, I believe,
and a pretty pale-blue colour, flowering in July, which
is always valuable. *C. cæruleus* is a beautiful dark-blue
colour ; it flowers earlier, and is not so hardy. *Cercis*,
or common Judas Tree, and *Buddleia globosa* both look
well on walls where there is room. *Vitis coignetiæ* is a
very handsome rapid grower, and covers quickly a barn,
a roof, or a dead tree. The claret-coloured Vine, with
its little bunches of black grapes, is very effective. The
grapes are used in France and Germany for darkening
the colour of wine. *Abelia rupestris*, a lovely little,
rather tender shrub, would grow admirably against low
greenhouse walls. Why are such spots generally left

quite empty by gardeners in large places ? The single
white McCartney Rose would do well in a similar situation, and for those who are in the country in June it
is well worth a place. *Aimée Vibert, Gloire des Rose-*
maines, and *Fallenberg* are delightful Roses for house or
pergola. Sweet Verbena (*Aloysia citriodora*)—Why, oh !
why, is this little shrub, which everyone is so fond of,
grown so little out of doors ? Practically, with a little
care, its roots are quite hardy, as in the very severe
winter of two years ago only one of mine, out of five
or six plants, was killed. It requires nothing but planting out late in May, watering, and not picking at first,
as the growth of the shoots makes the roots grow. It
may be picked in early autumn as much as you like,
but the summer growth should not be cut down to the
ground till the following spring. It is the easiest plant
possible to strike in spring, and there should be plants
of it planted in greenhouses, others grown in pots, and
brought on in stoves in spring ; but nearly all gardeners are satisfied with one little plant of it in a pot,
unless they are urged to increase it. Mock Orange
(*Philadelphus grandiflorus*) looks very well against a
warm wall in July, but should not be nailed in too tight.
Piptanthus nepalensis on a warm wall is admirable, but
rare ; I have only seen it once. *Schizophragma hydran-*
geoides is a good wall-plant. For those who can get it
to do on a half-shaded wall, is there any greater joy
to the south country gardener than the *Tropæolum*
speciosum ? There is an illustration of it in the
' English Flower Garden ' (Flame Nasturtium), where
it is depicted growing up strings. I think, however, it
looks better if grown over some light creeper, Jasmine
especially. It wants peat and moisture, and, above all,
it must be in a place the spade or fork never reaches,
as its thin little creeping white roots are easily disturbed,
and even mistaken for a weed and thrown away.

March 22nd.—Such a lovely spring day, in spite of its

cold wind ; it makes me long to be sixteen miles away in my little garden. Even here in London great pure white stately clouds are sailing over the blue. How lucky I am to be going away so soon ! I wish it gave half as much pleasure to the rest of the family as it does to me ; but one of the few advantages of old age is that we may be innocently selfish. A day like this makes me think of a little poem that appeared in the *Spectator* twenty years ago. It was written by a young clergyman's wife, who worked hard amidst the sordid blackness of a manufacturing town on the banks of the Tyne. My young friends will say, ' How morbid are Aunt T.'s quotations ! ' It is perhaps true ; but all bright, lovable, sympathetic souls had a touch of morbidness in the days that are gone, and these ' Notes ' have no meaning at all unless I try to give out in them the impressions received during forty years.

THE POET IN THE CITY.

The poet stood in the sombre town,
　　And spoke to his heart and said :
' O weary prison, devised by man !
　　O seasonless place and dead ! '
His heart was sad, for afar he heard
　　The sound of the spring's light tread.

He thought he saw in the pearly East
　　The pale March sun arise ;
The happy housewife beneath the thatch,
　　With hand above her eyes,
Look out to the cawing rooks, that built
　　So near to the quiet skies.

Out of the smoke and noise and sin
　　The heart of the poet cried :
' O God ! but to be Thy labourer there,
　　On the gentle hill's green side—
To leave the struggle of want and wealth,
　　And the battle of lust and pride ! '

He bent his ear, and he heard afar
　　The growing of tender things,
And his heart broke forth with the travailing earth
　　And shook with tremulous wings

Of sweet brown birds that had never known
The dirge of the city's sins.

And later, when all the earth was green
As the garden of the Lord—
Primroses opening their innocent faces,
Cowslips scattered abroad,
Blue-bells mimicking summer skies,
And the song of the thrush out-poured—

The changeless days were so sad to him
That the poet's heart beat strong,
And he struggled as some poor cagèd lark,
And he cried, ' How long—how long ?
I have missed a spring I can never see,
And the singing of birds is gone.'

But when the time of the roses came
And the nightingale hushed her lay,
The poet, still in the dusty town,
Went quietly on his way—
A poorer poet by just one spring,
And a richer man by one suffering.

I must begin to tell you about my old garden books, and how I first came to know about them, and then to collect them. Until lately I was absolutely ignorant of their existence, and had never seen an illustrated flower book of the last century. About fifteen years ago I was living in London, with apparently small prospect of ever living in the country again, or of ever possessing a garden of my own. When ' A Year in a Lancashire Garden,' by Henry A. Bright, was published in 1879, the book charmed me, and I thought it simple, unaffected, and original. I had not then seen Dr. Forbes Watson's delightful little book, ' Flowers and Gardens,' alluded to by Henry Bright. ' A Year in a Lancashire Garden ' has been much imitated, but, to my mind, none of the imitations possess the charm of the original. It is a fascinating chat about a garden to read in a town and dream over as I did. It revived in me, almost to longing, the old wish to have a garden, and I resolved, if it were ever realised, that every plant named by

Henry Bright I would get and try to grow. This I literally carried out when I came to live in Surrey. His joys have been my joys, and his failures have sometimes been mine too. In the 'Lancashire Garden' I was delighted to find a sentence which exactly expresses an opinion I had long held, but never met with in words before. As I agree with it even more strongly now than I did then, it is well I should quote it here, for the evil it denounces exists still, not only in England, but even more in several countries I have visited abroad : 'For the ordinary bedding-out of ordinary gardens I have a real contempt. It is at once gaudy and monotonous. A garden is left bare for eight months in the year, that for the four hottest months there shall be a blaze of the hottest colours. The same combination of the same flowers appear wherever you go—Calceolarias, Verbenas, and Zonal Pelargoniums, with a border of Pyrethrums or Cerastiums ; and that is about all. There is no thought and no imagination.' Yet twenty years ago this sort of garden was like Tory politics, or Church and State, and seemed to represent all that was considered respectable and desirable. I shall never forget the bombshell I seemed to fling into a family circle when I injudiciously and vehemently said that I hated parks and bedded-out gardens.

In Mr. Bright's book I first saw the mention of Curtis's 'Botanical Magazine,' and afterwards came across a few stray illustrations out of it. Many of these old gardening books were, I fear, cut up and sold for screens and scrap-books when there was no sale for the complete works. I was much struck with the beauty and delicacy of these hand-coloured flower plates, and so began my first interest in old flower books, which has led by degrees to my present collection. At one time I thought of giving some account of the Herbals and botanical works at the library of the South Kensington Natural History Museum, where there is a very fine collection, which begins with the early Herbals and includes botany and gardening books. This, however, proved to be too ambitious a work ; but a short account of my own books may be of some interest, for these, though far from being a large collection, extend over nearly three hundred years. The knowledge of the very existence of these beautifully illustrated Herbals and old gardening books is even now limited, though they are within reach of everybody at the Natural History Museum. Probably the reason why these books so suddenly fell out of all knowledge is owing to the letterpress, which is often in Latin, having, for one reason or another, become obsolete. No one now consults Herbals medically, or goes to old books for botanical instruction.

I will arrange the account of my books in chronological order, according to the date of their publication :—

1614. ' Hortus Floridus, by Rembertus Dodonæus and Carolus Clusius.' This is the earliest gardening book I possess. It was printed in Amsterdam, and is a real representation of cultivated garden flowers, not a Herbal in any sense. It has a frontispiece with the portraits of the two authors, which was common enough in the old Dutch books of the seventeenth and eighteenth centuries. Jupiter and Diana are represented on either side of the page, with wreaths of flowers hung along the top, and plants growing in pots placed at the bottom. The title of the book is in the centre. The plates are not coloured, but the flowers are very well drawn. There are two charming pictures of Dutch gardens surrounded by an arched wall with creepers, straight paths, and beds edged with box. In one a woman is gathering Tulips, dressed in the quaint fashion of the period, and a man is leaning over a wooden or stone railing looking at her. The number and variety of exotic flowers figured in the book is surprising. Besides all the ordinary spring bulbs which are now grown, there are Sunflowers, called Indian Golden Suns (Helianthuses, of course, all

came from America), Cannas, Marvels of Peru (called *Merveille d'Inde à diverses couleurs*), Nicotiana, etc. Insects are introduced on several of the plates, and in one or two instances mice are feeding on the bulbs which lie on the ground. The African *Agapanthus* is called *Narcissus marinus exoticus*. Both the Hellebores are here, and all the flowers are so well drawn as to be perfectly recognisable. The book is an oblong shape, bound in unstiffened white parchment. It is well preserved, though some Philistine lady of the last century has, with patient industry, pricked some of the flowers and insects all round for the purpose of taking the outlines for needlework. The book historically is certainly interesting. The text is in Latin, but even the unlearned reader is able to realise how horticulturally perfect may have been the gardens of Europe where Louis XIII. of France played as a child, and the number and richness of the flowers which our Prince Charles of Wales (his future brother-in-law) may have gazed at from his palace windows or enjoyed when gathered. This, perhaps, helped to nourish the great taste for art which Charles I., more than all our other kings, developed later in life.
1629. I have both the Parkinsons. The first published of the two has the following curious descriptive inscription written on a shield at the bottom of the title-page :—

PARADISI IN SOLE
PARADISUS TERRESTRIS.

A GARDEN OF ALL SORTS OF PLEASANT FLOWERS WHICH OUR
ENGLISH AYRE WILL PERMITT TO BE NOURSED UP :
WITH
A KITCHEN GARDEN OF ALL MANNER OF HERBES, RAVIES, AND FRUITES
FOR MEATE OR SAUSE USED WITH US,
AND
AN ORCHARD OF ALL SORTS OF FRUIT-BEARING TREES
AND SHRUBBS FIT FOR OUR LAND,
TOGETHER
WITH THE RIGHT ORDERINGE, PLANTING, AND PRESARVING
OF THEM, AND THEIR USES AND VERTUES
COLLECTED BY JOHN PARKINSON,
APOTHECARY OF LONDON

3

The picture on the title-page portrays the Garden of
Eden with Adam and Eve tending the flowers. The
outward edge is rimmed with spikes representing the
sun's rays. At the top is the eye of Providence, and
on each side a cherub symbolising the winds. In the
centre of the garden is the famous Vegetable Lamb,
supposed to be half animal and half plant. This curious
myth of the Middle Ages lingered on, and was actually
discussed as a matter of faith by scientific men towards
the end of the eighteenth century. The Borametz, or
Scythian Lamb, or Vegetable Lamb of Tartary, as
described by travellers, appears in both the frontispieces
of Parkinson's books. When studying the flower books
at the South Kensington Museum, I felt curious about
this tradition, which the Church of the Middle Ages
took up, making it a matter of faith that the Vegetable
Lamb grew in Paradise and was in some mysterious
way typical of the Christian Lamb. My brain was soon
cleared by finding at the Museum a book written by
Mr. Henry Lee, and published as late as 1887, giving an
excellent account of the whole tradition. This book,
called ' The Vegetable Lamb of Tartary,' contains several
pictures, reproduced from old books, of the lamb. Some
represent it growing, as Parkinson has it, on a stem,
from which it was supposed to eat the grass as far as it
could reach and then die. Another picture is of a tree
with large cocoons, which burst open and display a
lamb. The belief seems to have been that the lamb
was at the same time both a true animal and a living
plant. Mr. Lee carefully goes through the whole tradition, quoting all the known sources from which it arose.
According to him, about the middle of the seventeenth
century very little belief in the story of the Scythian
Lamb remained among men of letters, although it continued to be a subject of discussion and research for at
least a hundred and fifty years later. He sums up his
explanation with the following sentence :—' Tracing the

growth and transition of this story of the lamb-plant from a truthful rumour of a curious fact into a detailed history of an absurd fiction, I have no doubt whatever that it originated in early descriptions of the cotton plant, and the introduction of cotton from India into Western Asia and the adjoining parts of Eastern Europe.' All this seems so simple as explained by Mr. Lee, how the early travellers came back and said, ' In the far East there is a tree on which grows the most beautiful fine wool, and the natives weave their garments of it.' The Western mind could conceive of no wool except that of a lamb ; in this way the fiction grew, and was passed on from one writer to another. In a poem by Erasmus Darwin, published in 1781, of which more here-after, it is alluded to as a plant that grew on the steppes of the Volga in the following terms :—

> E'en round the Pole the flames of love aspire
> And icy bosoms feel the sacred fire.
> Cradled in snow and fanned by Arctic air,
> Shines, gentle Borametz, thy golden hair ;
> Rooted in earth, each cloven foot descends,
> And round and round her flexile neck she bends,
> Crops the grey coral moss and hoary thyme
> Or laps with rosy tongue the melting rime ;
> Eyes with mute tenderness her distant dam
> And seems to bleat—a ' vegetable lamb.'

Curiously enough, when in Norway last year, I came across an old wooden chair, and the back was carved in a way that seems to me conclusively to represent this old tradition. The design is a lamb enclosed in a circular cocoon, surrounded by branches and leaves. This chair I have now.

In the ' Nineteenth Century ' of January 1880, there appeared a very interesting article on Parkinson's ' Paradisi in Sole,' called ' Old-fashioned Gardening,' by Mrs. Kegan Paul. She describes the title-page, and says, ' The tree of knowledge, its fruit still unplucked by Adam, appears in the centre of the plate.' I thought we were told that Adam never did pick it, but received it from the hand of Eve ? But this is a trifling criticism on a useful and original article. Mrs. Paul makes a great many delightful quotations from Parkinson, and says that he is ' not content to deny that single flowers can be transformed into double " by the observation of the change of the Moone, the constellations or conjunctions of Planets or some other Starres or celestial bodies." Parkinson holds that such transformation could not be effected by the art of man.' In her condemnation of bedding-out and in her admiration of the old-fashioned English garden, read by the light of these sixteen years, Mrs. Paul's article is almost prophetic. The ' Paradisi in Sole ' is essentially a book describing a garden of ' pleasant flowers ' and with many interesting details about their cultivation. There is no allusion to medical matter at all, though, as usual, the botanist was a doctor. The woodcuts are rather coarser and rougher than in the Dutch book before described, but they are fairly drawn and generally like Nature. In a little book by Mrs. Ewing, called ' Mary's Meadow,' the author speaks a good deal of this book of Parkinson's, and in a footnote she alludes to the fact that the title is an absurd play upon words, after the fashion of Parkinson's day. Paradise is originally an Eastern word, meaning a park or pleasure ground. *Paradisi in sole Paradisus terrestris* means Park-in-son's Earthly Paradise !

1840. We now come to Parkinson's second book, ' The Theatre of Plants, or an Universal and Complete Herbal. Composed by John Parkinson, Apothecary of London and the King's Herbarist '—(' the King ' being Charles I., at the time just preceding his execution). The frontispiece is quite as curious in its way as the one in the ' Paradisi in Sole.' It has a portrait of old Parkinson in a skull-cap, looking very wise and holding a flower that looks like a Gaillardia. In the middle of the page is the title, with Adam on one side, dressed in the skin of a beast and holding a very fine spade, like the spades used in France to this day. This, I imagine, represents Toil, while Wisdom is personified on the other side by Solomon. He is clad in the conventional dress of the kings of the Middle Ages—a long cloak, a cape of ermine, a spiked crown, a sceptre, bare legs, and a pair of Roman sandals. At the top of the page is the eye of God with a Hebrew word written below it. At the four corners are four female figures representing Europe, Asia, Africa, and America. Europe, only, is in a chariot drawn by a pair of horses. Asia, riding a rhinoceros, wears a very short skirt and curious, pointed, curled shoes, not unlike the slippers still worn in Turkey, and a stiff headdress that resembles those used by women in the thirteenth century. Africa has no clothes, only a hat, and rides a zebra. America has a bow and arrow, and rides, also without clothes, a curious long-eared sheep. These ladies are surrounded by the vegetation supposed to be typical of each country. Among other plants, Asia has again the Vegetable Lamb before described, and Asia, not America, has the Indian Corn (Maize), which, I believe, is supposed to be as exclusively indigenous to America as Tobacco is. It appears to have been entirely unknown to the Old World, and has never been found with other corn in any of the old tombs, or alluded to in the classics. Its cultivation must have spread very quickly, and it is known all over the South of Europe as *Blé de Turquie* to this day. *Turquie* was the term used in the Middle Ages for describing anything foreign. When the early discoverers of Canada went up the St. Lawrence and reached the rapids, which still bear the name of *La Chine* rapids, they thought they had reached the China seas and joined the continent of Asia. It is, therefore, curious to note that Parkinson figures an American plant amongst the vegetation of Asia. The old Red Indian natives of North America used to sow the Maize with a fish on either side of the seed to propitiate their gods. No wonder it grew luxuriantly. Africa has in the foreground what appears to be a Stapelia, Aloes, and Date-palms. America has Cactuses, Pineapples, and the large Sunflower, being the vegetation rather of South than North America. As representing the geographical knowledge and art notions of the day, it is decidedly an interesting title-page. The woodcuts throughout the book are of the whole plant, root and all; but they are without much character, all about the same size, and less well-drawn than the flowers in the ' Paradisi.' The medical properties of the plants are described at length and with much detail, and are really curious. I wonder if our complicated prescriptions and remedies will some day sink to the level which the science of herbs has reached to-day. It would not be so very surprising if this should happen, considering how much the faith put in the modern drugs resembles the belief in cures as described in these old Herbals. At the Museum there is a great collection of Herbals of all nationalities, especially German. They are all much of the same kind, and illustrated in the same way as this one of Parkinson's, leading one to conjecture that the medical science throughout Europe at this time was about on a level.

1633. 'The Herbal or General Historie of Plants gathered by John Gerarde, of London, Master in Chirurgerie.' This edition of Gerarde's Herbal appeared between the publication of Parkinson's two books just described, but it is a reprint of an earlier edition, very much enlarged, and amended by Thomas Johnson, citizen and apothecary. The frontispiece is stately and serious. The title is on a shield in the middle, with a column on each side dividing it from two draped figures, Theophrastus on the left and Dioscorides on the right. Above these two figures, but divided from them by a line, are Ceres and Pomona, both fully draped. Ceres has a sheaf of wheat in her arms, and behind her grows the Indian corn. A ploughed field is spread out in the distance on her left. In the middle, between these figures, are growing plants and flowers and an orchard. At the bottom of the page is a fine portrait of Gerarde, holding a flower I do not recognise. He is dressed in the correct costume and ruffle of Charles I. On each side of him the spaces are filled by two vases of different shape and design, in which are various flowers arranged in a stiff and formal manner, typical of flower arrangements in that time and long after, as we see depicted by art in this and other countries. Nowhere on the page does there appear any representation of the Vegetable Lamb, nor can I find any reference to it in the text. On the other hand, however, there is an elaborate allusion to what Mr. Lee describes in his book on the Vegetable Lamb, before mentioned, as the companion superstition of the Barnacle Geese. Gerarde gives a most interesting and detailed account—too long, alas ! for me to quote—of having seen the barnacles and watched their development into tree-geese. He corroborates his own observation by quoting the like experience of others. He also states in all gravity that ' the shells wherein is bred the barnacle are taken up in a small island adjoining to Lancashire, half a mile from the mainland, called the Pile of Foulders.' Mr. Lee says : —' The growth and development of the story of " the Scythian Lamb " from the similarity of appearance of two really different objects may be best explained by comparing it with another natural-history myth which ran curiously parallel to it. I allude to the fable that Sir John Mandeville tells us he related to his Tartar acquaintances, viz., that of the " Barnacle Geese," which has never been surpassed as a specimen of ignorant credulity and persistent error.

' From the twelfth to the end of the seventeenth century it was implicitly and almost universally believed that in the western islands of Scotland certain geese, of which the nesting-places were never found, instead of being hatched from eggs, like other birds, were bred from " shell-fish " which grew on trees. Upon the shores where these geese abounded, pieces of timber and old trunks of trees covered with barnacles were often seen, which had been stranded by the sea. From between the partly opened shells of the barnacles protruded their plumose cirrhi, which in some degree resemble the feathers of a bird. Hence arose the belief that they contained real birds. The fishermen persuaded themselves that these birds within the shells were the geese whose origin they had been previously unable to discover, and that they were thus bred, instead of being hatched, like other birds, from eggs.' Mr. Lee states that the old botanist Gerarde had, in 1597, the audacity to assert that he had witnessed the transformation of the shell-fish into geese. What Gerarde states, as I read it, is that something like a bird fell out of the shell into the sea, ' where it gathereth feathers, and groweth to a fowle bigger than a mallard and lesser than a goose.' He distinctly says that if it fell on the ground it died.

The drawing of the plants throughout Gerarde's book is more delicate and finished than in Parkinson's.

1691. I have a little gardener's almanack of this date. My copy is the ' 8th edition, and has many useful additions.' This book is without illustrations except for a frontispiece of a young man and young woman admiring a garden through a doorway. The woman is attended by a page, who is holding a modern-looking sun-shade. This is curious, as umbrellas did not, I believe, come into general use till very much later.

1693. Evelyn publishes his translation of ' The Compleat Gard'ner, written by the famous Monsieur de la Quintinye, Chief Director of all the Gardens of the French King.' They must have been wonderful gardens, those of Louis XIV. ; and one of the most beautiful hand-coloured flower books in the library of the museum at South Kensington was executed by order of the king for

Madame de Montespan. This translation of Evelyn's has some interesting little illustrations of gardens, plans of beds, fruit-trees, pruning, &c. The frontispiece is a portrait of Evelyn in a hideous wig of the day.

1710. I have an English Herbal by William Salmon, doctor to Queen Anne. It contains a most fulsome dedication to the queen. The type of man who even in that century was capable of publishing such an effusion would be very likely, I think, to have caused the death of all Queen Anne's children, while quite convinced all the time that they died solely by the will of Almighty God. What a curious person that Queen Anne must have been, who allowed the great category of persecuting laws against the Catholics in Ireland to be framed in her reign; and whom Horace Walpole called ' Goody Anne, the wet-nurse of the Church ' ! The book is purely medical, and is supposed to be principally written for the use of doctors, but it describes flowering garden plants as well as the wild ones. It has a large, coarsely executed frontispiece, mostly torn out in my copy. The drawings of the plants show no artistic improvement over Parkinson's, but are much in the same style.

1739. ' New Improvements of Planting and Gardening, both Phylosophical and Practical, by Richard Bradley.' This is a small book with rather good copper-plates, and interesting as showing the researches and ideas of an intelligent man just previous to the illuminating of botany through the works of Linnæus, who in 1739 was only thirty-two. He knew that earthworms were hermaphrodites, but from a text of Scripture he was convinced that plants have their seeds in themselves, and that every plant contained in itself male and female powers. The common Aucuba, so long a puzzle to botanists, only received its green-leaved pollen-bearing mate from Japan towards the middle of this century. Before that it was only propagated by cuttings, and never bore any red berries. The gardening books of the last century are full of useful hints, as gardening was then practised and written about by men of the highest education ; and very often this was done solely for botanical and what they called ' philosophical ' reasons. Sometimes the childish earnestness of their ignorance concerning facts now known to every schoolchild accentuates the extraordinary advance and increased popularising of knowledge since that day.

1732. ' Hortus Elthamensis, à Johanne Jacobo Dillenio, M.D.' Two folio volumes published in London, and interesting as showing the general development of the improved power of illustrating. The plates are coloured by hand, and contain many figures of Cape Aloes, Geraniums, and other African plants, either depicted with their roots or as growing out of the ground. The text is in Latin.

1771. ' Uitgezochte Planten, by Christ. Jacob Trew, Georgius Dionysius Ehret, Joh. Jacob Haid.' The characteristic of this large folio is that it begins with very fine separate portraits of the three authors. One seems to have been the botanist, one the artist, and one the engraver. It was brought out at Amsterdam by subscription, as was so common with handsome books in those days. The book begins with a long list of subscribers. The flower-plates are extremely fine, very strongly coloured, and as fresh and bright as the day they were painted, each page being covered with a sheet of dark-grey thick hand-made paper, such as Turner loved to sketch upon. One of the things figured is the Japanese plant, *Bocconia cordata* (' Plumed Poppy,' Robinson calls it), which we have been in the habit of thinking a new plant in our gardens. Many of the plates are interesting and a few remarkable, and the botanical details of the flowers beautifully drawn, some natural size and some magnified.

1771. ' The Flora Londinensis, by William Curtis.' The first number was brought out by subscription on the above date. I have the two volumes of the first edition. It is the handsomest, the most artistic, and the best drawn of any English illustrated botanical books I have seen. I do not know who was the artist, but I imagine not Curtis himself. These plates have some of the qualities of Jacquin's drawings, of which more hereafter. How much they were in communication, a not uncommon custom of the time, I do not know. Curtis's first book was a translation of Linnæus's, with the title of ' An Introduction to the Knowledge of Insects.'

In 1773 Curtis was appointed lecturer of the Chelsea Garden. The plates of ' The Flora Londinensis ' are lovely large folio, and most delicately drawn and tinted. The text is in English, and is descriptive of the wild flowers and plants growing round London. No doubt the book was suggested to Curtis by Vaillant's ' Catalogue of Plants in the Environs of Paris.' It retains strongly the Herbal character, and the medical details of diseases are weird and extraordinary. The decision and particularity of the assurance that every disease to which flesh is heir will be relieved by the use of certain plants are quite surprising. The place where the innocent little wild plants are picked is always named, and it is pathetic to think of the growth of the city, and how the places mentioned are now densely covered with buildings and streets. The second edition, in five or six volumes, finished by Dr. Hooker, is far the more valuable and complete. Curtis began his ' Botanical Magazine, or Flower Garden Displayed ' in 1778. I have the first sixty-seven volumes of this lovely and best known of all the Old English gardening publications. It is purely horticultural. Every alternate page is an illustration, with the letterpress on the opposite side describing the nature of the plant, the country from which it comes, and its cultivation here. With the same truthful accuracy with which he tells the home of the wild plant, he names the nurseryman or amateur who has flowered the exotic.

The best drawings by far are in the early numbers, and were executed by Sowerby. The two who succeeded him were Sydenham Edwards and Dr. Hooker. Spode, the man who perfected the process of mixing bone-dust into the paste used for china in the early part of this century, used these illustrations a good deal for his pretty china dinner and dessert services, with the names of the flowers or plants marked at the back of the dishes.

1791. ' The Loves of the Plants, in two parts : The Botanic Garden and the Economy of Vegetation. A Poem by Erasmus Darwin,' seems to me one of the real curiosities of literature. It is unique, so far as I know, in its sincere desire to clothe the latest science in the garb of the Muse. The frontispiece, by Fuseli, is a drawing most characteristic of that artist and full of all his affectations. *Flora*, attired by the elements, is a striking example of the fashion and bad taste of the day, and yet it is full of ingenuity and skill in drawing. This frontispiece is well worth, by itself, the price I gave for the whole volume. Another print in the book, by the same artist, is called ' The Fertilisation of Egypt,' meaning, of course, the rising of the Nile. A huge unclothed man with a dog's head is praying to the star Sirius. A note explains this by saying ' the Abbé La Pluche observes that as Sirius, or the Dog-star, rose at the time of the commencement of the flood, its rising was watched by the Astronomers and notice given of the approach of the inundation by hanging the figure of Anubis, which was that of a man with a dog's head, in all the Egyptian temples.' Erasmus Darwin's mind was evidently fascinated, as was common with all the scientific men of the day, by the fertilisation of plants. In one of his notes he says, ' The vegetable passion of love is agreeably seen in the flower of the *Parnassia* (Grass of Parnassus), in which the males alternately approach and recede from the female ' (a practice not wholly unknown to many beside the innocent *Parnassia*), ' and in the flower of

Nigella.' We call it now Love-in-the-Mist, 'in which
the tall females bend down to their dwarf husbands ' (a
picture sometimes seen in modern drawing-rooms).
Darwin goes on to say, ' I was surprised this morning
to observe, amongst Sir Brooke Boothby's valuable collection of plants at Ashbourne, the manifest adultery of
several females of the plant *Collinsonia*, who had bent
themselves into contact with the males of the same plant
in their vicinity, neglectful of their own.' The plate and
note of *Gloriosa superba* I have mentioned elsewhere;
As an outcome of the extraordinary effect of Linnæus's
work on thinking minds at the end of the last century,
the book is of great interest, though we should not call
it poetry in the modern sense. Erasmus Darwin was
the grandfather of our great Darwin, who did for the
middle of this century so much more than even Linnæus
did for the end of the last.

1778. ' Miscellanea Austriaca, by Nicolai Josephi Jacquin.' This is the earliest Jacquin book that I have.
It is in two small volumes of note-books, with all the
illustrations at the end. The text is in Latin ; but this
is of no consequence, as Jacquin's books are all botanical,
not horticultural, and their botany is obsolete. This
remarkable man, Nicholas Joseph Jacquin, whose industry must have been untiring, was born at Leyden in
1727, and educated there at the University for the medical
profession. This meant in those days the highest botanical education which could be obtained. He went to
Vienna, at the suggestion of a friend, to practise medicine,
but when there his great botanical knowledge brought
him to the notice of Francis I. This emperor seems to
have been a great patron of botany and gardening, the
fashionable combination of the day. He sent Jacquin
to the West Indies for six years to collect plants for the
Schönbrunn Gardens, paying his expenses. Jacquin did
not die till 1817, leaving an unfinished work, ' Eclogæ
Plantarum Rariorum,' the only one of Jacquin's books

that has a German as well as a Latin text. The second volume was not published till 1844, by Edouardus Fenzl, long after Jacquin's death. The colour and painting are very inferior to Jacquin's work. Towards the end of the last century, in the midst of wars and revolutions, the crumbling of old methods of government and the change of social customs, an extraordinary band of able men all over Europe were quietly working in concert and with constant communication. Their object was to increase the knowledge of the science of botany by reproducing, with the greatest botanical exactness of detail, the plants imported from all parts of the world as they flowered in Europe for the first time in the various greenhouses and stoves. It is remarkable that the books of this period, even of different countries, very rarely illustrate the same plants. The botanical curiosity, the feeling of something new, rare, and not fully understood, which is such an incentive to the human mind, has gone for ever as far as this kind of simple botany is concerned. Of these highly gifted men, who worked on lines which can no more be repeated than the missals of the sixteenth century in Italy, Jacquin, no doubt, was the most artistically interesting. No one who has not seen his works can realise the beauty, the delicacy, the truth, the detail to which flower-painting can be brought. None of the other flower-painters that I know show anything like the same talent of throwing the flower on to the paper with endless variety, and of adapting the design to the size and growth of the particular plant. This result seems produced by his botanical exactness, and not, apparently, by any intention to make a beautiful picture. No two pages are ever filled in the same way. This does away entirely with the ordinary wearisome monotony of turning over drawings one after the other, with the flower right in the middle of the page. His books fetch a considerable price, and are difficult to procure. The one I sometimes see in English catalogues is in my possession,

five volumes of ' Collectanea ad Botanicam Chemiam et
Historiam naturalem, 1786.' My copy was a surplus
one at the British Museum, of which it bears the stamp
and date of sale, 1831. The plates maintain their usual
excellence and are nearly all coloured with a brilliancy
that has not suffered at all from time. Some are of wild
flowers, mosses, Lycopodiums, insects, and serpents. All
Jacquin's drawings stand out wonderfully on the paper,
but there is no shading, except that the modelling is
indicated by a stronger tone of the same colour ; and
the relief and value, without any tinting of the background, are most effective. In the case of the bushy
little Alpines the plant is spread out like seaweed and
the root drawn, which gives the whole growth and proportion of the plant.

1793. ' Oxalis Monographia ' is an exquisite study
of about a hundred Oxalises. Nearly all the plates are
coloured. Most of these delicate little plants with their
bulbous roots come from the Cape of Good Hope. Jacquin seems to have had a peculiar affection for them,
as, besides this monograph, he constantly figures them
in his miscellaneous works. I have often tried to procure his book on Stapelias, also a large family of Cape
plants rather like small Cactuses, but have never been
able to do so, and have only seen it at the Museum.

1797–1804. ' Plantarum Rariorum Horti Cæsarei
Schoenbrunnensis.' These four superb folios, containing
five hundred spotless plates by Jacquin, represent some
of his very finest work. The plates are all coloured, in a
much stronger and more finished way than in his other
books. Some of the plates are folded and larger than
the book, and others extend across the·whole width of
the book. As an example of the richness of the plates I
will describe one taken at random, which he calls *Vitis
vulpina*. The shoot of the vine starts from a short piece
of stronger branch at the very top of the page, and
curves to the bottom, turning up at the end with young

leaves and tendrils. This young shoot has two bunches
of the flower as it appears in spring. Quite at the top,
on the right, is a detached autumn leaf turning red, and
drawn from the back with every vein showing. Half-
way down, on the left, is a bunch of ripe purple grapes ;
with one pip, drawn life-size, at the side. Below this is
a single flower, highly magnified, with a drawing apart
showing pistil and stamen. There are ten life-sized
leaves on the branch, and the whole is contained on an
unfolded plate. A short botanical description of each
plant is added in Latin. The hand-made paper on
which these plates are printed puts to shame all that
we now produce. Many of the plants are named differently from what they are now. To those who have
never seen Jacquin's works these volumes are an absolute
revelation. At the same time his genius will always
appeal more to the artistic than to the scientific mind,
although in the biographical notices of him that I have
seen he is only mentioned as a doctor and a botanist.
At the Natural History Museum is a large and much-
valued collection of his letters and original drawings.

1794. ' Thirty-eight Plates with explanations, intended
to illustrate Linnæus' system of vegetables, and particularly adapted to the letters on the elements of Botany.
By Thomas Martin, Regius Professor of Botany in the
University of Cambridge.' These plates are beautifully
drawn, and exemplify very well the careful draughtsmanship of a botanist of the day. They are most faithfully
hand coloured, and are only inferior to the best from a
little want of gradation.

1794. I have the ' Life of Sir Charles Linnæus, by
D. H. Stoever, translated from the original German by
Joseph Trapp.' It is, I believe, the only biography of
him ever written. To this is added a copious list of his
works and a biographical sketch of his son, whose life
is an interesting example of talents shared by a father
and son. The son, who died unmarried at the early

age of forty-one, seems to have been a brilliant and
much-loved individual. Trapp dedicates his translation
to the Linnæan Society of London. It contains a portrait of the elder Linnæus, a cheerful, bright, up-looking
profile, with the curly wig of the day, and a large branch
stuck in his buttonhole, as was not uncommon in the
portraits of botanists. He was born in 1707, was the
son of a Swedish minister, and the grandson of a peasant.
His industry and energy must have been exceptional,
and he chose truth as his guide. His first book was the
' Flora of Lapland,' which was perhaps the reason why
that little Northern flower, Linnea borealis, is the plant
that has received his great name. He married at
twenty-seven, and his father-in-law seems to have put
small faith in his botany, and advised him to apply
himself more exclusively to the theoretical and practical
study of physic. After his marriage he made money as
a doctor in Stockholm, and it is not otherwise than
interesting to know that when attacked with very
severe gout at forty-three, and the doctors who attended
him began to despair of his recovery, he cured himself by
eating nothing but Strawberries for a time. Afterwards
he kept the gout entirely in check by taking a Strawberry
cure every summer. In several ways the book gives an
interesting picture of life in the last century. Linnæus's
books are characterised by religious sentiment, nevertheless they had the misfortune of being considered at
Rome as heretical and materialistic productions. In
1758 they were inserted in the catalogue of forbidden
books ; no one durst either print or sell them under
pain of having every copy confiscated or publicly burnt.
This proceeding was implicitly condemned during the
papacy of the excellent and truly enlightened Ganga-
nelli, Pope Clement XIV. Linnæus himself mentions
this occurrence in a letter to the Chevalier Thunberg
in the following terms :—' The Pope, who fifteen years ago
ordered those of my works that should be imported into

his dominions to be burnt, has dismissed the Professor of Botany who did not understand my system, and put another in his place, who is to give public lectures according to my method and theory.'

1797. ' The Botanist's Repository, by H. Andrews.' This is a rare book, I believe, and ought to be in ten quarto volumes. I have only the first eight. It contains coloured engravings only of new and rare plants, many of which cannot, I think, have flowered in England, as there are several Proteas, which are exceedingly difficult of cultivation under glass. Andrews' great fondness for plants from the Cape of Good Hope makes one almost think he must have been there—Gladioli, Ixias, and curious Cape Pelargoniums, which are the parents of all our greenhouse varieties. On the bottom of the title-page is a charming little drawing of that humble plant the Linnea borealis (' Twin Flower,' Mr. Robinson calls it), which I have never yet been lucky enough to flower. The design represents two little flowering branches raised on either side like two arms. I feel much drawn to the man Andrews, who so skilfully placed it there, just a hundred years ago, to do honour to his great master. Andrews' other book is ' The Heathery, or a Monograph of the Genus Erica.' Again I have only the small edition published in 1804. The folio one is very scarce. This is a pretty, interesting book, with moderately well-drawn plates, coloured by hand. The Heaths are such a large family, and nearly all apparently come from the Cape of Good Hope. I cannot understand why people who have several greenhouses should not grow more of these charming plants. They require a certain amount of special treatment, a very cool house and plenty of air. It seems such a pity that private gardeners only care to grow the few plants which they can exhibit for competition—markedly, just now, Orchids and Chrysanthemums. These Cape Heaths look lovely picked and wedged, or growing in the greenhouse, and, I should imagine, would do espe-cially well in houses by the sea. On the frontispiece of his book Andrews has a quaint picture of a green-house for growing his Heaths.

Towards the end of the year I will tell you about those of my books which belong to this century.

APRIL

Whims of the weather—Spring flowers—The herbaceous nursery—
Love for the garden—A light sprayer—Homely French receipts
—French gardening—The late frosts.

April 2nd.—We came down to our little Surrey garden,
only sixteen miles from London, for good yesterday ; and
though the wind be ever so cold and the skies ever so
grey, I yet feel that that which makes going to London
worth while is the joy of coming back again. The
ceaseless interest of a garden of this sort is in the variety,
not only of the plants, but in the actual growth caused
by the different seasons. This year the winter has been
very mild, and dry too, which is unusual—and then came
a very wet March, such as I do not remember since we
have lived in Surrey, these fourteen years. It is really
amusing to watch all that happens consequent on these
whims of the weather ; the early and late, the wet and
the dry, all making immense difference in the plants.
Some are successful one year, and some another.

Nothing is more charming just now than the Forsythias. They are absolutely hardy, but they flower
best on walls, even a north one, as the birds are extremely
fond of the buds and can get at them much better when
the plant is grown as a bush. The birds always seem to
be extraordinarily destructive in this garden ; but I see
that most gardeners, in their books, make the same
complaint, and rather apologise to the common-sense
of their readers for cherishing and feeding instead of
destroying them. In my garden I hang up on the

trees, the pump, or shaded railings, little boxes with
part of one side cut out for the birds to build in, and
with lids that lift up for me to have the pleasure of
looking at them. The fact is birds do quite as much
good as harm, though the harm is the more apparent ;
and who would have a garden without song ?

The Crown Imperials are in full flower. They, like
many other bulbs in this light soil, reproduce themselves
so quickly that they want to be constantly lifted, the
small bulbs taken away and put in a nursery (if you
wish to increase your stock), and the large ones replaced,
in a good bed of manure, where you want them to flower
the following year. It is best, if possible, to do this in
June, when the leaves have died down, but not quite
disappeared so that the place is lost ; one can, however, always find them in the autumn by their strong
smell when the earth is moved beside them.

The orange Crown Imperials do best here, so, of
course, I feel proudest of the pale yellow. Both colours
are unusually good this year. In my youth they were
rather sniffed at and called a cottage plant. I wonder
if anyone who thought them vulgar ever took the trouble
to pick off one of the down-hanging bells and turn it
up to see the six drops of clear water in the six white
cups with black rims ? I know nothing prettier or
more curious amongst flowers than this. The lovely
little *Omphalodes verna* ('Blue-eyed Mary,' Mr. Robinson
calls it) is in flower under my trees. The soil is too dry
for it to flourish very successfully, and yet it is always
worth growing everywhere. Next year I shall try lifting
it in March and putting it into pots. The great thing
is to remember that it divides and propagates much
better in early spring than in autumn. The graceful,
pale grey anemone *Robinsoniana* is doing better this
year. Now that it has taken hold, I hope it may spread.

All the early tulips and some of the later are out ;
what delicious things they are ! None are better than

Gesneriana greigi and *sylvestris*. The beautiful Parrot Tulips will come later. *Ornithogalum nutans* is a weed most people dread to get into their borders, and not unnaturally ; but if put in a place where spreading does no harm, or planted in grass, where it does not flourish very much, it is a bulb well worth growing. It blooms better if divided every two or three years. The flowers are very lovely when cut, and, like all their tribe, they last well in water, looking most refined and uncommon, and are especially good to send to London. I do not make many remarks here on the lovely family of spring bulbs —Tulips, Scillas, Hyacinths, Daffodils, and Narcisses— for the same reason that I passed casually over the forced ones in February. We can all grow these easily enough by marking the catalogue and paying the bill. Anybody who does not understand their cultivation will find every detail on the subject in the older gardening books, as I have stated before. Of all the Dutch nurserymen from whom I have bought bulbs, J. J. Thoolen at Overveen, near Haarlem, is the cheapest, though I do not say that he is better or worse than any other. In my experience, all the finer kinds of bulbs are better for taking up in June or July, well dried in the sun, and planted again in September. When they are planted in grass they must, of course, be left alone to take their chance. Nothing can be more delightful than the spring bulbs. I grow them in every way I can—in pots, in beds, in borders, and in the grass.

Besides the Bulbs, the Arums, and the Azaleas, I have in the little greenhouse next the drawing-room several very pretty *Primula sieboldii :* they remain in the frames in pots during the summer, to die down entirely, and are re-potted in the autumn. They are hardy, and will grow out of doors, but the blooms do not then reach to such perfection. There is a large box filled with the last of the Neapolitan Violets and a pan of *Saxifraga wallacei*, one of the most effective of the

smaller Saxifrages. I never succeeded with it out of
doors till I divided it in June, planting it in the shade,
and in October I replaced it in the sunny bed for spring
flowering. In that way it can be increased to any
amount. This treatment I pursue with many plants :
—*Heuchera sanguinea*, one of the most precious of the
Canadian flowers, and the best worth cultivating, especially in small gardens. The pretty *Saxifraga granulata
flore pleno* disappeared year after year till treated more
or less in this way. In June, when the leaves die down,
the little bulblets are taken up and planted in groups in
a shady place. They make their leaves in October,
when it is easy to move them back into the border or
on to the rockery where they are to flower. The double
flower is of a very pure white, and its long stalk adapts
it well for glass vases and table decoration. The large
sweet-smelling double white Rocket, which I mentioned
before as growing so well in the damp Hertfordshire
garden, defeated me altogether for some years ; it made
a fair growth of leaves, but never flowered. Now it
succeeds perfectly. After flowering, we break it up,
put it into a shady place, and replant it in the borders
in the autumn. All this sounds very troublesome, but
it is really not so at all, as it is so quickly done. The
only trouble is remembering when to do the things ;
but that soon comes with practice, and the time of
year always recalls what was done the year before to
the true gardener. Everybody recognises this treatment
as necessary for violets, double and single—which,
indeed, do not flower well without it. The invaluable
Imantophyllums, which began to flower in the warm
greenhouse in January, are doing so still : so are the
Arums, which people insist on calling ' Lilies.' They
are not lilies at all, but belong to the same family as
the ' Lords and Ladies ' and ' Cuckoo Pint ' of our
hedges. The large greenhouse Arums come from the
Cape, where they are an absolute weed, appearing

88 POT-POURRI FROM A SURREY GARDEN.

wherever the ground is disturbed or turned up. They are there called Pig Lilies, perhaps because they feed the pigs on the roots. In the damp places, I am told, they are magnificent, growing finer and larger than they ever do in pots in England ; at the same time, when they come up in dry and heathy places, they are perfect miniature plants with delicate little flowers like shells. Arums in pots require lots of water while growing and flowering, and are better for a saucer to hold it.

A beautiful crimson Amaryllis, which I brought back from Guernsey some years ago, is in flower. It has never flowered before ; but we understand so much better than we did the drying and ripening in the sun of all the Cape bulbs, and this makes the whole difference to their flowering.

April 3rd.—This is the time of year when we make up our nursery, which I consider one of the most important gardening acts of the whole year, and one most fruitful in results. We take up, from wherever they happen to have been left last autumn, herbaceous Phloxes, early outdoor Chrysanthemums, and Michaelmas Daisies. These are broken up into small pieces, according to the number of plants that are likely to be wanted in the borders or to give away, and planted in rows in a half-shady corner of the kitchen garden. Here they are left to grow and increase till some wet day in July, when they are planted in bold masses where they are to flower. They really move better in dry weather than in wet, and I say a wet day merely because it reduces the trouble of watering, which is all the attention they require. They fill up bare places and holes in the borders, and flower as they never did with us in the old days when they were left alone. This treatment especially suits the Phloxes, which is curious, as they are moved when just coming into flower. The rows in the spring must be labelled with the names and colours, as the different hues of the flowers war with each other if promiscuously massed. The Michaelmas Daisies flower earlier in this way than when left to starve in a dry border or shrubbery, but one can always leave some in unfavourable places to flower late.

April 4th.—All the Linums and Linarias (*see* Mr. Robinson's book) are useful for house and table decoration, and are very suitable for small gardens. The common blue Flax is a lovely thing ; so is the white French Willow-weed (*Epilobium*), which is most useful, and flowers earlier in the year than the common lilac one.

As a single plant, for beauty of growth and foliage there are few things as lovely as the common Hemp plant (*Cannabis sativa*). It is an annual, easily grown in April in a pot or box, and planted out.

In gardening, as in most things, it is thought that is really required, and that wonderful thing which is called ' a blind god '—love. But blind love is mere passion. Real love in every form, even towards animals and plants, is watchful and ever seeing, never missing for a moment what is for the good and the advantage of the beloved. In walking round and round the garden, with a practised eye one soon sees when a plant is getting on well or the contrary. When a plant is doing badly, it means the conditions are unfavourable, and it is then our duty to find out why. In my garden the usual cause of failure is dryness, and many and many a plant has been saved, since I understood this, by a timely mulching or a good can of water. When things are coming into flower, especially early Alpines, Gentians, etc., it is quite safe to water, even in cold weather, early in the year. Do they not flourish where the ice-water drips upon them from the first melting of the snows under the spring sun ? Early spring plants do badly in our soil ; but were I there, to watch and to water just at the right time, I feel sure they would look more flourishing.

A most beautiful light sprayer for watering small plants is easily made in the following way :—Take a piece of sheet zinc five or six inches long and four or five inches wide. Cut a piece half an inch wide on each side of the zinc to within an inch of the middle, so making a little band attached to the main piece, and fold this tightly round the spout of the watering-pot ; bend the zinc sprayer upwards in the middle in a way to enable the water from the pot to flow over it in a continuous sheet.

Sorrel is a vegetable seldom grown in English gar-. dens, and still seldomer properly dressed by English cooks, and yet it is excellent, either cut up in the white soup called ' Bonne femme,' or dressed like Spinach, or purée'd as thin as a thick sauce. With veal, cooked in all ways, it is especially good. When the summer gets on and it is old, it is desirable to add a little Lettuce with it to soften it, as it gets too sour. It is one of those vegetables never quite so good in towns, as it is best freshly picked, and if faded should be revived in water before cooking. The receipts for cooking it in ' Dainty Dishes ' are quite right.

For those who keep cows, or who can have plenty of good fresh cream, the following, I think, will be found a really excellent pudding :—

Creme Brulée.—Boil one pint of cream for one minute, pour it on the yelks of four very fresh eggs well beaten, then put it again on the fire and let it just come to the boil. Pour it into the dish in which it is to be served, and let it get cold. Strew a thick crust of powdered sugar over it, put it in a slow oven for ten minutes, then brown it with a salamander, and serve it cold.

April 5th.—We started to-day to spend a week in a French country house, sleeping one night on our way at beautiful Chartres, which, as I am not writing a guide-book, I shall not describe. The weather was bitterly

cold; and when we humbly asked at the hotel for
some hot water, the answer we got was 'On n'échauffe
plus.' The French submit more meekly than we do
to this kind of regulation, which is curious, as they are
so much more sensible, as a rule, than we are in most of
the details of life. I was interested to see in the small
court of the hotel a quantity of most flourishing Hepat-
icas. These flowers, Mr. Bright tells us, defeated all
his efforts in his Lancashire garden. I have tried them
in various aspects, but they make a sorry show with
me in Surrey. In this little back-yard they shone in the
sunshine, pink and blue, double and single. I suppose
the secret is that they do not mind cold, but they want
sun. I wonder if anyone is very successful with them
in England? How I remember them, in the days of
my youth, pushing through the dead leaves in the little
oak woods in the valleys up the country behind Nice,
then, as now, 'Le pays du Soleil,' but probably long
since all changed into villas and gardens instead of
woods and fields.

A French country house! How different it all is!
In some ways we manage best, in others they do. This
was rather a cosmopolitan than a typically French house,
and yet in a country how traditions linger and customs
cling! We saw and did many interesting things, thanks
to the cordial hospitality and kindness of our host and
hostess. I, however, will only allude to certain domestic
details which I learnt during my stay, and which may
instruct you as they did me. What interested me much
from a housekeeping point of view was, not only the
excellence of the cooking, as that now can be seen elsewhere, but the management of the kitchen. It seems a
small thing to state as an example, but I was told that
no French housekeeper who at all respects herself would
ever allow lard to come into her house. Everything is
fried in what they call *graisse*, and we call suet. Five or
six pounds are bought from the butcher—anywhere in

England they will let you have it at sixpence a pound. This is boiled for two or three hours, skimmed and strained, and poured into jars ready for use, taking the place of lard when butter or oil are not used. Since I came home I have never had any lard in my house. Many people here do not know that dripping can be cleared by frying some pieces of raw potato in it till they turn brown ; this will clarify it nicely.

All chickens, game, birds of any kind, are roasted far more slowly than with us, and at wood fires. The livers, gizzards, &c., are chopped up and put inside the bird. It is always basted with butter, which is poured round the bird when sent to table. This is a very great improvement with all birds, especially fowls, on the pale watery gravy or the thick tasteless sauce as served in England. Our method of sticking the liver and gizzard into the wing is a useless waste, for they shrivel into a hardened mass before our fierce coal fires. The French, if they do not think the livers, etc., necessary for improving the gravy in the roasting often make them the foundation of a pie or side-dish. This cutting up the liver and basting with butter is a hint well worth remembering, and should be universally applied in the roasting of all birds. I noticed that all roast meat was basted with fat or butter, and the gravy served just as it was, without straining or clarifying, with all the goodness of the meat in it. This we have practised ever since at home, with great approval. Many people would object to this as greasy. I only say, ' Try it.'

A very good, easily made French soup is as follows :—

Potage Paysanne.—Cut one large onion into dice, put them into a stewpan with two ounces of butter, and fry a nice golden colour. Then take a half-inch-thick slice of bread toasted to the same colour ; break it into small pieces, and put them into the stewpan with a pint of good stock. Simmer gently for thirty-five minutes, then serve. Quantity for four persons.

The following receipt for a tame duck I can thoroughly recommend; if you follow it exactly, it cannot go wrong :—

Caneton à l'Orange.—Take a good fat duck, clean it out, and put the liver apart. Singe the duck, and clean it very carefully. Then mince the liver with a little onion and some grated bacon or ham, add salt and pepper. Put the stuffing inside the duck. Now close the opening of the duck ; leave the skin of the neck long, and bring it round under the duck to close the tail. Spread on the table a clean pudding-cloth, and roll the duck in this rather tightly, to preserve the shape. Tie up the two ends of the cloth with string. Put into a stewpan, with boiling salted water. Continue to boil it quietly for one hour for an ordinary duck, one hour and ten minutes if large ; it will then be cooked, and ought to be a good pink colour. (Chickens boiled in the same way are excellent.) Take three oranges, peel them with a spoon, cut the peel in quarters, taking out *all* the white ; shred the peel as if for Julienne soup ; put it into water for seven or eight minutes, drain on a cloth. Take the rest of the orange, removing all the white ; put the pulp into a good *reduced* stock half glazed. Add Spanish sauce (*see* ' Dainty Dishes '), two or three spoonfuls, and a little red wine—port is best. Pass through a sieve, and then add the chips of orange-peel. Unpack the duck, serve on a dish, surround it with pieces of orange ; put a little sauce over the duck and the rest in a sauce-boat.

Another good and useful receipt is the following :—

French Pie.—Cut up 2 lbs. of lean veal, 2 lbs. of bacon, and 2 lbs. of lean pork, in very thin slices. Place them in layers in a fireproof pie-dish. Moisten with stock, and chop up a little herb and very little onion, and put it between the slices of meat. Cover with a sham crust of flour and water. Take all the cuttings, parings, bones, etc. ; cook these in water or weak stock, and reduce to a large teacupful.

When the pie has baked some time slowly, take it out, take off the crust and pour in the teacupful of stock. When it has cooled, it improves the appearance of the dish to put some well-made aspic jelly (*see* ' Dainty Dishes ') on the top.

As it was the end of Lent, I had the chance of seeing several *maigre* dishes. All the good cooking which hung about monasteries and convents was swept out of England by the Reformation. It has returned only in my life-time, for gastronomic or health reasons rather than for religious mortification. The old object was to make tasty and palatable what the rules of the Church allowed. The French have a real talent for making good dishes out of nothing, and this they share with no other nation in the world. Ox-tails are not used to make soup in France, or were not ; but when the French refugees came over here, they found ox-tails were thrown away and were very cheap. They immediately utilised them, and made the excellent ox-tail soup which we use in England to this day. The black cooks of America, I am told, never spoil good materials, and they cook good things excellently. The English have a peculiar gift for taking the taste out of the best materials that are to be found in the world. A few terrible tricks of the trade are answerable for a good deal of this—iron pots and spoons ; soda thrown into many things ; water poured over roasted meat for gravy ; soups cleared with the white of eggs. This will spoil the best soup in the world, not only taking away all flavour of meat and vegetables, but supplying a taste that is not unlike the smell of a dirty cloth. Of late, in the effort to keep pace with foreign cooking, things in England have grown too messy, and I sometimes regret the real Old English dishes of my childhood. The system of trying to make one thing look like another is very objectionable, I

think, and wanting in good taste. But I must return
to my *maigre* receipts. The details can be found in
' Dainty Dishes.'

Vol-au-vent au Maigre.—Make a high Vol-au-vent
crust. Prepare some quenelles made of fish—any white
fish would do (lemon-soles, whiting, haddock, gurnet,
&c.) ; some white bottled mushrooms preserved in salt,
not vinegar (this is most important) ; some small pieces
of boiled fish. Mix these together in a white sauce made
of butter, flour (slightly cooked first, but not coloured) ;
then add the milk, warm the whole together, and pour
it into the crust.

A rather nice cake for luncheon can be made as
follows :—Take three eggs, put them into the scale and
weigh against them three equal parts of flour, sugar, and
butter. Then break the eggs and put the yelks into a
basin, melt the butter, add the flour and sugar, and mix
the whole. At the last moment add the whites of the
eggs, beat slightly, and put it into the oven in a round
flat tin with a thin rim. Serve it on a large round
plate. Fresh-water fish, so rare now in England, though
the traces of tanks and ponds are always to be found in
the neighbourhood of old abbeys and monasteries, are
still much eaten in the country in France. Pike and
carp marinaded are constantly seen at table. Marinading
is far too little done in England ; it is most useful for
many things—hares, venison, beef, and grouse—and it
preserves the meat for some time, if that is what is
wanted. It is described in ' Dainty Dishes,' but I give
you also the following receipt :—

German Receipt for Roast Hare.—Take a bottle
of common white wine (or any remnants of already
opened bottles) ; cut up onions, carrots, herbs, bay-leaf,
a clove or two ; and pour the whole over the raw hare
in a shallow baking-pan, basting it well every few hours
in a cool place for two or three days. Then prepare the
hare. Take off the head, lard the hare well, and put it into

the roasting-pan with a little dripping and more onions, carrots, herbs, salt, and pepper. When roasted, take it out of the oven, pour off all the grease, and replace it by half a breakfast-cupful of thick sour cream, which is to be mixed with the gravy at the bottom of the pan. Replace it in the oven, baste well with the mixture, and serve just as it is, pouring the sauce over the hare.

Chervil is always used in France for spring decoration of fish, cold meat, &c. It is much hardier and more easily grown than Parsley, and lives through the coldest weather if covered up with sticks and fern. In severe winters Parsley sometimes fails in English gardens.

The life in the little French town near which we were was like a page out of a volume of Balzac's 'Vie de Province,' so full of character, and, in a sense, so far away and old-fashioned.

I had the privilege of visiting and hearing the story of one of that charming type, the French old maid. I sat in her kitchen whilst her *bonne* prepared the Sunday dinner for herself, an adopted child, and the inevitable male friend, be he doctor, notary, or priest. The soup was *maigre* and economical :—One large onion cut up and fried in butter in a saucepan over a very slow fire till a nice yellow-brown. Then the saucepan filled up with boiling water from a kettle, and allowed to cook half an hour. Then strained, and a sufficient quantity of Vermicelli added. Cook for fifteen or twenty minutes more, and serve. A chicken, prepared as before described, was roasted for an hour and a half before a slow wood fire, basted with butter all the time, and served with the butter round it as gravy. The salad was carefully picked young Watercress (never used by itself for salads in England), with oil and vinegar, and a hard-boiled egg cut into small quarters laid on the top. (Few know that Watercress can be grown in ordinary garden soil, in half-shade, if sown every spring.)

The wine was good, and the sweets came from the pastry-cook.

During our short stay in France I saw several gardens, but nothing at all interesting. As we drove through the villages I noticed specimens of a white variety of *Iberis gibraltarica* (Candytuft) grown in pots, carefully pruned and cared for, standing in the windows of the cottages. Managed in this way, it made a very charming spring pot-plant. I have never seen it so treated in England. It is not quite hardy. I brought home cuttings, but they all died. I have now several plants which I have grown from seed. From their appearance I do not think they will flower well till they are two or three years old ; they will want hard cutting back directly after flowering.

It was early in the year, and no sort of spring gardening was aimed at in the large bare beds cut in rather coarse grass. I think turf is overdone in England ; but why it should be attempted at all where it grows badly, and is rarely successful, I cannot imagine. How infinitely prettier it would be to have earth planted with shrubs and low-growing, creeping plants, with grass paths ! The shrubs that I saw in France seemed to me as much overpruned—indeed stiffly cut back in spring—as they are under-pruned in England.

April 16th.—We returned home last night. At this time of year how a week or ten days changes the growth in one's garden ! I must confess that sometimes, coming home after dark, I have taken a hand-candle to inspect some special favourite.

Buddleia globosa is well worth growing, even in a small garden. It has many merits besides its golden balls, which so charmed Mr. Bright, and which here, at any rate, I think rather disappointing. The growth is lovely ; and the tone of the green unusual, mixing well with many summer flowers. It lasts a long time in water in the hottest weather. The more you cut it, the

4

better it seems to do. It was killed to the ground in the cold winter of '94–95, but broke up from the roots as strong as ever. Some plants do this; others never recover. The shrubby Veronicas never do break up from the roots here. My large Arbutus, killed the same winter, threw up a few shoots, but never did any good, and died the next year. I think the shrubby Veronicas so well worth growing that I have five or six varieties; and as they are not quite hardy, I keep pots of cuttings every winter. This we do also with three or four nominally hardy Cistuses, though they are, a little more difficult to strike. *Helianthemums* or Rock-roses are well worth growing from seed in a sunny dry situation. I know nothing more charming than these delicate bright-flowered little plants blazing and blinking in the sunshine. I have a double-flowered scarlet Rock-rose, not figured in any of my books and which I have rarely seen in gardens. It flowers persistently for many months.

April 17th.—We have had lately a severely cold week —Blackthorn winter indeed. How the poor garden shrivels and shrinks, and seems to lose all its colour !

Many years ago, in a volume of Tennyson given me by Owen Meredith, he wrote on the fly-leaf the following little poem, full of sympathy for the gardener :—

In Nature can aught be unnatural ?
 If so, it is surely the frost,
That cometh by night and spreadeth death's pall
 On the promise of summer which spring hath lost.
  In a clear spring night
  Such a frost pass'd light
 Over the budding earth, like a ghost.

But the flowers that perish'd
 Were those alone
Which, in haste to be cherish'd
 And loved and known,
 Had too soon to the sun all their beauty shown.
  Lightly vested,
  Amorous-breasted
Blossom of almond, blossom of peach—
 Impatient children, with hearts unsteady,

So young, and yet more precocious each
  Than the leaves of the summer, and blushing already
These perished because too soon they lived ;
But the oak-flower, self-restrained, survived ;
  ' If the sun would win me,' she thought, ' he must
  Wait for me, wooing me warmly the while ;
For a flower's a fool, if a flower would trust
  Her whole sweet being to one first smile.'

MAY

May 1st.—I have not mentioned during these spring months the cultivation of the kitchen garden. I leave that entirely to my gardener, only helping throughout the year by looking up in Vilmorin's book (mentioned in January) any special vegetables which are not generally cultivated in England, and noting any deficiency in quantity or quality. No one can expect everything to be equally successful every season, as an unfortunate sowing, a dry fortnight, a late frost, or a cold wind are answerable for a good deal in any garden. It is always some consolation if one finds one's failures are shared by one's neighbours, because then it is more likely to be from some atmospheric cause than from one's own bad cultivation. All the same, the best gardeners have the fewest failures.

We do not sow Sunflowers and many autumn-flowering annuals before the first week in May. For out-of-the-way hardy and half-hardy seeds I find no one is more to be relied on than Mr. Thompson of Ipswich. His packets of seed are not so large nor so expensive as those of some other first-class nurserymen, a great advantage for amateurs. His catalogue is one of the best —simple, concise, and clear, and giving all the information really wanted, except perhaps by beginners. These, however, are equally depressed and bewildered by every catalogue and every gardening book.

Nothing is so delightful as the first warm days, which come sometimes at the beginning, sometimes later in May. By this time all the March seeds are well up, the whole garden teems with life, and all Nature seems full of joy. The following little poem, which was in a May *Pall Mall* two years ago, expresses so charmingly the joyousness of spring that I copied it out :—

BABY SEED SONG

Little brown seed, oh ! little brown brother,
  Are you awake in the dark ?
Here we lie cosily, close to each other ;
  Hark to the song of the lark—
' Waken ! ' the lark says, ' waken and dress you,
  Put on your green coats and gay.
Blue sky will shine on you, sunshine caress you—
  Waken ! 'tis morning—'tis May ! '

Little brown seed, oh ! little brown brother,
  What kind of flower will you be ?
I'll be a poppy—all white, like my mother ;
  Do be a poppy, like me.
What ! you're a sunflower ? How I shall miss you
  When you're grown golden and high !
But I shall send all the bees up to kiss you ;
  Little brown brother, good-bye.

May 3rd.—It seems almost useless to describe my garden. Though I myself am so very fond of it, there is no reason anyone else should understand why I love it ; and when I read the description of the gardens that other people love, I wonder I can bear with it at all. It is surrounded, as I said before, with large forest trees ; and that most objectionable of conifers, a Wellingtonia, grows almost in the middle of the garden. I cannot cut it down, as this would deprive the lawn-tennis ground of the only shade it has. How I long to turn that lawn-tennis ground into a sunk Dutch garden, with its low red wall all round it ! Yet I know I should miss them very much if I no longer heard the cries of the lawn-tennis game or the more recent click of the croquet-balls. The top of the low wall, in front of the south side of the house, is a long bed of Tea Roses. Mr. Robinson names all the best sorts, so I need not do so. They do not flourish very well with us, I confess, and yet certainly better than any other Roses. It is their first flowering in June that is not very good. From August to October they are a great delight, flowering at intervals during all that time, and sending up long lovely shoots of brown leaves, that one can gather without scruple, as they are sure to be injured by the winter frosts ; and the more the blooms are cut, the more they flower. At the other side of the lawn-tennis ground I have a little rockery, the system of which I can recommend to anyone who wants room and various aspects for plants without blocking out the rest of the garden or the distance beyond. We dug a large deep hole in the ground, carrying up gradually a small irregular path to the level of the ground on each side, roughly placing pieces of flat stone on each side of the path (to form steps) and all round the hole at the bottom. We kept the earth from falling by facing it with a wall of stones, stuck flatly and irregularly into the earth ; this makes an excellent cool and deep root-bed for many Alpine and other plants. When it rains, there is a natural tendency for the water to drain down in all directions into the hole at the bottom. This hole had been dug deeper in the middle, and puddled with a little clay, not cement ; and large stones were laid in the bottom, to retain the water longer than it naturally would remain in our sand. For really dry weather some pipes are laid on underground to a tap in another part of the garden, from which the water runs into a tub at the top of the rockery for watering, and the over-

flow falls into the hole. In this way our tiny water-
bed is kept moist in the dryest weather.

We grow in the water one of the most beautiful of
our river plants, the *Ranunculus lingua*, or Water Butter-
cup. It has a noble growth and large, shining, yellow
flowers, which bloom for a long time. Its only fault
is that, if given the position it likes, it grows and increases with weed-like rapidity, and in a small space
must be ruthlessly thinned out when it begins to grow
in spring, and often later as well. We have in the hole
Japanese Primulas and Japanese Iris (*Kempferi*), though
they do not flower as well as in the dry bed above,
which is the hottest, dryest, most sunny place in the
garden ; and the only attention they get, after being
planted in good leaf mould, is some copious waterings
when the flower-buds are formed. They have the largest,
finest flowers I have ever seen in England. I must not
forget our native Forget-me-nots, which, Tennyson says,
' grow for happy lovers.' It is a much more persistent
flowerer than the garden kind. In his ' Lancashire
Garden ' Mr. Bright praises very much the *Primula
japonica*, and nothing can be more charming and unusual than the whorled growth of its flower-stems. He
calls the blossoms crimson ; I call them dark magenta
—at any rate, they have that purple tinge which spoils
so many reds. Where they really look well is in a
moist ditch or on the damp half-shaded edge of a wood.
If the ground is prepared for them, and the white kind
planted too, they sow themselves in endless variety of
tone from dark to light ; but they are not especially
suited for beds or mixing with other plants, and from
their colour are not worth growing in pots.

All round the top of the hole described above is a
raised bed, left irregular in places from the throwing-up
of the earth that was dug out. The whole thing is on
a very small scale in my garden, but it partakes slightly
of the nature of the rockeries at Kew, which anyone

interested in this kind of gardening can see, and by seeing learn. The great point of making a rockery is to have large mounds of good earth, and then lay stones on them, making terraces and little flat beds, stoned over to retain the moisture and prevent the earth being washed away. The old idea was to have stumps of trees or mounds of stones and brick, and then fill in the interstices with earth. This is no good at all ; the plants have no depth of earth, and perish. The trouble of such gardening consists only in the constant hand-weeding that it requires. This must be done by some-one more or less experienced, as very often the most precious plant looks like a small weed, while in other cases many planted things are no better than weeds if left alone, and quickly choke and destroy all their less vigorous neighbours.

Weeding! What it means to us all! The worry of seeing the weeds, the labour of taking them up, the way they flourish at busy times, and the dangers that come from zeal without knowledge! When we first went to live in the country, an affectionate member of the family, who hates weeds and untidiness of all kinds, set to work to tear up ruthlessly every annual that had been sown, and with pride said, ' At any rate, I have cleared that bit of ground.' Weeding, if tiring, is also a fascinating employment ; and so is spudding. The first is best done in dry weather, the second in moist. I am all for reducing lawns and turf, except for paths, in small gardens ; but what there is of grass should be well kept, and free from weeds. A quantity of daisies showing up their white faces, though pretty in theory, are in fact very unbecoming to the borders on a sunshiny summer's day.

The longest side of the house faces west. How I love it because of this ! To my mind, every country house is dull that does not face west, and have its principal view that way. Modern civilisation forbids us to enjoy the sunrise, but the varied effects of the sunset sky glorify everything—the most commonplace gable or the ugliest chimney-stack, a Scotch fir or an open field, which assumes a green under an evening primrose sky that it never has at any other time. The sky is like the sea for its ever-changefulness. You may watch sunsets most carefully every day in the year, and never will you see twice exactly the same effect. How we all know, and notice after midsummer, that marching south of the sun at setting-time! The old fellow in June sets right away to the north, over the Common, changing groups of trees and a little distant hill to purple and blue. At the autumn equinox he looks straight in at the windows as he goes down between the stems of the two tall fir-trees. Who, when forced to come into dinner on a summer's evening, does not appreciate a west dining-room with tall panes of glass which give the power to measure the gradations of the sky, from the deep grey-blue of night's garments at the top, to the bright gold, streaked with purple and crimson, at the base—the earth growing mysteriously dark all the while, and the evening star shining brighter every minute? Architects tell you, and men say, they prefer that a house should face south-east. I do not at all agree with them; the effects of evening to me are too much to give up for any other advantage in the world, real or imaginary. It is far easier to make some other room into a breakfast-room, to catch the morning sun in winter, than to change your dining-room in the summer for the sake of the sunsets. To the west, then, I have my fountain, level with the turf, and with only the ornament of some special plants. To the right of the fountain is a large bed of carnations, slightly raised and terraced with stones, to give good depth of rich soil, unrobbed of moisture from the strong-growing shrubs behind, that are especially necessary for protection from the north and east. I strongly advise that on first coming to a new place you should never cut down much till you have given all the consideration possible to that matter of protection. I cannot repeat too often that wind-swept gardens can never be really satisfactory to the gardener. On the left of the fountain, cut in the grass, are the two long borders, far the most difficult part of the garden to keep as I should wish them to be. They should be always gay and bright, the highest plants planted down the middle ; and even they should be unequal in height. All plants that grow forward into the grass must be kept for other beds edged with stone or gravel. Borders cut in grass must be luxuriant and not untidy, and filled principally with plants which in their non-flowering season are not unsightly. It is for such borders that the seed beds and the reserve garden are so indispensable. On the left of these borders are a few specimen plants cut in the grass :—A *Polygonum cuspidatum*, which is a joy from the first starting of its marvellous quick spring growth to its flowering-time, and to the day when its yellow autumn leaves leave the bare red-brown branches standing alone after the first frosts of October ; a Siberian Crab, beautiful with blossom in spring and with fruit in autumn ; also that lovely autumn-flowering shrub *Desmodium penduliflorum*, which has to be cut down every year, and which is never seen to advantage in a border because of its feathery and spreading growth. Behind these again, and facing due north and shaded from the south, is a large bed of the old Moss-Rose, which in this position does exceedingly well. The large branches are partly pegged down, and they are not pruned back very hard. Behind the fountain, away from the house, are bamboos, Japanese grasses, and low-growing, shrubby Spiræas ; the smallest gardens should not be without some of these, more especially *S. thunbergi*, so precious for its miniature early flowers and its lovely decorative foliage, and very useful for picking and sending away. *Clethra* (Sweet Pepper Bush) is also

a useful little shrub, as it flowers in July, when watering
helps it to bloom well. But I have only to refer you
again and again to the 'English Flower Garden.' If
you study this, you will never lack variety or plenty,
whatever your soil, or your situation, or your aspect—
no, nor even your nearness to that deadly enemy of
plant life, a smoky town.

A lovely spring-flowering shrub is *Exochorda grandiflora*. I can most conscientiously say, 'Get it.' It is
perfectly hardy; the flowers, full-blown and in bud,
are of an exquisitely pure white, and the foliage is light-
green, delicate, and refined.

One of the most precious of May flowers, and one not
nearly enough grown, is the early Dutch Honeysuckle.
It is nearly white, though it dies off yellow. I have
named it in the lists, but it deserves, if only for picking,
a place in every garden. Being an early bloomer, it
requires a warm place, and would do admirably against
the low wall of any greenhouse. Those precious front-
ages to greenhouses, in large places and in what I call
'gardeners' gardens,' are so often left unused, neat,
empty, and bare. On these wasted places many lovely
things would grow, and none better than this beautiful
Dutch Honeysuckle, with its double circles of blooms,
its excellent travelling qualities, and its powerful sweet
scent, unsurpassed by anything. It is, I suppose, like
many things, better for good feeding. It wants nothing
but cutting back hard as soon as it has made its summer
growth, after flowering, to keep it well in its place. It
flowers profusely year after year, and it is easily increased
by summer layering.

Old Man or Southernwood (*Artemisia abrotanum*) ought
never to be forgotten. It grows easily from cuttings
stuck into the ground in any of the early summer months.
I am told that it is an especial favourite with the London
poor. Perhaps its strong smell brings back any chance
association with the country and the cottage garden.

It reminds one of the old story of the poor Irishman, when the Lady Bountiful of the place had transformed his cabin into the graceful neatness of an English cottage. He gazed half-indignantly and half-gratefully on the change. ' It is all very kind,' said he, ' but the good lady does not know how dear to a poor man is everything that reminds him of the time when he played, instead of working. These great folks do not understand us.' But, after all, are we not all like that ? Does not sweet Nature herself throw a veil over the storms of middle-life and soften memories, which become sharp, vivid, and clear only concerning our young days and the time when ' we played,' full of buoyant hope for all that lay before us ?

I have always wished for a sundial in the middle of my grass walks where they widen into a circle. Even in an unpretending modern garden I do not think a sun-dial is affected—or, at any rate, not very—and I long to write round the top of it my favourite among the old Italian mottoes :—' I only mark the bright hours.' To the left of my long borders are four large, most useful, square beds, divided by narrow green paths. These are planted and sown, and renewed three or four times a year ; and I always wonder how anyone gets on without such kinds of beds. The Love-in-the-Mist and *Gypsophila gracilis* are sown broadcast here together twice a year, in March and in September. I always save my own seed of Love-in-the-Mist ; but in doing that, you must be careful to mark the best, largest, and bluest flowers. Then what you keep is far better than what you can buy ; but, unless you take this trouble, seeds grown in one place degenerate. To the right of the long borders are two large Rose beds with Roses—old-fashioned rather than very large ones. The Hybrid Perpetuals do so badly in the light soil ; but here are *Gloria Mundi*, Cottage-maid, the dear little pink *Rose de Meaux*, the large white Cabbage, and so on. Beyond the Rose beds is a covered walk, made with stems of small fir-trees bound together with wire—an attempt at a pergola, but not by any means as solid as I should like. On this grow vines, hardy climbing Roses, Honeysuckles, and a dark claret-coloured Vine (which looks well), *Aristolochia*, Clematis (various), and, to make a little brightness in spring, two Kerrias. The single one, which is the original Japanese plant, is very uncommon, and yet so pretty—much better for wedging than the double kind, the old Jews-mallow of cottage gardens.

All these plants want constant watching, pruning, manuring, chalking, mulching. One ought always to be on the watch to see if things do not look well, and why they do not. The great thing to remember is, that if a plant is worth growing at all it is worth growing healthily. A Daisy or a Dandelion, fine, healthy, and robust, as they hold up their heads in the spring sunshine, give more pleasure and are better worth looking at than the finest flower one knows that looks starved, drooping and perishing at the flowering-time. With many plants here, if not watered at the flowering-time, the buds droop and the flowers never expand at all.

We have been eating lately, as Spinach, and found it quite delicious, the leaves of the Chicory, which Sutton calls ' Christmas Salad.' It is a first-rate plant all through the winter, an excellent salad, and now so good, useful, and wholesome to eat cooked. It should be dressed as recommended for Spinach in ' Dainty Dishes.'

This is the time to make Rhubarb jam ; if carefully made, and a little ginger added, it is very good indeed.

To my mind, few flowers please the eye as the Tulip does.

T. gesneriana, with its handsome long stem and brilliant flower, gives me especial delight. The Tulip is a member of the Lily family, and has an interesting history, which I read one day in a newspaper. It is a native of Asia Minor, and was brought from Constantinople in 1557. It was first flowered in England in 1559 by the wife of an apothecary. She had procured the first bulb from a grateful sailor who had brought it home in return for attentions during sickness, by which his life was saved. It was all he had, like the widow's mite, but it was a source of great profit to the wife of the apothecary, who tenderly cultivated it, and sold the bulbs for a guinea each after she had, by good care, procured a sufficient stock of them.

May 5th.—The garden looks dull just now ; but four weeks of no rain always produce that effect on this soil. When the showers do come, everything revives in the most extraordinary way, partly from the earth being so warm and dry. The only rather showy things in the garden are some early red Rhododendrons, and they look droopy ; a Siberian Crab, which has been one mass of snowy-white blossoms for a fortnight ; and a most desirable little shrub called *Deutzia elegans*, quite hardy, totally unaffected by our coldest winters, flowering every year, and wanting no attention except the cutting-back every year after flowering. Berberises I do not find quite so hardy as one expects them to be, but this very likely is because they do not grow very robust, owing to the dryness of the soil. *B. Darwinii* was nearly killed by the severe winter, but is now flowering profusely, and is a lovely and desirable shrub. The whole charm of flowering shrubs, to my mind, depends on their being given lots of room, and sufficient care being taken of them to make them individually healthy plants. The dear little pink *Daphne Cneorum* is doing well, but I have myself often given it a canful of water during the last fortnight. It is very much strengthened if, after the flowering, you layer a certain number of the branches, covering them with a little peat ; this enables you to increase your stock of plants, and improves the size of your specimen plant.

All this last month we have been eating the thinnings

of seedling Lettuces as salad, and they are most delicious. All kinds of Lettuces seem to eat equally well ;
they are grown in boxes in a frame. I first thought of
eating them from seeing that they were thrown away to
give room for those that were going to be planted out.
I now purposely grow them in extra quantities, and in
succession, so that my salads may never fall short. Even
out of doors, in the summer, we sometimes grow them if
our large Lettuces run to seed. They make infinitely
better salad than the tough little brown Cos Lettuces,
grown with such care in frames all through the winter.
All the year round I always mix the salad on the table
myself, using nothing but oil, vinegar, salt, and pepper ;
and I always have brought to table, on a separate little
plate, some herbs, Tarragon, Chervil, and some very
young Onions ; these I cut up over the Lettuces before
I mix in the oil and vinegar. If you have no young
Onions, Chive-tops do very well. These herbs are an
immense addition to any salad, but are far from universally used in England, though they are quite easy
to grow, for anyone who has a kitchen garden, even a
small one. The Tarragon, however, and the Onions have
to be grown in the conservatory in the winter. Many
young gardeners do not know that the secret of young
Potatoes being good, and not watery, is to take them
out of the ground several days before you boil them. A
little Mint chopped on to young Potatoes instead of
Parsley makes a pleasant change ; but then we English
like Mint, and it is very different here from the Mint
grown in dry countries, which is just like Peppermint.
The French have a way of boiling Asparagus which is
especially good for the thin green Asparagus so common
in our English gardens :—You tie them into a bundle,
and put them, stalk downwards, into a fairly deep saucepan. In this way the heads are only cooked by the
steam, and do not become soppy.

May 10th.—I have a friend who to-day writes she is

having iron rings driven into an old stone house round
the windows so as to hold pots of Carnations and Geraniums, to hang down as they do in Tyrol and Switzerland. This will look pretty, no doubt, if it answers ;
but in our cold and windy summers I am sure they
would do better if one pot were sunk inside another
with some moss between, so that the evaporation caused
by the wind, which freezes the roots, should not be so
great. Abroad the pots are frequently glazed either all
the way down or part of the way down ; this stops
evaporation. So many greenhouse plants, when they
are ' stood out,' as the gardeners say, get injured by the
cold winds on the pots, which does far more harm than
the wind on the leaves. One of the best and simplest
remedies is to dig moderately deep trenches with a
raised border round them of turf or boards, and stand
the pots in these, instead of on the open ground. Sheets
of corrugated iron cut to convenient sizes make excellent
movable shelters for plants from the north-east wind.
Shelter in all forms, without taking too much out of
the soil, as trees and shrubs do, is the great secret of
success in all kinds of gardening. I should spend my life
in inventing shelters if I lived on the East Coast ; but I
confess that temporary protections are not very pretty.
Another good method of obtaining shelter is to use
common hurdles of iron or wood, or flat laths with Gorse
or Bracken twisted into them. When all your hand-
lights are in use in Spring, a good deal of protection from
frost may be given to the seed beds by sheets of newspaper held down by a stone or two ; muslin sewn over
a zinc wire-coop will keep out six or seven degrees of
frost. Dried Bracken spread over frames is even better
for keeping out frost than matting, and is nearly as
easily removed.

May 11th.—Epimediums are charming little plants
with lovely, graceful foliage, and are well worth growing
if you have a moist and shady corner. *E. pinnatum* is

perhaps the best, and has long clusters of small yellow flowers ; the leaves are very pretty, and mix well with any flowers.

Aloysia citriodora (Sweet Verbena) is a plant that is a universal favourite. I have never known anyone, not even those who dislike strongly scented flowers, not be delighted with the delicious refreshing smell of its leaves, which they retain long after they are dried. Yet you go to house after house, and find no plants growing out of doors. Their cultivation is simple, and they require but little care to make them quite hardy ; out of five or six plants which I have out of doors, only one died in the hard winter two years ago. If you have any small plants in your greenhouse (if not, buy them at sixpence apiece), put them out at the end of May, after hardening off, in a warm sunny place, either close to a wall or under the shelter of a wall. Water them, if the weather is dry ; and do not pick them much the first year, as their roots correspond to the top growth. Cut off the flowers as they appear. When injured by the frost, never cut the branches down till quite late in the following year. It is this cutting-back that causes the death of so many plants ; the larger stems are hollow, and the water in them either rots or freezes the roots. In November cover the roots of the Verbena with a heap of dry ashes ; this is all the care they require, and they will break up stronger and finer each year. I have kept plants in this way year after year, even in an open border. I believe they would grow in London gardens as long as they have plenty of sun ; and if the plant is weak when they begin to grow in the spring, it would be well to pick off some of the shoots. The cuttings strike quite easily all through the summer in sand in a greenhouse or under a bell-glass.

May 14th.—I suppose it is the same with everything in life that one really cares about, and you must not, any of you, be surprised if you have moments in your gardening life of such profound depression and disappointment that you will almost wish you had been content to leave everything alone and have no garden at all. This is especially the case in a district affected by smoke or wind, or in a very light sandy soil. Five weeks without a drop of rain, and everything bursts into flower and as quickly goes off. Two or three days ago the lilacs were quite beautiful, having responded well to last year's pruning ; now they are faded and scentless, and almost ugly. The German Irises, too, were blooming well, with long healthy stalks. I find that what helps them here is to grow the small pieces one buys from the nurseryman for two or three years in rich garden soil, where they grow quickly, making roots and leaves. After that I move them into some dry border facing east or south, and I find that they then flower as well as one can possibly desire. The beautiful pale-blue *Anemone apennina* is now nodding its little blue heads under my big trees. In the far-away days of my childhood—it must have been in the 'Forties—a really typical man-of-the-world presented my mother with four well-bound volumes of Mrs. Hemans' poems. Imagine any man giving such a present now ! And yet she wrote some pretty things, of which the following is a specimen, and certainly it is quite as good as many modern flower-poems :—

TO THE BLUE ANEMONE.

Flower of starry clearness bright,
Quivering urn of coloured light,
Hast thou drawn thy cup's rich dye
From the intenseness of the sky ?
From a long, long fervent gaze
Through the year's first golden days
Up that blue and silent deep
Where, like things of sculptured sleep,
Alabaster clouds repose
With the sunshine on their snows ?
Thither was thy heart's love turning,
Like a censer ever burning,
Till the purple heavens in thee
Set their smile, anemone ?

Or can those warm tints be caught
Each from some quick glow of thought ?
So much of bright soul there seems
In thy bendings and thy gleams,
So much thy sweet life resembles
That which feels and weeps and trembles,
I could deem thee spirit-filled
As a reed by music thrilled
When thy being I behold
In each loving breath unfold,
Or, like woman's willowy form,
Shrink before the gathering storm,
I could ask a voice from thee,
Delicate anemone.

Flower, thou seem'st not born to die,
With thy radiant purity,
But to melt in air away,
Mingling with the soft spring day.
When the crystal heavens are still,
And faint azure veils each hill,
And the lime-leaf does not move,
Save to songs that stir the grove,
And earth all glorified is seen,
As imaged in some lake serene—
Then thy vanishing should be,
Pure and meek anemone.

Flower, the laurel still may shed
Brightness round the victor's head,
And the rose in beauty's hair
Still its festal glory wear,
And the willow leaves droop o'er
Brows which love sustains no more
But thy living rays refined,
Thou, the trembler of the wind,
Thou, the spiritual flower,
Sentient of each breeze and shower,
Thou, rejoicing in the skies,
And transpierced with all their dyes,
Breathing vase, with light o'erflowing,
Gem-like to thy centre glowing—
Thou the poet's type shall be,
Flower of soul, anemone.

May 16th.—None of the small cheap bulbs are better worth growing than the Alliums, white and yellow. They increase themselves rapidly, and are quite hardy, though the white ones force well and are useful. People

object to them because the stalks smell of garlic at the
time of picking, but it goes off as soon as they are put
into water ; and the flowers are lovely, delicate, and
useful, and have the great merit I mention so often of
remaining a long time fresh in water. We leave some
of the bulbs in the ground, and take up others. Those
that are taken up and dried in the sun flower best the
following year ; and the finest bulbs can be planted
together, the yellow making a fine splotch of colour just
as the yellow Alyssum is over. The smaller the garden,
the more essential it is to get a succession in colour.
Avoid many white flowers in small gardens ; in roomy
gardens with shady corners nothing looks better than
the common single white and purple Rocket, raised
from seed and planted in bold groups. It will grow in
very dry places, but it soon gets untidy, and has to be
cut back, which it does not seem to mind at all

Tiarella cordifolia (' Foam-flower,' Mr. Robinson calls
it) is a little Canadian plant which ought never to be
left out of any garden.

May 19th.—This is the first day of one of the great
gardening interests and treats in the year—the Royal
Horticultural Show in the Temple Gardens. I go every
year now, and should be sorry to miss it. How odd it
seems, that for years and years I never went to a flower
show, or knew anything about them, and now they have
become one of the interests of my life ! The great
attraction this year is the revival of what are called
old-fashioned late single Tulips—Breeders, Flames, &c.
Those who like to buy the bulbs, ordering them carefully by the catalogue, may have their gardens gay with
Tulips for over two months, certainly the whole of April
and May. The quantity of Apples, for so late in the
season, was what struck me as almost the most remarkable thing at the show. One of the great growers told
me that he had tried every conceivable plan for keeping
Apples, but that nothing answered so well as laying them

simply on open, well-aired shelves in a fruit-house that was kept free from frost.

Tradescantia virginica (Spiderworts) are plants that do admirably in light soils, and flower two or three times in the summer, wanting nothing beyond thinning-out and transplanting, and dividing in the autumn. The pale-blue and the white are even more beautiful than the dark-blue and the red-purple; but they are all worth having, with their quaint-shaped flowers, so unlike other things. Every year, towards the end of May, I put in cuttings of Lavender and Rosemary. If the weather is dry, they are what gardeners call 'puddled-in,' which means that the ground is very much wetted first. In this way I have a constant supply of young plants. Rosemary is only really hardy with us if planted under the protection of large shrubs; the keen winds of March cut them off in the open. Many other plants can be increased in the same way—early flowering shrubs such as *Ribes sanguinum*, the Forsythias, &c. Last spring, in Suffolk, I saw a charming little garden-hedge made of *Ribes sanguinum*, all one brilliant mass of its flowers. This is quite worth trying; its success would depend on its being sharply pruned back the moment after flowering and before its seeds ripen. If your cuttings take, you can make your hedge in October. It is rather a repetition of the well-known and often-seen Sweetbriar hedge, which is all the better in a light soil for cutting back the young growths in July as well as for the spring pruning. It is a very good plan this month to take off some of the shoots—apt to be too numerous—that sprout on the pruned-back creepers, such as White Jasmine, Vines of all kinds, and *Bignonia radicans*, which handsome old garden favourite buds so late that the flowers do not expand unless treated in this way.

May 22nd.—Not the smallest and dryest garden should be without *Stachys lanata*, a white woolly-leaved plant, called Rabbit's Ears by cottage children, and particularly attractive to some people, who through life retain the love of a child for something woolly and soft. Certain characteristics are always reminding us, especially in some women, even when old, that they were once children. These leaves were formerly used as edgings to beds in a very objectionable way ; but when grown in large clumps, they are most useful for picking. When cut, they go on growing in water, as Buttercups and Forget-me-nots do, and mix very well with many flowers, especially with *Narcissus poeticus,* any of the German Irises, and the lovely white *Scilla campanulata,* a cheap bulb, of which we can hardly have too many. There· is a blue and a pink kind, but the white is the most lovely ; and, in my opinion, all three are better worth growing than the usual Hyacinths, double or single. I think the people who live in the country in spring would find it more satisfactory to grow their greenhouse bulbs in large, open pans, several together, and covered with some of the mossy Saxifrages, than the usual two or three in a pot that gardeners are so fond of. If the pan has no hole at the bottom for drainage, you must put in lots of crocks, and be careful not to over-water ; but bulbs like their roots moist.

I made a curious experiment with the little double *Prunus.* One moved last autumn, and one moved last spring out of the nursery into a sunny, sheltered border, are both covered with bloom, and lovely objects. Another plant, which was left in a sunny border for a year, has no bloom on it at all, though it is quite healthy. This is one more proof of how much is to be done with reserve gardens and moving in this light dry soil. Next month I shall choose a wet day, and move them all back again into the nursery. The white Dog-tooth Violet and the various Fritillarias are very satisfactory things. They like shade and a certain amount of moisture, but it is not necessary for their cultivation ; they will grow anywhere. The common *Saxifraga*, London Pride, is a most desirable, useful plant ; it is the better for dividing every two years. It travels well picked, and is so pretty and decorative in water ; it looks well with large red Oriental Poppies, with no green at all. *Silene*, too, looks well with it in small glasses, for a change.

Deutzia crenata is a charming shrub, and flowering well this year. Unless the garden is very small, anyone who lives in the country in spring ought to have it. There is so little room for shrubs in a very small plot of ground, and no garden can be beautiful except when the lie of the ground and the surrounding circumstances are beautiful. The only ambition that can be indulged in with a small flat ground is to grow the greatest number of healthy plants possible in the least amount of space, and so secure continuous and varied flowers for nine months of the year.

The planning and laying-out of a small garden without great natural advantages ought to be as practical and simple as possible, a mere improvement on the cottage garden :—A small, straight path of brick or paving-stone, or grass or gravel, though that is the least desirable of all to my mind. Let beds be on either side. If you have shrubs round the edge of the garden to hide the paling, have a grass path in front of the shrubs, and then square or long beds in the middle. Never have a small lawn with beds cut in that ; nothing gives so much labour and so little satisfaction as beds cut out of grass, and what makes them uglier still is bordering them again with some plant. The flowers are much better out in the open, away from the moisture-devouring shrubs. In gardening, as in many things in life, let your wits improve on what is rather below you ; never look at the squire's big garden in your neighbourhood, and then try and imitate it in small. Nothing makes a more charming edging for beds, if you have gravel paths, than large flat stones ; they retain the moisture, and many small, low-growing things feather over the stones and look very well indeed.

May 28th.—After a great deal of practice I really think I have evolved a way of packing cut flowers which is both economical and satisfactory. I collect all the linen-draper's and milliner's cardboard boxes that I possibly can ; while these remain good, my friends send them back to me by parcel post. The flowers are picked over-night, and put into large pans of water, keeping each kind in separate bunches. In the morning they are dried, and the different bunches are rolled up, fairly tightly, in newspaper—the great point being to exclude the air entirely both from the stalks and flowers. These bundles are then laid flat in the boxes ; the tighter they are packed, without actually crushing them, the better they travel. The lid is then put on, the box tied up with string, and sent to the station in time for an early train.

When friends themselves take away the flowers, a box is unnecessary, as the separate bundles can be tied up together in some large sheets of newspaper.

May 29th.—An excellent fish sauce is to beat some cream, and drop into it a little anchovy sauce from a quite recently opened bottle. It is served cold, in a little deep dish, not in a sauce-boat.

Here is an Italian receipt for Risotto :—Take a saucepan that holds about a quart, cut up a fair-sized onion into very small pieces, let it brown to a good golden colour in some fresh butter. Add the rice, raw and well washed, and let it cook slowly, stirring well for about five minutes. Add the saffron (half a thimbleful, well pounded), pour in the stock by degrees as needed by the quantity of rice. When the rice is done, draw it to one side, and add some grated Parmesan cheese. Stir it gently and serve, sprinkling some Parmesan on the top.

A good breakfast or lunch dish is called 'Convent Eggs':—Boil four eggs for ten minutes. Put them in cold water. Peel, and slice thin, one onion. Put into a frying-pan 1 oz. of butter; when melted, add the onion and fry white. Then add a teaspoonful of flour; mix it well. Add about half a pint of milk, till it forms a nice white sauce, half a teaspoonful of salt, and a quarter ditto of pepper. When nicely done, add the eggs—cut into six pieces each, crossways. Toss them up; when hot, serve on toast.

Gascony Butter.—Take equal quantities of parsley (picked from the stalk and parboiled), of anchovies (washed, boned, and pounded), and of fresh butter. Mix the ingredients well together, and pass them through a hair-sieve. Make into pats or balls, ice them, and serve with hot dry toast.

Here is an old Indian receipt for curry powder:— 1 lb. of coriander seed, ½ oz. of red chilli, 1 oz. of black pepper, 4 oz. of cummin seed, 3 oz. of fenniquick, 1 lb. of turmeric, 1 oz. of dry ginger, and 1 oz. of poppy seed.

For making curry, take 1½ lb. of meat cut into dice (mutton is perhaps the best), 2 oz. of butter, 1 large onion (the size of a large potato) and a large apple, one dessertspoonful and a half of curry powder, and a teacupful of stock. First melt the butter; then fry the onion and apple, cut small, till quite brown. Then add the curry powder; then the meat, cut into small pieces, and fry it in the above till quite brown, turning the meat constantly to keep it from burning. Then put the whole into a saucepan, add the stock, and place it near the fire to simmer for 3½ or 4 hours. If it gets too dry, add a little more stock. Mutton wants no butter added at the end, but chickens and rabbits do.

To boil Patna Rice for Curry.—Put 3 quarts of spring water in a saucepan to boil, and add ½ lb. of rice. Let it boil as fast as possible, with the lid off. Keep skimming it all the time. When done (which means that it is soft, but with a little hardness left in the middle), strain it off on to a sieve, and then let cold water run on it till it becomes quite cold. Put it back into the saucepan without water, to get hot enough for table. It should take 1 hour to get hot; it will be a bad colour if hurried.

Curry of Ham Toast.—This receipt is useful to finish up an old ham :—8 oz. of lean ham chopped very fine, 1 teaspoonful of Harvey and 1 of Worcester sauce, 1 teaspoonful of curry paste, a small piece of butter, a good tablespoonful of white sauce, and 2 tablespoonfuls of thick cream. All these should be mixed together and heated. Cut some rounds of toast, and serve very hot.

The following receipt for bottling green Gooseberries I think you will find useful. The great point is to pick them just at the right moment, when neither too large nor too small. And much depends on waxing the corks well ; so I add the receipt for that.

Bottled Green Gooseberries.—Pick off noses and stalks, but be careful not to burst the berries. Then fill some wide-mouthed bottles quite full, tie over the mouths paper with pricked holes, stand the bottles in boiling water, and just let the fruit turn colour (no sugar or anything with the fruit). Take the bottles out, and cork and seal them. The old way was to bury them head downwards in a garden border ; but if well sealed, to keep out all air, I do not believe that is necessary. Green Currants are excellent done the same way, and Morella Cherries, small Plums, and Damsons ; only these must be ripe.

Wax for Bottles.—2 parts of beeswax, 1 part of resin, 1 part powdered colour (Venetian red). Melt the beeswax and resin in an old iron saucepan. (Only melt, do not boil.) Then stir in the colour and let it cool a little, both to avoid the pungent vapours and to thicken slightly. Dip the corked tops of the bottles while holding them horizontally over the pot, and turn them round, so as to run the extra stuff into the joint; they are the better for a second dip. Leave the remains of the wax to harden in the pot, which should be used for this purpose only. It can be melted again at any time, and more added as wanted.

May 30th.—A good deal of real gardening pleasure and satisfactory ornamental effect is to be had from growing plants in pots and tubs, vases and vessels of all kinds, both in small and big gardens. I use large Sea-kale pots, when they are no longer wanted for the Sea-kale, by turning them upside down, putting two bits of slate in the bottom of the pot, some drainage and a few lumps of turf, and filling it up with really good soil. As a variety a Rhubarb-pot is useful. If you live near a pottery, they will turn you out pots to any shape you fancy. Flat ones, like those used by house-painters, make a pleasant change, especially for small bulbs; also petroleum casks cut in two, burnt inside, then tarred and painted. It must never, of course, be in any case forgotten to have holes large enough to make good drainage. I use butter casks treated in the same way, and have some little oak tubs in which bullion came from America. These are very strong; and some water-loving plants do much better in wood, since the evaporation in summer is not nearly so rapid as from the earthenware. That is an important thing to remember, both as regards sun and wind. If the plants are at all delicate, and brought out of a greenhouse, the pots, when standing out, ought to be either quite sunk into the earth or shaded. This cannot, of course, be done in the case of pots placed on a wall or terrace, or on a stand; constant care about watering is, therefore, essential. Even in wet weather they often want more water if the sun comes out, as the rain wets the leaves, but hardly affects the soil at all. On the Continent, where all kinds of pot-cultivation have been longer practised than in England, flower-pots are often glazed outside, which keeps the plants much moister, and makes less necessity for frequent watering. The French, especially, understand much better than we do the potting-on of plants. They begin by putting seeds into pots no bigger than a thimble, and sinking them in boxes with cocoanut fibre ; the little plants are then potted-on very gradually, never injuring the roots at all. The merciless way in which gardeners often tear off the roots collected at the bottom of a pot is most injurious to the plant. The large red jars that still bring oil from Italy, covered with their delightful coarse wicker-work, are useful ornaments in some gardens. They are glazed inside, and boring a hole in the bottom of them is not very easy work. They have to be more than half filled with drainage ; and plants do not do well in them for more than one season, as the surface of earth exposed at the top is so small. In old days the oil merchants in the suburbs of London used to cut them in two vertically, and stick them against their houses above their shops, as an advertisement or ornament. Enthusiastic amateurs will find that they get two very nice pots by sawing them in half horizontally, just below the sham handles. The top part, when reversed, requires the same treatment as was recommended for the Sea-kale pots. Many different things may be grown for standing out of doors in the large pots and tubs above described, and one plant may succeed another. The first rule, I think, is to grow in them those plants which do not grow especially well in your own local soil. To put into a pot what is flourishing much better in a bed a few yards off is, to my mind, a mistake.

I grow in pots large old plants of Geraniums—Henry Jacoby is especially good. They are kept on in the greenhouse from year to year, their roots tied up in moss and crowded into a pot or box with no earth and very little water through the winter ; early in April they are potted-up and protected by mats in a pit, as we have no room for them in the greenhouse. This causes them

to be somewhat pot-bound, and they flower brilliantly
during the latter part of the summer. French Mar-
guerites (the yellow and the white) with large leaves are
good pot-plants early in the year—far prettier than the
narrow-leaved kinds. A double Pomegranate I have
had for many years in a pot ; and if pruned out in the
summer, it flowers well. The large, old-fashioned, oak-
leaved, sticky Cape Sweet Geranium, which has a handsomer flower than the other kinds, makes a very good
outdoor pot-plant. In potting-up strong, growing plants
that are to remain in the pots for some time, it is useful
to put some broken-up bones with the crocks at the
bottom of the pots for the roots to cling to them.

Fuchsias, especially the old-fashioned *fulgens*, are
satisfactory. Carnations—Raby Castle, Countess of
Paris, and Mrs. Reynolds Hole—I grow in pots, and
they do extremely well ; they must be layered early in
July, and answer best if potted up in September and
just protected from severe frosts. This year we took
up a large clump of Montbretias out of a dry sunny
bed of Cape bulbs in the kitchen garden, just as they
were coming through the ground, and dropped them
into a large Sea-kale pot. They flowered exceedingly
well, and in September we put them back in the dry
border to die down. In fine summers Myrtles and
Oleanders flower well with us in tubs, not in the open
ground. We treat Oleanders as they do in Germany—
cut them back moderately in October, and dry them
off, keeping them in a coach-house, warm shed, or
wherever severe frosts will not reach them. When
quite dry, they stand a moderate amount of frost. Then
in March they are brought out, the ground is stirred and
mulched, and they are taken into a greenhouse and
brought on a bit. In May they are thickly covered with
good strong horse-manure and copiously watered. At
the end of the month they are stood out in the open
on a low wall. During May, June, and July they cannot

have too much water ; after that they want much less, or the leaves turn yellow and drop off. *Campanula pyramidalis* (*see* ' English Flower Garden '), a biennial, does well in pots, if shaded—blue and white both in one pot, or apart. The seedlings have to be potted up in autumn (plants a year old) ; as with the Canterbury Bells, if you cut off the fading flowers the flowering season is much prolonged. Canterbury Bells (*Campanula medium*) make charming pot-plants for large rooms or corridors in May or June. They are annuals, and the seed can be sown out of doors in March or April, keeping the seedlings well thinned, transplanting in the autumn, and potting-up the following spring (*see* ' English Flower Garden '). If strong crowns of *Campanula persicifolia* are potted up in autumn, they force beautifully in a moderate greenhouse in spring, and are most satisfactory for picking or otherwise.

Some years I grow *Solanum jasminoides* over bent wires in pots ; they are rather pretty. *Clethra* (Sweet Pepper Bush), a small North American shrub, we lifted from the reserve garden in June and put into a pot, and it flowered very well. The variety of plants which can be experimented upon for growing in pots out of doors in summer is almost endless. Love-lies-bleeding (*Amaranthus caudatus*) is an annual ; but if sown in January, and very well grown-on as a fine single specimen plant, it looks handsome and uncommon in a green glazed pot or small tub. Nothing we grow in pots is more satisfactory than the old-fashioned *Calceolaria amplexicaulis*. It does not grow to any perfection in the beds, the soil being too dry ; but, potted, it makes a splendid show through the late summer and autumn months. A red-brown kind, little grown now, which I brought from Ireland, and which I cannot name, also succeeds very well. They both want potting-up in good soil in April. The shrubby Veronicas (*Speciosa rubra*, *Imperialis*, and the variegated *Andersoni*) I grow in pots because they flower beautifully in the autumn ; and the drowsy bumble-bees love to lie on them, in the sunshine, when the *Sedum spectabile* is passing away. They are not quite hardy with us, as they cannot withstand the long, dry, cold springs. This in itself justifies the growing them in pots ; in mild, damp districts they are large shrubs. The small bushy Michaelmas Daisies we put into pots at the end of July, and they fill up blank spaces on the wall late in the year.

The blue Cape *Agapanthus* everybody grows in tubs. They have to be rather pot-bound and kept dry in the winter, to flower well ; as the flower-buds form, they want to be well watered and a weekly dose of liquid manure. Hydrangeas I find difficult to grow when planted out. The common kinds do exceedingly well in tubs, in half-shady places, if they get a good deal of water. A variegated half-hardy shrub called *Procosma variegata* makes a showy and yet restrained pot-plant. Large standard Myrtles I have had covered with blooms in August in tubs. My large old plant, which I had had many years, was killed this spring by being turned out of the room it had wintered in too early, because we came from London sooner than usual. The great difficulty in small places is housing these large plants in winter. They do not want much protection, but they must have some ; and the death of large old plants is grievous. We have just built a new greenhouse, which we are going to try with no heating beyond a lamp-stove in very cold weather. If I lived in the country in the winter, I should grow small Evergreens in pots and try various experiments, which are of no use to me, as I live in London. In many cases the plants would not get injured by frost if one pot were sunk inside another.

JUNE

Hands and fingers after weeding—Shrub-pruning—Boxes for birds—
Robins in greenhouse—'Burning Bush'—Two Polygonums—
Strawberries—Geraniums and cuttings—Cactuses—Freesia bulbs
—*Gloriosa superba*—Luncheon dishes—Cucumbers.

June 2nd.—It must be admitted that one of the great
drawbacks to gardening and weeding is the state into
which the hands and fingers get. Unfortunately, one's
hands belong not only to oneself, but to the family, who
do not scruple to tell the gardening amateur that her
appearance is 'revolting.' Constant washing and always
keeping them smooth and soft by a never-failing use of
vaseline—or, still better, a mixture of glycerine and
starch, kept ready on the washstand to use after washing
and before drying the hands—are the best remedies
I know. Old dog-skin or old kid gloves are better for
weeding than the so-called gardening gloves; and for
many purposes the wash-leather housemaid's glove,
sold at any village shop, is invaluable. Good gardeners
tell you never to cut flowers except with a sharp knife.
This is good advice for shrubs or pot-plants, the clean
cut being better for the plants; but I advise that the
knife should be on a steel chain a foot or so long, with
a good pair of garden hook-shaped scissors at the other
end—for the cutting of annuals or lately planted plants
with a knife, in light soil, is very much to be avoided. The
smallest pull loosens the roots, and immediate death,
in hot weather, is the result. Another advantage of
knife and scissors together on the chain is that they are

more easy to find when mislaid, or lost in the warm and bushy heart of some plant.

June 4th.—Now, and even a little earlier, is the great pruning-time of the year for all spring-flowering shrubs. No doubt this cutting-out may be especially important in a light soil such as ours, where things flower themselves to death, like pot-bound plants. It is rather tiresome work ; it requires one person to cut out the old wood and slightly cut back the topmost branches with a long-handled nipper, and another to stand at a little distance and give directions. Without this precaution, the tree or shrub would often become lop-sided and unsightly. It is impossible for the man who is cutting to see what should be taken out. *Choisya ternata* must be gone over and cut back severely, in spite of all one may have gathered from it while in flower. Also with Lilacs, Laburnums, Weigelias, Crab-apples, Double Cherries, Viburnum, and *Pyrus japonica*, this pruning—at any rate, in light soils—must never be neglected or forgotten. Very often only a little cutting-out is required. If it is done too late, it does more harm than good, and injures next year's bloom. *Clematis montana* succeeds much better if the young growth is cut off every year, which prevents it from getting tangled and matted, and all going to leaf instead of blossom. It is the same with Honeysuckles and Brooms. We sow the Brooms— white, yellow, and red and yellow—every year. They can always be transplanted when quite young to where they are to flower, and a good supply of young plants is so useful.

The bird-boxes this spring have been well used by my little couples. Fly-catchers and Wrens never fail ; but this year we have had rather an uncommon bird, a Red-start, and in the nest are seven eggs, though Bewick asserts that they only lay four or five. The eggs are pretty in colour, like the Hedge-sparrow's. The Red-start's eggs are a little longer and narrower in shape than

5

the Hedge-sparrow's. A pair of Robins have hatched out three families this year in my greenhouse—fourteen young Robins ! They began early in March, and built on a top-shelf ; when the little ones were hatched, the old birds were so tame that they did not mind at all our putting the nest into a deep pot and placing it near the window for them to feed their young more conveniently. We also thought that in the pot it would attract less the attention of a terrible bird-killing old cat we have. He stays near a nest, scratching, till the parent birds are in such a frenzy of agitation and fear that they kick the young ones out of the nest ; he then devours them at his leisure.

To those who have room I recommend the Venetian Sumach (*Rhus cotinus*), but it is not worth growing if it is crowded up. The most perfect way to grow it is to put the young plant in a well and richly made hole in the lawn, or at the edge of a shrubbery, the formality of which you wish to break. As it grows, cut away the turf from under it, and mulch it every winter ; this makes it grow quickly. When it gets into a good big plant, leave off mulching, and dress it with chalk, which will make it flower and bear its lovely feathery seeds in July. In a good sunny situation it will turn a flaming red colour, which is the reason for its English name of the ' Burning Bush.' It does better in moderately damp soils than with us, but a little care will make it grow anywhere. It is well adapted for picking and putting into water, as the leaves have a faint aromatic smell ; but it is not suited to very small gardens, for it spreads and takes up too much room. Crowding spoils its great characteristic of rooting into the ground all round.

The finer sorts of Clematis (*see* ' English Flower Garden ') only do fairly well in our soil ; and till I gave them plenty of chalk they often died. All the large *Jackmani* tribe (*see* nurserymen's catalogues) want cutting back to the ground very early in the year, before they begin to break in the spring ; but they are worth all care and trouble. Many gardeners do not agree with me, but I am very fond of specimen plants grown in holes cut in grass, if they are planted with care, to group with shrubs behind them, and so as not to present a dotted-about appearance. In large gardens there are places enough—in shrubberies, by the side of water, or elsewhere—where these single specimens can grow healthily. In really small gardens they take too much room. In medium-sized gardens they become a feature and an interest. Several plants, besides the Venetian Sumach before mentioned, are such fine growers that they are well worth an individual place to show them off :—

Polygonum cuspidatum and *P. sacchalinense* are very effective, and grow splendidly in dry soils if the outside suckers are pulled out every spring ; they want no other care. *Bocconia cordata* (Plume Poppy), a Japanese plant, also wants no other treatment ; and in this way the old shoots grow up finer and stronger each year. They are herbaceous, like the Polygonums, and it is best not to cut down their hollow stems till the spring. *Leycesteria formosa* has a good growth ; its uncommon brown flowers come late in the summer. (*Kerria japonica*, especially the single one mentioned before ; the Privets, the golden one and the Alexandrian are the best.) Tamarisks, so seldom grown away from the sea, which are very pretty, especially the one with tiny pink flowers that come out in the spring (*T. parviflora*, I believe it is called) ; and many hardy Bamboos can all be grown separately as specimen plants ; as also the two Eulalias, *japonica* and *zebrina*, the tall Japanese grasses. The *Arundo donax* is the lovely tall cane that grows in the ditches in Italy. But beware how you move it, if once you get it to grow ; it does not at all like being disturbed. *Acanthus* in full sun is very handsome, and grows large in rather a moist place ; so does the Giant Parsnip, but it is only a biennial.

June 9th.—The Strawberry season is beginning. For many years this fruit was poison to me ; now it gives me pleasure to think that I live almost entirely upon it for some weeks in the summer, eating it three times a day, and very little else, according to the practice of Linnæus, as quoted in March. It is of great importance that anyone who has room to grow strawberries at all should grow several varieties—early, medium, or late (*see* catalogues). For ices, creams, jams, &c., I greatly recommend some of the high-flavoured, old-fashioned Hautboys ; they are not very easy to get. The fruit grown on heavy soils round London for the market is often very tasteless ; but one most work away with books and experience to get good Strawberries, and a fairly long succession of them. In growing Strawberries, everything depends on making some new rows every year ; layering the runners early, too, makes a great difference in the young plants the next year. ' Dainty Dishes ' has some instructive old-fashioned receipts for Strawberry jam. Strawberries make an excellent compote if boiling syrup is poured over them. Raspberries are much better treated in this way. Currants require stewing. It improves all summer compotes to ice them well before serving.

I do not at all despise planting out the old-fashioned scarlet and crimson Geraniums—Pelargoniums, they ought to be called. Old plants are very much better than the small cuttings ; but I have a few of these as well, and pots full of cuttings of the sweet-leaved kinds, of which there are so many varieties, and which are planted out the first week in June. Among red Geraniums, nothing is so fine and satisfactory as Henry Jacoby ; it is a very steady bloomer, and has a fine rich colour. When you are planting out your Geraniums and cuttings, do not forget that some must be kept back in their pots and given constant care and attention all through the summer for late autumn and winter flowering in the greenhouse. We keep our plants for winter in a cold frame through the summer, and carefully pick off the flower-buds. Raspail is an excellent double variety for winter picking. One the nurserymen call ' Raspail Improved ' is perhaps what it professes to be, though I do not see very much difference. It is because I live in London in the winter that I so much recommend double Geraniums, as the flowers of the single kind require to be gummed before they are packed. If not, they arrive only a little heap of scarlet petals in the paper, beautiful and lovely, but quite useless for putting into water.

My old books taught me to take an interest in Cactuses, which in the early part of the century were much grown. They are very easy of cultivation, and well worth growing for those who spend June and July in their gardens. A succession must be aimed at, as the drawback is that the blooms only last a short time. The old *Cereus speciosissimus* surpasses in beauty and splendour any garden plant I know, with its brilliant scarlet petals shot with the richest purple and its handsome white tassel of stamens. Another beautiful flower is the large white night-flowering *Cactus ;* and if brought, when just about to bloom, into the hall or sitting-room, its delicious perfume pervades the whole house for twenty-four hours, if not for longer. Although Cactuses are very easy to cultivate, yet what they require they must have, or they do not flower at all, and then gardeners throw them away. Wholesome neglect is better than too much misdirected care ; they want to be kept very dry, and not too warm all through the winter, but quite free from frost. In April they are re-potted, if they seem to require it ; but that is seldom. Once started into growth, they want heat, light, sun, a little nourishment, and plenty of watering and syringing, with rain-water if possible ; hard chalky water is bad for them. When they have done flowering, I plant them out in a good warm border till the middle of August. This does them a lot of good, and helps them very much to make new growth ; they should be well syringed overhead while growing. Anyone really interested in Cactuses will learn all they want to know in a little book called 'Cactus Culture for Amateurs,' by W. Watson. The old and long-neglected taste for growing Cactuses is certainly reviving, and some of the finest kinds can be grown with very little trouble or expense. Mr. Watson is Assistant Curator of the Royal Botanic Gardens at Kew, where there is a large collection of Cactuses. He writes as one who knows, and the book is full of practical instructions.

I have a great many Stapelias, South African plants rather resembling miniature Cactuses in their growth, and requiring the same treatment. They are very curious, and are described in a modern book translated from the German, called the ' Natural History of Plants,' as belonging to a group of plants called ' indoloid.' Sometimes the scent of these South African Stapelias resembles that of decomposing mammalian flesh, sometimes of rotten fish, &c. This, of course, attracts insects. Flowers provided with indoloid scents resemble animal corpses in their colouring, having usually livid spots, violet streaks, and red-brown veins on a greenish or a fawn-coloured background. All the same, the flowers are to me curious and rather beautiful, so entirely unlike anything else.

This month is the time to sort out the Freesia bulbs that have been drying in the sun, in their pots, laid on one side on the shelf of the greenhouse. The largest bulbs are re-potted now or in July in good strong loamy soil, but hardly watered at all till they begin to show through the earth. The next-sized bulbs are potted a month later. When the quite small ones are put into a

box to grow on for next year they are too small to flower.
Early potting-up of Freesias is very important if they are
to flower early.

June 20th.—For anyone with a small stove or warm
greenhouse I can thoroughly recommend the growing of
the *Gloriosa superba* or Creeping Lily. It is a lovely
and curious flower ; it lasts very long in water, and
flowers continuously for two or three months. Its cultivation is simple enough : buy the bulbs in April, pot
them up in good Lily soil (*see* Johnson's ' Gardener's Dictionary' for this and all other greenhouse and stove
cultivation of plants), start them in heat, and grow them
up wires or thin branching sticks, or anything that gives
them support ; water them well while growing ; and as
they begin to go off after flowering, and the leaves turn
yellow, dry them gradually till they have quite died
down. Then lay the pots on their sides, and keep them
quite dry, but in a warm temperature, till you re-pot
them the following spring. The flowers are lovely—
crimson and yellow, with crinkled, turned-back petals,
and they wedge so well in small flat vases.

In the last century the disciples of Linnæus took great
pleasure botanically in this plant, as the pistil bends at
nearly right angles in a most curious way, to insert its
stigma amongst the stamens ; and it is a good illustration of the sex of plants. It is figured in that old book
I alluded to in March of Erasmus Darwin's, called the
' Botanic Garden,' and in the poem named ' The Loves
of the Plants ' it is thus spoken of :—

> Proud Gloriosa led three chosen swains,
> The blushing captives of her virgin chains,
> When Time's rude hand a bark of wrinkles spread
> Round her weak limbs, and silver'd o'er her head ;
> Three other youths her riper years engage,
> The flatter'd victims of her wily age.

I must acknowledge that I have watched attentively
a great many blooms of ' proud Gloriosa,' and have

admired her immensely, but I never could see the difference in the length of the stamens, or that first one set of
three and then the other set of three came to maturity.

I consider it quite as essential for amateurs who really
care about their gardens to grow out-of-the-way plants
in the greenhouse and conservatory as in the garden.
Why should only just a few easily grown and eternally
repeated plants, everywhere the same, be alone chosen
from the wonderful and beautiful and abundant supply
that Nature provides us with, while many rarer sorts,
with a little care and knowledge, are quite suitable for
growing under glass ? A study of Veitch's or Cannell's
catalogues, and looking up the names in Johnson's
' Gardener's Dictionary,' makes a selection quite easy,
even if you cannot visit any of the first-class excellent
nurseries in summer, or if you do not possess any of the
old illustrated books.

June 27th.—For those who live in the country, or
those who spend the early summer months in towns and
have their flowers sent up, no family of plants are more
useful than the Campanulas (all described in the ' English
Flower Garden '). Perhaps the one we could least do
without is the beautiful *C. persicifolia*. It takes little
room, is a true perennial, and divides well in the autumn.
In light soils it flowers better if treated as a biennial and
sown in a seed bed annually, so as to have a good supply
of young plants every year. The seed sown in June or
July can be planted out in October and potted up the
autumn of the second year for flowering in pots in the early
spring in a greenhouse. They are then good strong
plants, and several can be put in one fairly large pot.
C. grandis is a stronger and coarser plant. It is far
more beautiful for picking if grown in a poor soil and
under the shade of bushes or trees. But it is hardly
worth growing in a small garden, though it is what I
call a friend among plants ; it gives a good deal, and
requires so little, and looks cool and beautiful when

picked and placed by itself in a large glass bowl filled
with water. Its tiny rosette-like leaf-growth is also useful, attractive, and ornamental, especially in the autumn.
It travels as well as the other Campanulas, only it must
be picked in bud. The flowers expand well in water ;
so do those of the common Canterbury Bell.

As a summer luncheon dish this Mayonnaise soufflé of
crab is rather out of the common :—Slightly butter the
lining of a soufflé-case, pin a buttered band of paper
round rather high, and season the eatable part of a crab
with pepper, salt, oil, and vinegar ; whip some nice aspic
jelly, and put a little in the bottom of the lining. Make
a bed of Mayonnaise sauce on the top of the aspic, put in
the crab, then some more chopped aspic ; it should be
about three inches above the tin lining. Stand it in the
ice-box till wanted. Put the lining in the case, sprinkle
with fried breadcrumbs, and serve with a plate of chopped
aspic jelly apart.

A less complicated luncheon dish is as follows :—
Take some ripe tomatoes, equal-sized ; cut a round hole
and scoop out a portion of the middle, fill in with cold
minced chicken and Mayonnaise sauce, put some aspic
in the dish, and serve the tomatoes, on round pieces of
fried bread, cold.

The following fresh chutney is good with any roast
or cold meat :—Equal parts of cucumber, onion, and
sultanas chopped very fine, some salt and cayenne.
Moisten with vinegar, and press for two hours. It will
keep some time : when wanted for use, warm in a little
gravy and let it get cold.

A very much prettier way than the usual English one
of serving cauliflower is to break it up in pieces large
enough for one helping ; boil them very lightly, so that
they should be quite firm and dry, almost crisp. It quite
spoils them if they are soft and sodden. Serve apart,
in a good-sized boat, some white creamy sauce into which
you grate a little Parmesan cheese.

Small pieces of cauliflower put into clear soup, and Parmesan cheese handed apart, is a good way of using up cauliflowers that are just beginning to run to seed.

Young onions boiled in clear soup give it an unusual and gelatinous consistency.

Raw sliced cucumber is quite a different dish if cut very thin and soaked in salt and water for two or three hours before it is wanted. It is then drained and pressed, and served with oil, vinegar, and pepper, in the usual way.

There are several ways of cooking cucumbers ; I suggest the following :—Peel and cut up a cucumber into pieces about two inches long, and divide each piece into two. Soak them for two or three hours in brown sugar and vinegar. Stew them in a little stock, and serve them as a vegetable.

Another way is to stew these pieces in a little butter. Make the sauce apart by boiling the peel in a little milk and butter, rub it through a fine sieve, mix in a little yelk of egg, and pour over the pieces.

A third way is to take a large old cucumber, peel it, cut off the two ends, and boil it very lightly. When done, make an incision down the middle, not quite to the two ends. Scoop out the seeds, and fill in the hollow with a light stuffing of suet, herbs, breadcrumbs, and egg. Serve it whole, like a rolly-poly pudding, with a yellow Dutch sauce round it.

I find, all through the year, that a compote is a much more popular way of cooking fruit than in a tart. The great secret of making compotes is to stew some fruits, and only to pour boiling syrup over others. For instance, Red Currants are not good unless stewed for some time in an earthenware dish in the oven. Raspberries are quite spoilt by this treatment.

JULY

July 6th.—One of the prettiest weeds that we have in our modern gardens, and which alternates between being our greatest joy and our greatest torment, is the Welsh Poppy. It succeeds so well in this dry soil that it sows itself everywhere ; but when it stands up, with its profusion of yellow flowers well above its bed of bright green leaves, in some fortunate situation where it can not only be spared, but encouraged and admired, it is a real pleasure. It is not a Poppy at all, but a *Meconopsis*. It is quite easy to distinguish between the two, once having grasped the fact that the seed-vessels of the entire Poppy tribe are flat on the top, whereas the seed-vessels of the *Meconopsis* are pointed. There are several varieties of *Meconopsis*, all very desirable, and to be found, as usual, well described in the ' English Flower Garden.'

Their cultivation is a little more difficult than that of the ordinary annual and biennial, so one hardly ever sees them anywhere, but they are well worth the little extra trouble. Among the many small plants of easy cultivation and persistent flowering, Astrantias are very useful, especially in light soils, where things flower and are over so quickly. There are several shades ; I have a pink and a green. They have a most refined beauty of their own, and last well in water. They are best grown from seed, and are well worth every care. Any soil will suit them, and they will grow in half-shade or full sun.

Some dry summers Green Peas do very badly with us ; they dry up so quickly. We all know the hesitating remark to the cook : ' The Peas were not so good last night.' ' No, m'm, they are getting old.' When they do get old, the following is an original French receipt for stewed Peas, which is very good indeed :—Put the Peas into a saucepan with a good-sized Cabbage Lettuce cut up, a white Onion, a sprig of Parsley, four ounces of butter kneaded with flour ; put the butter in small lumps on the Peas, also a very little salt and a piece of white sugar. Cover the saucepan, and let it simmer slowly for about three-quarters of an hour.

Currants ripen very early with us. It is a good plan, in order to keep them for eating when other fruit is not so plentiful, to tie the whole bush up in coarse muslin just as the Currants are getting ripe. This protects them from birds and from insects, and they hang well on into September, and are perfectly good. Black Currants will not stand the same treatment.

The following is a good receipt for Red Currant jelly, one of the preserves best worth making at home :— Gather the Currants on a dry day. Strip them off their stalks, and squeeze the juice through a cloth. Leave the juice to stand in the cellar for twenty-four hours ; then pour it into another cloth, carefully leaving the thick sediment behind. For each pound of juice allow one pound of powdered white sugar (not bought ready pounded, but done at home). Put the juice on the fire in the preserving-pan, and keep stirring it from the first with a silver spoon, adding the sugar, which should be standing close by, in spoonfuls. When the sugar is all added and dissolved, it will be necessary to take off the rising scum with a flat sieve-spoon, very well scalded and cleaned previously ; and by placing a little jelly on a saucer it will be seen by the consistency when it has jellied. As soon as there is a sign of this take the pan off the fire, let it stand five or ten minutes, and fill the jelly glasses, which should previously have been well sulphured, and be standing ready face downwards. Next day they should be covered with rounds of paper soaked in brandy. Half a teaspoonful of brandy should be sprinkled over each glass, and then they should be tied or gummed up in the usual way.

July 8th.—I consider no trouble too great, whether the garden be large or small, to grow the beautiful stately Madonna Lily (*Lilium candidum*). It requires very different treatment from other Lilies, and flourishes in rich, heavy soils in full sun, where many Lilies would fail. Gardening books often tell you it is fatal to move these Lilies, but I think this has arisen from gardeners moving or disturbing them when they have ' done ' their orders in October or November, and when the Lilies have made an autumn growth ; moving them then is fatal. When I used to leave them alone, they made an excellent top growth in spring, but dried up and died down without flowering. What I now do when they begin to die down some time this month, whether they have flowered or not, is to dig them up carefully with a fork, remove all offsets, re-make and manure the ground well, mixing with it some brick rubbish or chalk, and then replace the large bulbs, planting them rather deep, and not too close together. In this way every bulb flowers. A little liquid manure helps them to open well when they are in bud the following June. The small offsets are put into a nursery apart, and many of them will flower the following year in a way that does admirably for picking.

A few years ago I brought from Paris some bulbs of *Ornithogalum pyramidale,* the flower-spikes of which are sold at the end of May in the Paris flower market under the name of *L'épée de la Vierge.* I have never seen the plant grown anywhere in England as I have grown it, and yet in every way it is quite one of the most satisfactory flowers for picking that I know. If you gather it just as one flower is coming out, the whole of the long spike grows and flowers in water up to the very top, bending and curling about, and assuming the most graceful curves. No one can grow a better flower plant to send to London. It has one fault in the garden—the leaves droop and turn rather spotty and yellow before the flower comes quite to its prime ; but this defect can indeed be forgiven for the sake of its many merits. I cultivate it nearly as I do the above-mentioned Lilies ; only, when the bulbs are dug up, we place the small ones at once in a nursery, but the large ones are well dried in the sun and not replanted till October. A mulching when they begin to show through in the spring does them good. Mr. Barr sells the bulbs, but I cannot say if his are as fine as those I brought from Paris six or seven years ago. I know no summer-flowering shrub so beautiful as the *Hydrangea paniculata grandiflora*. I have tried over and over again to grow it, but it does badly and then dies. It is not the soil only, for I once saw a magnificent specimen growing under a wall at Ascot, where the soil is the same as ours. I suppose it never has had quite a good enough place. It should be cut back hard every spring, and, when growing freely, wants much watering ; I am told that constant applications of soot-water do it good. I daresay I shall succeed in time.

July 10th.—This is about the time we move our things from the reserve garden, spoken of before, and from the late-sown seed beds, and plant into the borders and square beds those amiable autumn annuals that do not seem to mind moving at all, such as French Marigolds, Tagetes, Everlastings, Scabious, &c. The Phloxes, Michaelmas Daisies, and early low-growing Chrysanthemums, grown in the reserve garden, move just as well in warm, dry weather as in wet, only, of course, they must be well and continuously watered till the weather changes and they have taken hold. The large *Sedum spectabile*, so loved by the bees in September, also moves perfectly in the same way, and, in a large mass, makes a very handsome autumn plant. I am sure that the system of reserve garden and moving plants and seedlings in July can be extended and experimented upon to almost any extent. Next year I must try it with the *Veronica spicata*—white, blue, and pink. They are very pretty things when flowering well and healthily, and they come into bloom at a time of year when herbaceous plants are scarce. *Campanula turbinata*, blue and white, are useful for the same reason.

Alstrœmerias do very well on dry, light soil ; they want mulching in spring, but are no trouble at all when once established. *A. aurantiaca* is the easiest to grow, but *A. chilensis* is the most beautiful. The seeds of the best flowers are worth keeping and sowing, to improve the colour and size of the flowers. The white one I have not yet succeeded in making grow from seeds, but I saw it at the Horticultural Show, and it was most beautiful and delicate. I find that buying the bulbous rootlets dried is no use at all, they do not grow. They do not mind moving in August after flowering, and they are best increased as Lilies of the Valley are—by digging out square pieces, filling in with good soil and dropping in the pieces cut out where they are wanted somewhere else without disturbing the earth that clings to them. If you ever try to force your own Lilies of the Valley, pick out the best crowns, but never put them into the greenhouse till frost has been on them, and never mulch outdoor Lilies of the Valley before March, and then only with leaf mould. As Lilies are an early spring flower, you will find they do better under a wall facing east than anywhere else.

July 14th.—How beautiful are the really hot, lovely

English summer's days. They come sometimes, and they are exquisite; nothing beats them. Why, oh! why, can I never enjoy such things without that tinge of sadness which moderns call morbidness? It does no good, but I think of someone who is ill, or of those masses and masses of people in that dreary great city so close. As I enjoy my garden alone, with the beauty and the flowers, the flood of summer light and the intense pleasure of it, I long to do something, and longing generally resolves itself into picking flowers for somebody. This little poem by Paul Verlaine seems to give the colour of it all, and the pain :—

LA VIE

Le ciel est par-dessus le toit,
  Si bleu, si calme !
Un arbre par-dessus le toit
  Berce sa palme.

La cloche dans le ciel qu'on voit
  Doucement tinte,
Un oiseau sur l'arbre qu'on voit
  Chante sa plainte.

Mon Dieu, mon Dieu, la vie est là
  Simple et tranquille ;
Cette paisible rumeur-là
  Vient de la ville.

Qu'as-tu fait, O toi que voilà,
  Pleurant sans cesse—
Dis, qu'as-tu fait, toi que voilà,
  De ta jeunesse ?

July 15th.—July is a very busy month in all gardens. The borders must be cleared and replanted, the seeds of perennials have to be gathered and sown, and many other things require attention. The *Delphiniums* may bravely be cut down after flowering ; it does them no harm, and they often break again and have stray flowering sprays in the autumn. Some of the best seed should be sown every year. The same with the Verbascums ;

JULY. 145

if cut down, they flower again, in rather a different way, but very charmingly, in the autumn. July is also the great time for sowing perennials, or perennials that are treated as biennials ; and when you have fine flowers or good colours, it is quite worth while to mark the flowers by tying a piece of bass or coloured wool round the stalk. These little white ties are recognised and respected by the gardeners while clearing the borders, a work which it is essential to do in July. I sow a great many things every year, and find them most useful— *Gaillardias, Coreopsis lanceolata,* Snapdragons (*Antirrhinums*). Oh, how useful and beautiful are the tall yellow and the tall white Snapdragons ! They can be played with in so many ways : potted up in the autumn, grown and flowered in a greenhouse, cut back and planted out in the spring to flower again, admirable to send away ; in fact, they have endless merits, and in a large clump in front of some dark corner or shrub they look very handsome indeed. They are lovely picked and on the dinner-table, especially the yellow Snapdragons, but, like many other things, they just want a little care and cultivation, which they often do not get ; and they ought to be sown every April, and again in July. The smaller the garden, the more essential are these plants for people who like having flowers to pick ; but I warn everyone against those terrible inventions of seedsmen, the Dwarf *Antirrhinums ;* they have all the attributes of a dwarf, and are impish and ugly. The flower is far too large for the stalk, and they are, to my mind, entirely without merit. July is the time I take up both the English and the Spanish Irises, which makes them do ever so much better. The English Irises are best planted again at once, only taking off the small bulbs. The Spanish Irises are best dried in the sun and replanted in September. In both cases the small bulbs are planted in rows in the kitchen garden ; they take up little room, and in this way the stock is increased. In our soil, unless treated in this way, they dwindle, cease flowering, and ultimately disappear. I lost many from not knowing this in my early gardening days, when I was certainly green in judgment. The Spanish Iris likes a dry place in full sun ; the English Iris does best in half-shade, and likes moisture if it can get it, but flowers well without ; the leaves are what suffer most from dryness— long, succulent, moisture-loving things that they are.

July 17th.—We have had a most unusually hot dry summer, and to go into the garden is absolute pain to me, for all the trouble and labour of the year seem more or less wasted. Plants are miserably forced into bloom, to go off almost immediately ; and it is little consolation to know a week's rain will make many plants beautiful again, for the especial beauty of early summer is over. July and August are always trying months here. The soil is so very light, and one must pay the penalty ; even the heavy soils, I am told, are suffering much this year (1896).

One ought, too, to study with great interest and take note of what survives, and even does better in these very dry years. That handsome, rather coarse-growing perennial, *Buphthalmum cordifolium,* now called *Telekia speciosa*—as if one such name were not enough for a stout-growing composite—looked shrivelled and unhappy last month, but it has flowered better than usual, and it is a handsome plant. The pretty feathery *Gypsophila paniculata* never suffers from dryness, it has such a splendid big tap-root. The *Gaillardias,* moved from the seed bed in spring, have done very well in full sun.

The *Coreopsis grandiflora* blazes in the sunlight. I save a little seed from the largest flowers of both of these, and sow them every year, so as to have a continual supply of young plants. It is not to avoid buying fresh seeds that I mark the best flowers of some, but because by this means, and by saving only from the best flowers, I get really better plants.

My Carnations are much less good than usual this year, but I cannot blame the weather for this. I stupidly followed the advice in some of the gardening papers last year of leaving the layers on the old plants till April. I shall never do so again; here it does not answer at all; but I shall layer them as early as possible, take them off in October, and make up the bed then. It is a very good plan to plant a row of young Carnation plants in the kitchen garden, some distance apart, so that they may be layered earlier than in the beds.

July 25th.—Not the least delightful part, in my opinion, of the growing knowledge of gardening is the appreciative visiting of the gardens of others. On first going into a garden one knows by instinct, as a hound scents the fox, if it is going to be interesting or not. One's eyes are sharp, and a joyful glow of satisfaction comes over one on seeing something not by any means necessarily new, but unknown to oneself. When looking through old books or modern catalogues, one feels one has nothing in one's garden, but I must confess that visiting other people's gardens very often makes me feel I really have a very fair collection. A notebook is a most important companion on gardening expeditions. I use metallic paper, to ensure a permanent record, and an ordinary pencil. I write the date and name of the place, then jot down the names of plants and general observations. I have also kept a kind of gardening journal for many years, making notes three or four times in the month, and on the opposite page I keep lists of any plants I buy or bring home from friends, with the date; noting the deaths the following year is instructive. I have lately had a rain-gauge given me. This is a great interest and amusement, especially where rain-water is always in demand and often running short. I did not know the importance of rain-water when first we came to live here; and though we have lots of roofing, we are not sufficiently provided with underground tanks.

Our small ones are supplemented now as much as possible by petroleum barrels sunk into the ground, and
the watershoot from the roof allowed to pour into them.
You can connect this first barrel with others by a little
piece of lead piping, and so increase the storage.

For those who have not got very good memories for
the names of plants, I strongly recommend them, if they
can draw, to make a little coloured sketch, however
small, on the page of a gardening book next the name
of the plant. This will be found a great help to the
memory ; I began gardening so late in life that I had
to get all the help I could. I have lately been visiting
what I call intelligent gardens, and will make a few
remarks about them. In one place where Roses grow
well I saw a beautiful specimen of La Marque Rose—
one of the most satisfactory Roses for a wall. Everyone
ought to try and grow it who has room and a fairly good
Rose soil. The long flowering branches were cut a yard
or more in length. At the end of each branch was a
beautiful bunch of pure, cream-white Roses, seven or
eight in number, with buds in between, and pale, healthy
green leaves down the stem. Two such branches in a
narrow-necked vase, bronze or blue or dark green, are
an ornament to which nothing can be added for any
room, be it in a cottage or a palace. As a decoration
for a large dinner-table, nothing can be better than
these Roses when they are in their prime, which, unfortunately, is but for a very short time.

In the old days of bedding-out, lawns used to be cut
up into beds and patterns. Now the fashion has changed,
and bedding-out has become so generally condemned that
most people have levelled and turfed-over the rounds,
stars, crescents, and oblongs that used to enliven their
lawns for a short time, at any rate, every autumn. As
a result of this reaction, there are now an immense
number of large, dull lawns, which as a rule slope slightly
away from the house, and often to the south. They are

wet in rain, and dry and brown in hot weather. They have their weekly shave with the mowing-machine, and lie baking in the sunshine. The poor plants, which would flower and do well in the open, are planted at the edges of the shrubberies, where—in a light soil, at any rate— they are robbed and starved into ugliness and failure by their stronger neighbours.

There are several ways of breaking up lawns. One is by turning the lawns into grass paths, along which the machine runs easily, and making all the rest into open, informally shaped beds. These can be planted in every kind of way—in bold masses of one thing alone, or at most in mixtures of two, such as Roses and Violas ; Azaleas and Lilies ; Carnations and more Violas, or mossy Saxifrages ; Campanulas in succession, tall and low-growing ; a bold group of Bamboos and *Bocconia cordata ;* or simply with a selection of a few low-growing shrubs ; and so on *ad infinitum.* Another way, and one that finds small favour with gardeners, and with considerable reason, because of the trouble of turning the mowing-machine round the plants, is to break up the lawn with sunshine-loving specimen plants—Mulberries, Savins, Sumachs, clumps of creeping Ayrshire Roses and Honeysuckles, poles covered with claret-coloured Vines, Clematis, &c. Yet another way is to have a double pergola running all round the lawn in a square, or only down both sides, with a grass path, broad and stately, underneath the pergola. This can be made of stone or brick, oak-trees or fir-poles ; or, if wanted very light, of Japanese large Bamboos—to be got now in London, I believe. These Bamboos look best if two, three, or five are blocked together unequally, with different-sized openings in between, and used as supports for fruit-trees and flowering shrubs of all kinds. As these plants grow, bamboos and wires have to be put across the top to support the creepers. In the middle is a large square of grass ; the openings are left turfed, but where the supports are put into the ground a narrow bed must be made for the plants. This enables them to be manured, chalked, watered, and generally cared for. I now come to what is, in my idea, by far the most enchanting plan for breaking up a lawn, which is to sink a small Dutch garden in the middle of it. The size of the Dutch garden must, of course, be in proportion to that of the lawn. If the proportion cannot be kept, it would be better to leave it alone. It should have a red-brick wall all round it, and be oblong or square, as suits the situation. The entrances to it are by brick steps, one in the middle of each of the four sides. The height of the wall is about three feet from the ground on the outside, and five feet on the inside. Along these walls, on the inside, are rather wide beds, bordered by paths made of rows of large, square red tiles, laid flat and not quite joining, so that tiny alpines and mosses may grow in between them at their own sweet will. If preferred, this narrow path can be made of bricks or broken paving-stones. The object of this path, besides the convenience of standing dry to pick the flowers or weed the beds, is that the front of the bed can be planted in groups, not in rows, with all sorts of low-growing things :—Alyssums, Aubrietias, Forget-me-nots, Pinks of all kinds, Saxi-frages, and mosses. On the side shaded by the wall and facing north small ferns, Campanulas, and shade-loving plants are the only ones that will do well. Prim-roses, Auriculas, and the spring-flowering bulbs and Irises do best on the side facing east ; and the summer and autumn plants like to face west and north, as they weary of the hot sun all the summer through. All the year round this little garden can be kept a pleasure and a joy by a little management, and by planting and re-planting from the greenhouse, the seed-beds, or the reserve garden. The wall looks best if entirely planted with Tea-roses. As they grow, they send up long waving branches, which beautifully break the hard line of the wall. The middle of the walled garden is grass, and the mowing machine can never cut or injure the plants, feather forward as they will on to the tiled path between the beds and the grass. In the centre there can be a sundial on a square base ; or, if you have water laid on, a small square or oblong cement tank let into the ground, quite level with the grass, as a fountain and to be handy for watering. All day long the water in the tank is warmed by the sunshine. This kind of fountain is an enormous improvement, I think, to small suburban gardens, and it is prettier oblong than square. The fountain must be made of cement and six or eight feet deep. If the garden slopes at all, the overflow from the fountain can be guided by small watercourses on to different beds. I have pockets of cement made at irregular intervals at the edges of the fountain to hold water-plants and such things, which then appear reflected on the surface of the water, not as they grow against a dark shrub or a group of Italian Canes of Bamboos, but against the blue sky above them—an endless pleasure to those who notice such things. A piece of water, however small, and the sound of water falling from a small fountain, or even from a raised tap if the tank is near a wall, is such an added enjoyment to life on a hot summer's day, not to mention the infinite superiority for watering of having water that has been exposed to the sun and air. If not artificially fed, gold-fish live and breed healthily in these tanks.

Water-plants, such as the Sweet-smelling Rush, the flowering Rush *Butomus umbellatus*, the Water-lily, the Cape pond-weed *Aponogeton*, can all be grown in tanks if the plants are planted in baskets or hampers, not pots, and let down to the bottom. They give food for the fish, and keep them healthy ; a tank also serves as a dip for swallows on the wing, and as a breeding-place for the beautiful blue dragon-fly.

To go back to the Dutch garden. I think at the

corners of, or on each side of, the entrances there may
be pots with plants in them, or balls of stone, or anything else in character with the rest of the stone or brick
work, which should be formal and slightly constrained
in design, as I consider all brickwork in a garden close
to a house ought to be. If planted as I described, no
two such gardens would ever be the least alike ; no
law could bind them, and no wind destroy them.

One of the most perfect ways of laying out a long flat
piece of ground I have ever seen was in a garden in
Salisbury. One long, very long, broad grass path, right
down the middle ; wide herbaceous borders on each side,
with low plants in front and tall ones behind ; and at
the back of these again, on each side, was the kitchen
garden—Gooseberries, Currants, and Raspberries, and in
between all the usual kitchen-garden vegetables ; beyond that was a small cinder-path, and then a wall on
either side, shutting off the neighbours. One wall faced
nearly north and the other nearly south. The long garden, stretching from the house eastward and westward,
was ended by the river ; the tall spires of the cathedral
towered behind the house. I have often thought that
the same disposition of an oblong piece of ground would
turn a depressing laurel-planted suburban garden into
a thing of joy and beauty, even without the cathedral
towers and the swift, clear, running river.

One of the most beautiful of late summer plants—I
see my friends often fail with it—is the *Lobelia cardinalis*
and *L. fulgens*, Queen Victoria. It is generally injured
by kindness, sown in the early spring, drawn up in greenhouses, and planted out weak and straggling, when it
does nothing. It is a North American bog-plant, where
it lies frost-bound for months, so it is not cold that kills
it ; but it likes a long rest. I generally take up my old
plants and keep them very dry in a box in a frame,
planting them out at the end of March or early in April,
before they begin to grow at all. It is letting them

grow on in the boxes that brings the disease and rust. Every year we sow a small patch of both kinds out of doors in June or July, and these young plants survive the winter perfectly. Dear youth ! What a power it is to those that have it, even among plants ! In spring these plants are put where they are wanted to flower. If they are in a dry place, I am bound to say they require plenty of water when once they really begin to grow. They look very well in autumn growing out of a fine spreading base of Mrs. Sinkins Pink, which must be divided in the autumn, leaving spaces for the planting of the Lobelia in spring.

This is the time when the plants before named, which were put into the reserve garden in the spring—early Chrysanthemums, Phloxes, Michaelmas Daisies—are brought to fill up bare places in the border. If the borders have been planted as before advised, the colours must be arranged according to the several groups. Two plants of the Daisy tribe—one blue-violet with a yellow middle, called *Erigeron speciosus ;* the other a bright yellow, though some are paler than others, called *Anthemis tinctoria*—are invaluable in dry borders. They grow easily from seed, and are very amiable about being moved.

July 27th.—Watering outdoor plants not in pots or tubs is a question about which people differ much. Gardeners as a rule are against it, and it certainly kills perennial plants and small shrubs if begun and left off, or even if improperly done. But in a dry soil many a plant is saved by watering it thoroughly once or twice a week, more especially if the flower-buds are formed. My experience is that under those circumstances watering hurts nothing, but it has a tendency to draw the roots to the surface, which is very undesirable with perennials, both for heat in summer and cold in winter. With any precious plant newly planted, and which looks thirsty, a very good and safe plan is to sink a flower-pot in the ground, just above the plant if the ground slopes at all. Fill this with water, and let it soak gradually away, to the cooling and refreshing of the roots. After the plant has been well soaked, one filling of the pot a day, in the morning, is sufficient. All plants that have been planted out, after being removed from a reserve garden or seed bed, must be watered ; and once you begin, whether in kitchen or flower garden, you must go on till it rains steadily and well ; a slight shower is no good.

A very good shading protection for small plants or delicate seedlings is to get the village blacksmith to make you some flower-pots—he will understand that—in perforated zinc such as would be used for larder windows, &c. Reverse one of these over the plant, to protect it from sun and wind.

The mention of blacksmith reminds me that the parings and raspings of horses' hoofs, which can be purchased for very little, put into a tub of water and allowed to decompose, make a very excellent and nourishing liquid manure. It should not be applied too strong.

July 30*th.*—Two shrubs are now flowering in the garden which in this month of the year are valuable. One is called *Clethra* (Sweet Pepper Bush), mentioned in May for pot-cultivation, and useful, as it stands pulling about and changing ; it is quite hardy, but in dry places it is the better for watering when coming into flower. The other is called Pavia or *Æsculus parvifolia* (Dwarf Horse Chestnut), a handsome and valuable hardy tree from North America. It does not grow fast, and takes little room ; it has long spikes of flowers with bright pink stamens, is refined and sweet, and very pretty when gathered and wedged (*see* Appendix), though it would not look well in a room in any other way. I have had it several years, and it flowers every year ; its handsome and yet restrained growth is a great advantage in a small garden.

AUGUST

Gilbert White—The decline of vegetable culture in the Middle Ages—
Preserving French Beans and Scarlet Runners—Scotch gardens—
Tropæolum speciosum—Crimson-berried Elder—The coast of Suther-
land—The abuse of coarse Creepers.

August 1st.—I cannot allow a summer to go by without
referring to that dear old classic, Gilbert White's ' Natural
History of Selborne.' Even now I do not quite know
why I am so fond of these letters, except that they show
strongly the observant eye and the genuine love of
Nature which are so sympathetic to me. When I was
young my mother gave me the book to read, and it
bored me considerably. I thought the long speculations
about the hibernating of birds—Swifts, Swallows, and
others—so tiresome ; especially as I knew for sure that
they migrated. I, almost a child, knew that. In those
days I just panted for what was coming ; the saying
' old days ' to me meant the present, which was older
than the past and growing each day, as I grew myself, to
greater maturity. I did not understand what people
meant by referring to the days which were behind as
' the old days,' for they represented to me the youth of
time. I longed to live the day after to-morrow before
it came, if only that were possible. Everything new
interested me ; I thought the world was moving so fast ;
and now that my life is nearly over, it is as if nothing
had happened. Progress is indeed like the old Greek
pattern, a continuous unbroken line, but curling back
and inwards for long periods before it starts a new de-

velopment. Just now even the enthusiastic and the young are trying to live in the past—a whole generation conservative in its youth. I suppose it is all right, but it seems to lack the generous impulses of the generation nourished on the teachings of Mill and Bright. How true it is that Liberalism is not a principle, but an attitude of mind! And the old Greek pattern will start its long line forward again some day.

Now that hope is over for me, the old times, with their edifying lessons, interest me most ; and so I try to understand the evolution of the present as taught through knowledge of the past, rather than breathlessly to grasp the future. My mother was so kind and sensible with me. So many parents are apt to be irritated by daughters who bound forward in life as children pick flowers in a field, always thinking there are many more and much finer ones just a little further on.

Though it is now little over a hundred years since Gilbert White died, his pictures of the change within his memory in the general condition of the poor, and of the improvement in agriculture, gardens and health, seem most strange. Leprosy still existed in Selborne, though it was much on the decline. He attributes this partly to improved food and partly to wearing clean linen instead of dirty woollen garments. As to the produce of a garden, he adds, ' Every middle-aged person of observation may perceive, within his own memory, both in town and country, how vastly the consumption of vegetables is increased. Green stalls in cities now support multitudes in a comfortable state, while gardeners get fortunes. Potatoes have prevailed in this district, by means of premiums, within these twenty years only, and are much esteemed here now by the poor, who would scarce have ventured to taste them in the last reign.

' Our Saxon ancestors certainly had some sort of Cabbage, because they call the month of February " Sprout-cale " ; but long after their days the cultivation of

gardens was little attended to. The religious, being men
of leisure, and keeping up a constant correspondence
with Italy, were the first people among us who had
gardens and fruit trees in any perfection, within the
walls of their abbeys and priories. The barons neglected
every pursuit that did not lead to war or tend to the
pleasure of the chase.'

It seems to me from this exceedingly probable that
gardens declined very much in England after the Reformation, and no doubt the eating of vegetables, like the
eating of fish, may have been considered Popish. Even
in my childhood I can remember that salad was rarely
seen at any but the tables of the very wealthy, who had
foreign cooks, and then it was covered with a rich cream
sauce, full of mustard, which was supposed to make it
digestible. This superstition of the day was pointedly
brought forward in some letters I found of my grand-
mother's to my father at Oxford, strongly recommending him to take mustard-seeds before his meals as very
helpful to digestion.

I am far from suggesting that the Reformation had,
on the whole, an injurious effect on England, but indirectly in many ways it seems to have led to curious
and even pernicious results. Among the most peculiar
of these was the increase of piracy in Elizabeth's reign.
The following account, given in Froude's 'English Sea-
men in the Sixteenth Century,' will explain what I
mean :—' In harbour there were still a score of large
ships, but they were dismantled and rotting ; of artillery
fit for sea work there was none. The men were not to
be had, and, as Sir William Cecil said, to fit out ships
without men was to set armour on stakes on the seashore. The mariners of England were otherwise engaged
and in a way that did not please Cecil. He was the
ablest Minister that Elizabeth had. He saw at once
that on the Navy the prosperity and even the liberty of
England must eventually depend. If England were to

remain Protestant, it was not by Articles of religion or Acts of Uniformity that she could be saved, without a fleet at the back of them. But he was old-fashioned. He believed in law and order, and he has left a curious paper of reflections on the situation. The ships' companies in Henry VIII.'s days were recruited from the fishing smacks, but the Reformation itself had destroyed the fishing trade. In old times, Cecil said, no flesh was eaten on fish days. The King himself could not have license. Now to eat beef or mutton on fish days was the test of a true believer. . . . The fishermen had taken to privateering because the fasts of the Church were neglected. He saw it was so. He recorded his own opinion that piracy, as he called it, was detestable, and could not last. He was to find that it could last, that it was to form the special discipline of the generation whose business it would be to fight the Spaniards. But he struggled hard against the unwelcome conclusion. He tried to revive lawful trade by a Navigation Act. He tried to restore the fisheries by Act of Parliament. He introduced a Bill recommending godly abstinence as a means to virtue, making the eating of meat on Fridays and Saturdays a misdemeanour, and adding Wednesday as a half fish day. The House of Commons laughed at him as bringing back Popish mummeries. To please the Protestants he inserted a clause that the statute was politically meant for the increase of fishermen and mariners, not for any superstition in the choice of meats ' but it was no use. The Act was called in mockery " Cecil's Fast," and the recovery of the fisheries had to wait till the natural inclination of human stomachs for fresh whiting and salt cod should revive in itself.'

I have made this long extract because it seems to me to throw an exceedingly interesting side-light on the non-cultivation, and above all on the bad cooking, of vegetables, which extended to a great degree into my childhood. Even to-day, in spite of the increased quantity of vegetables and their comparative cheapness, it is rare to see them in any variety in English family life ; and I am told that at ordinary clubs Potatoes and Brussels Sprouts represent in winter the vegetable kingdom. What is still more remarkable is that the absence of vegetables has now extended to all the principal foreign hotels, with the probable notion of suiting the English taste.

In the early Protestant days meat was no doubt eaten with a religious zeal, and the cultivation and cooking of vegetables was utterly neglected. The old gardens of the monasteries ran to ruin even quicker than the fish-ponds. It became a point of national honour to disregard the methods of cooking vegetables which had been brought by the monks, who were men of taste, from France and Italy. Proper cooking alone makes ordinary vegetables palatable, and improves even the very best. The extraordinary development of the vegetable, fruit, and flower trade is one of the most marked changes of my lifetime. When I was young, it was impossible in the West End of London to buy any flowers at all in the streets or shops. If we did not winter in the South of France, but remained in London, we had to go to some nursery gardens that lay between Rutland Gate and Kensington in order to buy a few Violets.

Froude says, about another strange effect of the Reformation. ' It probably, more than any other cause, stopped the development of painting in England. Holbein had no pupils. Zuccaro left the country in disgust. All portraits that remain were painted by foreigners.' The worst kings from the political point of view have been the best from that of painting. Charles I. was no exception to the rule, and his magnificent gallery was sold by Parliament in 1645 for 38,000l., apparently without protest.

Of all the months in the year, this is perhaps the one in which the keenest amateur can best afford to leave home ; and if I do not go away, it is the one I can best spare to my gardener for his holiday. In August hope, as far as the year is concerned, is over. There is nothing that imperatively requires doing ; nearly all there is to do can be as well done in July or September. After deciding to leave home I gave instructions that the young French Beans and Scarlet Runners should be picked over, almost daily, so that none should grow coarse and old ; and that the cook should lay them separately, as they were brought in, in large earthenware pans—a handful of Beans and then a handful of salt, and so on till the pan was full. This is an excellent method ; and I have eaten them, preserved in this way, all through the winter. I believe this is done everywhere abroad, but never in England, where the waste, both in the kitchen and the garden, is, as we all acknowledge, a national vice. Of course the Beans in the salt must not be allowed to get touched by frost in the autumn. When wanted, they are taken out, well soaked (to prevent their being too salt), boiled in the ordinary way—cut up or whole, as we like them best—then drained, and warmed up in fresh butter, a squeeze of lemon and a little chopped Parsley on the top. They can also be cooked with a white cream sauce. All this is well described for fresh Beans in ' Dainty Dishes.' I think these salted Beans have more flavour than the tinned ones, or than those that come from Madeira in the winter. Besides, the principle of utilising everything in a garden should never be lost sight of.

This year fate took us to the North, to Northumberland, the home of my maternal family, from which my mother in her youth, with the whole large family, travelled twice a year on the old North Road to London and back in carriages and coaches. One of my mother's aunts used to tell a story of how in her youth she had had her hair dressed in London to appear at a Newcastle ball, and she added with pride, ' When I entered the ball-room I had my reward.'

I was surprised to find that the great changes that have come over our Southern gardens by the re-introducing the old-fashioned flowers and the old methods of cultivating them are much less noticeable in the North. Apparently changes work slower in the North than around London. I wonder why this is ? People there have the same books, the same newspapers, and the same climatic advantage as in Scotland, which makes the herbaceous plants grow to great perfection, and flower much longer than in the South. One would have thought the fashion which has so influenced us would have influenced them. I saw in many places long borders planted with rows of red, violet, white, yellow, and purple—vistas of what used to be called ribbon-borders, very unpicturesque at the best, and nearly always unsatisfactory. Why they ever came in, and why they have lasted so long it is difficult to understand. The gardens of rich and poor, big house and villa, were planted on the same system—perennials in lines, annuals in lines, Mignonette in lines ; and where long lines were not possible, the planting was in rows round the shrubberies, which is, I think, the ugliest thing I know. If shrubberies are planted with flowers at all, I like large holes cut back, which makes a good protection, and plants introduced in bold groups. I did not see one garden while I was away—whose owners ought to have known better—where things were what I call well planted, in good bold masses of colour ; whereas near Dublin more than two years ago I found the best herbaceous border I have ever seen. The way of planting in this Dublin border, with all the reds in one place, and the blues, the yellows, and the whites kept apart as much as possible, was as superior to the dotted arrangement as the dotted system is to the line, in my opinion. I even saw in some places this year what I as a child had remembered as old mixed borders, turned into that terrible gardening absurdity, carpet-bedding—the pride, I suppose, of the

6

gardener and the admiration of his friends. This is
never to be seen now in Surrey, I think, except in certain
beds at Hampton Court; and why it is continued there
I find it hard to understand, unless it is that it really
does give pleasure to Londoners, and certainly in its
way it is carried out to great perfection.

I had always heard of the brilliant beauty of Scotch
gardens, and the moment I saw them I understood why
it was. The seasons are so late that all the summer
flowers bloom together; May and June of the South
merge into July and August in Scotland, and everything
is in flower at once. No wonder the gardens look bright;
besides, the damp air makes the colours more beautiful
and the scent stronger.

It is, I think, very interesting to the gardener, where-
ever he goes, to see how the common everyday things
flourish more in one place than another. The Highlands seem to be the home of the Gooseberry—such old
and hoary bushes, more or less covered by grey Lichens,
but laden none the less with little hairy Gooseberries,
both red and green, and full of flavour. There, too, the
beautiful *Tropæolum speciosum*, South American stranger
as it is, flames and flourishes and luxuriates everywhere,
growing too, as it will not do in the South, in full sunshine. The seed is so lovely in Scotland, almost as
beautiful as the flower itself—three dark steel-blue
seeds set in the dying flower, which turns a rich brown.
Was ever anything more daintily beautiful to be seen?
It can be grown up strings, as in the picture in the
' English Flower Garden '; but I do not think that is
as pretty as rambling with its delicate growth over some
light creeper, such as Jasmine or Rose, as I recommended
before. I did not see in the Highlands, rather to my
surprise, though I believe it is planted in some places,
the beautiful crimson-berried Elder, *Sambucus racemosa*.
This was the one remarkable plant-feature I saw in
Norway last year. I was there too late to see the wild

flowers. It had not been imported very long, they told us, and it adorned all the stations (there is only one short railway in Norway), throwing out long branches covered with bunches of crimson berries, which are shaped like the black bunches on the Privet rather than like the flat berries of the common Elder. At a distance the plant looks, when covered with ripe berries, like a beautiful Crimson Rambler. It is singularly effective, and I have never seen it in England. I imagine this must be because, if it grew and berried ever so well in damp places, the birds would soon clear off all the fruit. In Norway there seem to be no small birds, for there the berries hung for weeks and weeks, in crimson loveliness. The shrub is about the height of Lilac bushes ; the berries grow on the old wood, and the growth of the year is a most brilliant green. It is a plant that more people should try to grow in damp situations.

We were far North, up in Sutherland, where the great storm of two years ago laid bare miles and miles of forest. I never saw a more curious sight—pathetic and sad too, in a way. The poor trees, which had from their youth up been accustomed to storms from the south and west, had sent out long roots, and buried them deep under rocks and stones, which gave them firm hold to resist the blast. But on this November morning two years ago the snow was on the tree-tops, which made them heavy, and the furious gale swept on them from the north, and down they fell in thousands—whole hillsides laid bare, without one tree left standing, all torn up by the roots. It will be many years before the countryside is cleared of its own fallen timber.

We lived a mile from the sea. The Sutherland coast is tame enough, but beautifully desolate—no travellers, no tourists, nothing to disturb the solitude. I am not very fond of the East Coast, as there in the afternoon one is only able to enjoy reflected sunshine. It always reminds me of friends as they grow cold ; they expect us to be warmed by the sunshine of yesterday. Once I went down alone to the shore ; it was a beautiful evening, with hundreds of shades of pearly greys and pinks reflected on sand and wave—an evening to make mean things noble and costly things ridiculous, an evening that humbles one down to the very dust, and yet lifts one clean off one's feet with enthusiasm and exultation. I remember years ago a friend of mine telling me she had met Jenny Lind, who had then just left the stage, at a quiet South Coast seaside bathing-place. Jenny Lind was sitting on the steps of a bathing-machine, and my friend began talking to her and asking her ' if she did not think she would miss terribly the excitement of acting.' ' Very likely,' she answered, ' but I had ceased to be able to admire that,' pointing to the great gold sun going down in its glory, ' and I had ceased to be able to read this,' tapping a Bible that lay on her knees. ' Don't you think it was time to give it up ? '

I had not been five minutes on this lonely Sutherland shore before I counted quite ten wild sea-birds of different kinds flying around, screaming to each other, and floating about on the tiny waves that broke gently on the sand. I suppose few can hear that sound of the waves without thinking of Tennyson's ' Break, break, break.' A little poem of Emerson's, much less known, is a great favourite of mine, full as it is of a tender double meaning :—

The delicate shells lay on the shore ;
The bubbles of the latest wave
Fresh pearl to their enamel gave,
And the bellowing of the savage sea
Greeted their safe escape to me.
I wiped away the weeds and foam,
And brought my sea-born treasures home ;
But the poor, unsightly, noisome things
Had left their beauty on the shore
With the sun and the sand and the wild uproar.

I feel these lines reproach me for my many quotations.

AUGUST. 165

Have we any right to pick beautiful things out of books and quote them without their context ? I suspect not, and I beg you all to consider, if you find them deficient, that it is I who have taken them away from ' the sun and the sand and the wild uproar.'

In the grounds of the great castle we were near was a very interesting museum. What an excellent thing is a private museum in a large place ! It would be a great advantage, I think, if it were started on many estates, or even in villages, as then the barbaric things and various specimens of natural history which different members of a family bring home might be kept where they are of distinct interest, instead of crowding up a modern sitting-room, where they look totally inappropriate and even ugly.

There had always been a tradition that one of the ships belonging to the Spanish Armada had been wrecked off this coast, but no treasure had ever been found. Two years ago, when the river was low, a cow went into the mud to drink, and came out with a splendid Spanish old gold coin of the time of the Armada stuck in her hoof. Nothing more was discovered, but as the river was tidal it was a curious confirmation of the old tradition. On our way South we could not help noticing how far more beautiful Scotland is than Norway. The Heather was unusually fine this year. We stayed a night in Edinburgh, which gave me an opportunity of seeing the pictures in the National Gallery. I wonder if many tourists visit it ? The morning I was there I did not see two people in the gallery. Besides the Rae-burns, which are of world-wide fame, several pictures stand out with peculiar interest, especially the life-sized Gainsborough of the young Mrs. Grahame. She sat for this picture as a bride, but before it came home she was dead and her husband had gone to the wars. When he came back, he never had the courage to open the case which contained his young wife's portrait. On his death, many long years after it was painted, it was opened by his heirs, and inside the case was the little white slipper she had left with the painter to help him to finish his picture. The portrait was given to the Edinburgh Gallery, and the slipper was kept by the family. It is worth noting that an oil picture should have remained so long shut up and apparently not deteriorated in any way. There is a lovely Greuze, one of the prettiest I have ever seen, a child of about fourteen crying over a dead canary ; an exquisite little Boucher of Mme. de Pompadour ; a large picture by the eighteenth-century Venetian painter Tiepolo, whose works are rarely seen out of Venice. The picture gives one more impression of his power and cleverness than it delights one with its beauty. The expression, character, and sex are described by the power of the brush as completely as by the word-painting of a Paul Bourget novel. What added to my interest in Tiepolo was the revival of admiration his works have lately had among young French painters. I was immensely pleased at seeing a portrait of the painter Martin, by himself—a red-haired youth, with the cold dreamy eyes of the artistic temperament, a mouth rather sensual than passionate, a fine brow, and a slightly receding chin, which gave a touch of weakness to the face. All my life I have so admired his wildly imaginative illustrations of the Bible, Milton, &c. The impression given by the portrait is of a touching, interesting face, with that look of sorrow which so appeals to one, especially in the young. The gods do not always remember that those whom they love should die young. Poor Martin did not die till middle life, and went mad, I believe.

On leaving Edinburgh we returned to Tweed-side, where we saw several of the old Border towers and the really fine ' stately homes ' of England. Here I was struck by the same mistake which prevails in the South. The walls and shapes of fine old houses are ruined by allowing, even on the southern and western aspects, a rampageous growth of coarse creepers, such as Ivy, the common Virginia Creeper, and *Ampelopsis veitchii*. This last is the most insidious and destructive of all, as no kitten compared to a cat, and no baby donkey compared to an old one, could ever more completely change its character from youth to age than does this creeper. When first planted, the tiny, delicate growth that creeps up the mullioned windows is as pretty and harmless as anything can be ; but in a year or two all this turns into a huge mass of green leaves of an even shape and size, smothering up any less strong-growing creeper and destroying all outline of the house itself, its tiny feet sticking so fast to the stone or brick work that, if you try to pull them away, small particles of the wall itself come with them. Besides the temptation of its beautiful early growth, one must admit that for ten days the red and bronze and gold of its autumn tints go far to compensate for its many defects during the rest of the year. But this pleasure is easily retained by allowing it to grow over some ugly barn or northern wall, which has no architecture to injure or hide, and where flowering creepers would not flower. No one who has ever been to America and seen Boston can forget the dreary effect of house after house covered from cellar to roof with this luxuriant, overpowering ' Vine,' as every Creeper is called in America. The true name of the *Ampelopsis* is *Tricuspidata ;* but the Americans call it Japanese Ivy, in memory of where it comes from. If anything could accentuate the ugliness of the general effect, it is the square holes cut for the windows in this evenly green foliage. Everything is worth having in London that will grow there, but, with this picture in my mind, may I urge all who have any influence to make some protest against the fashionable use of this creeper, which seems to prevail from South to North of Great Britain ? Just before I left home I saw with consternation that every delicate brick turret of Hampton Court Palace had been carefully planted with *Ampelopsis*. For the present it looks harmless enough to all but the prophetic eye of a gardener, but in a few years the sharp lines of the delicate masonry will be entirely veiled by its luxuriant and monotonous growth. Surely fine and historical buildings are very much better left without creepers. In the case of ordinary modern houses with bare walls it is infinitely better to cover them with some of the endless variety of shrubs, creepers, and plants, which can be chosen to flower in succession through the whole year —from the *Chimonanthus fragrans*, which pushes forth its sweet-scented brown flowers in January, to the bare branches of the *Jasminum nudiflorum*, whose yellow stars light up a December fog.

Returning from Scotland, we spent a few days near Lancaster. The town is picturesquely situated. It is full of sketching possibilities for those who delight, as Turner did, in the glorification of commonplace objects by the veiling and unveiling of smoke, and in the constant colour-changes produced by the same. A very handsome bridge crosses the broad Lune, and carries the Preston and Kendal canal. This is one of the curious historical records of the waste of a people's money, and absolutely dead speculation. This canal was just finished, with its magnificent engineering, at great expense and with high hopes of its usefulness, immediately before the railways came and rendered it almost useless. Sleepy barges glide along it, profiting by its dignified engineering, and creeping under its countless bridges as they never could have done had it been ceaselessly ploughed by small steamers, as was intended. I do not exactly know why, but it brought back to my mind—from a consecutiveness of idea, I suppose—the elaborate fortifications of Quebec, the pride of George III.'s heart, upon which had been spent the nation's money and labour, and which were scarcely finished when the developments of modern warfare rendered them useless. Not very far from Lancaster, at Levens, is the famous example of topiary gardening which figures in the last edition of the ' English Flower Garden.' I was unfortunately prevented from going to see it by deluges of rain.

SEPTEMBER

Weeds we alternately love and hate—*Amaryllis belladonna*—First touch of frost—Colour-blindness—Special annuals—Autumn seed-sowing —Re-planting Carnation layers—Planting drives and approaches to small houses—' Wild gardening '—Double Violets—Salvias—Baby chickens—Pigeons.

September 11th.—In talking of the Welsh Poppy in July I spoke of it as one of the plants which are such weeds that at times one says, ' Oh, I wish I had never introduced the horrible thing into the garden at all ! ' Another of these is the *Campanula ranunculus*, or Creeping Bell-flower—' creeping,' not because of its growth, but because of its root. After rain in July, August, or September, or even much later, I know nothing more lovely than the way it throws up its flower-stems, quite in unexpected places. These when picked and fixed in vases in the Japanese way are most graceful, and last a long time in water. Another terrible weed is the wild annual Balsam, *Impatiens glandulifera*, which sows itself in the most audacious and triumphant manner ; but it takes little root-hold, and is easy to pull up in the spring. What a wonderfully handsome, yet delicate, plant it is ! with its beautiful flowers, its long pointed leaves, its red square stems, its seed-vessels shaped like buds, which burst with a crack and scatter the seeds far and wide. Were the plant difficult to grow, no garden or greenhouse would be without it. It deserves a place, even if reduced to one plant, in every moderate-sized garden ; it looks especially well grown as a single plant in good soil. To add to its perfections it has a delicate, sweet smell, and does well in water. Gardeners will always look upon it, with a show of reason, as a horrid weed ; but flower-lovers will never be without it. The little yellow Fumitory is invaluable for walls and dry places and under shrubs, always looking fresh and green and flourishing, however dry the weather or apparently unfavourable the situation. It is a weed, but it keeps away other weeds, which, as the old nurse said, was the great use of mothers—they kept away stepmothers. Another low-growing, fast-spreading small plant I strongly recommend is the *Polygonum affine.* It has pink flowers, which continue in bloom many weeks ; it can be increased with the greatest facility by division, and it is a good border plant, as the leaves take beautiful colours in the autumn. The hardy *Plumbago larpentæ* is a first-rate plant for a sunny, dry place, and its bright-blue flowers continue till the frost comes. *Tradescantia virginica* is a plant constantly turned out of borders, as it spreads so fast ; but all it requires is severe thinning in the spring, and again sometimes in the summer. I have four shades— the ordinary blue, a deep red-purple shade, a pale grey, and a pure white ; they are lovely flowers, and interesting through their unusual shape. All these last-mentioned plants are well worth growing in even the smallest gardens.

September 15*th.*—I have flowered out of doors this year for the first time the beautiful *Amaryllis belladonna.* Anyone who has a garden, or a wall or a corner near a greenhouse, where the conditions for growing this Lily can be carried out, ought to spare no effort to make it successful. The instructions have been clearly given in the 'English Flower Garden,' but I have found two other things helped the growth—one is planting them by the wall of the greenhouse where the warm pipes run ; and the other is, when the leaves have died down in June, and the earth is weeded and raked, to cover the beds where the bulbs are planted with pieces of glass, so that the rains of July, which are so frequent, should not damp the bulbs before they are ready to start into flower in September. When the flower-buds appear, a dose of liquid manure may be given them ; and a little fern to protect their leaves in early spring is desirable. I know nothing more beautiful than the fine, pink, Lily-like flower on its thick, rich brown stem when brought into a room.

September 16*th.*—About this date is when we look, here in the South, for the first sign of cold, or even for frost. The weather must be watched, and any half-hardy things that have not done flowering are best taken up, potted, and encouraged to go on flowering. The drought this year kept many things back. My Tuberoses and the sweet-smelling white Bouvardia— the one best worth growing, especially outside—I must now take up, and they will go on flowering in the green-house. The pink and red Bouvardias are pretty, but have no sweet scent, like the white ; the pink ones are a true pink, and that is always worth cultivating for a greenhouse, where every shade of magenta should be excluded. I am sure many of the eye-shocks we receive with regard to colour—both in dress, in rooms, and in the arrangement of flowers—is not so much owing to what would be called bad taste as to various degrees of colour-blindness. An inability to see colours at all, much less to see the shades truly and correctly, is far more common than we imagine, and is one of the things that should be tested in children, as—though probably the defect cannot be cured, any more than short sight, which is now so much helped by glasses, &c.—any good oculist would give advice as to the best method of cultivating the eye to be true as regards colour. The improvement in the arrangement of cut flowers in the last twenty years is very great indeed, and in almost every family there is one member at least who gives it real love and attention ; but I hardly ever see a greenhouse, large or small, that is not left entirely to the tender mercy of the gardener, who thinks of nothing, and quite rightly, but of his plants being healthy. He spots everything about —red, white, blue, grey, yellow—and often in the very midst he places some well-grown but terrible blue-pink or magenta Pelargonium, which puts everything out of tone. In the greenhouse, as in the garden, two things are to be aimed at—form and colour : and in a greenhouse one must be sure to add plants that give forth a sweet smell. To get the colour good, you must keep the plants in groups, the same colours as much as possible together, a bold mass of yellow, red, or blue, dividing them with green or nearly-green plants. *Cryptomeria japonica* makes a charming greenhouse shrub, and will grow in very small pots, and not grow quickly ; it is, however, only one of many. Another small green growth that is very pretty, and easy to grow and increase by division, is *Pilea muscosa*. For smell I know nothing more delicious than the mixture of *Lilium auratum* and *Humea elegans ;* but lately I have had to give up that tiresome though charming half-hardy biennial, as, like the Hollyhocks, it is so apt to get a disease, its leaves growing spotty and falling off. In the ' English Flower Garden ' it is said that this happens from sowing it too early the previous year. A thick-leaved plant called *Rochea falcata* I find a useful greenhouse plant. It has to be two or three years old before it flowers, but is easy to increase from cuttings in July. I tried drying it off like the Cactuses, but that does not answer ; it requires a warm greenhouse all the winter and a little water. For baskets in the greenhouse I use *Fuchsia procumbens ;* it has a lovely little miniature flower, and later a pretty fruit three times as big as the flower. *Campanula garganica* (blue, and the white one too) and *Convolvulus mauritanicus* are lovely basket plants. The last-named, nearly hardy, is from North Africa, and easy to increase from division or cuttings. The Cape

Mesembryanthemums are pretty basket plants, and do well in a sunny greenhouse. Small, old-fashioned Ivy-leaved Geraniums grow prettily in baskets. But the flowers are endless that can be grown in this way ; some require a saucer to keep in the moisture, others do not. Nothing, however, will teach all this but experience and constant reference to the books.

Among the immense mass of annuals advertised in catalogues it is often so difficult to make up one's mind what to have. I live, luckily for me, not far from Mr. Barr's Nursery at Long Ditton, and this gives me a chance of seeing a variety of plants and annuals for which no private garden would have room. Two little half-hardy annuals that flowered this year for a very long time seem to me well worth growing, *Alonsoa linifolia* and *A. Warscewiczii.* I do wish such small flowers would have less break-jaw names. They are low-growing (about a foot or a foot and a half high), rather delicate-looking little plants ; but so bright in colour, one scarlet and the other scarlet and orange. They are very effective if grown in a good large clump. *Bartonia aurea* is a picturesque-growing yellow summer annual, which does well in this light soil.

Limnanthes Douglasii, a Californian annual, is much loved of bees in spring, and, if sown early in the autumn, flowers in May. Wallflowers require sowing very early for the following year ; also all the Primrose and Poly-anthus tribe are all better sown in April. I know nothing more puzzling in gardening than the times of sowing annuals and biennials to make them successful, and I imagine they must have different treatment in different soils and climates. Constant practice and study are required. All the autumn things do best here sown late in April or at the beginning of May ; otherwise they come in too early. Early annuals and late annuals are worth growing in this light soil ; but Poppies, *Salpiglossis*, Mignonette, and Sweet-peas are, I think, almost the only summer annuals we make room for every year. *Eschscholtzias* and Musk sow themselves and only have to be thinned. The common Hemp (*Cannabis sativa*) is a lovely foliage-plant when well grown and not crowded up.

It is all-important to remember in the sowing of seeds from January to September, be it in heat or out of doors, and whether perennials, biennials, annuals, or greenhouse plants, that what we want is not a quantity of seedlings all germinating into life in masses, but a few fine healthy plants. The larger and cheaper the packet of seed, the more thinly they should be sown. In the case of rare and delicate plants it is well to sow only one seed in each pot, the smallest that can be got (I have never seen any so small as the French ones), sink them in a box with cocoanut fibre, which prevents the necessity of constant watering. Seedlings, like all other plants, are the better for using nothing but rain-water, if possible. If the sowing is done in a seed bed out of doors, and if the weather is very dry, it is best to soak the ground well first before sowing, and then cover the tiny seed beds with fine gravel, leaving the small stones in, as they give great protection to the seeds from the heat of the sun. We have all noticed the vigour with which self-sown seeds grow in a gravel path. Towards the end of this month, or at the beginning of the next, is the time to take the early layers off the Carnations and to re-make the beds, or, at any rate, to plant them in clearly-named rows in the kitchen garden, so that they may be carefully moved in the spring with a ball of earth. I find that the beds made up in early autumn do much the best, though one is loath to disturb Carnations which may go on occasionally throwing up a flower, or whose foliage, in any case, is so very beautiful half through the winter if the weather keeps mild.

September 15*th.*—Everyone who lives at all in the neighbourhood of suburban residences must be struck with the extraordinary sameness of the shrubberies which surround these houses and gardens, especially those which are almost invariably planted along the approaches. First of all you generally find the road waving and twisting—to give, I suppose, an impression of greater length—edged by a foot or two of grass, ugly in itself and laborious to keep tidy. The shrubs are roughly clipped back, chiefly at the bottom, while as they grow upwards the top branches out of reach are left to overhang the road. This clipping, without any regard to the good of the shrub, whether evergreen or deciduous, all treated in exactly the same way, makes a hideous hard wall of green, more or less imperfect. A still uglier way, though more modern, is to keep the shrubs apart by cutting them back in round, pudding-shaped nobs. This method has not one redeeming quality, to my mind. When you arrive in front of the house, the road terminates in a most unmanageable and impracticable circle, surrounding a green plot of grass with more or less the same clipped shrubs all round. This plot of grass is sometimes broken up with standard Rose-trees, or small beds with Geraniums, or basket beds, all very inappropriate, adding much to the gardener's labour, but not contributing in any way to any beauty of form or colour. Instead of this drive round a grass plot or the circular bed of shrubs, I think most people would find their approach more simple and dignified if that road were straightened where it is possible, and ended in a large square or oblong of gravel at right angles to the house, sufficiently roomy for carriages to turn with ease. The sides could then be planted with borders or shrubberies, or merely turfed, according to the taste of the owner and the space at his command. When the soil is light, and the drive up long enough, it is well to plant it with the wild growth of the neighbouring common—Box, Holly, Broom, Ling, Honeysuckle, Blackberries. These will never grow into a wall and require very little weeding and attention.

Now a word about the original planting. When you take a new house, it generally happens that the first wish is to gain privacy by planting out a neighbour or a road. In light soils the common Rhododendron grows nearly as quickly, if planted in peat, as the Laurel or the Portugal Laurel. It is decidedly prettier, and does not suffer in the same way in severe winters from frost. I believe that some people prefer Laurels to other shrubs ; but it must be remembered that Laurels make rootgrowth like trees, take all moisture out of the soil, and starve other shrubs near them. *Rhododendrons*, on the other hand, grow very much on the surface, are easily transplanted at any time during the summer, and can be increased by layering. When screening is necessary, the first object must, of course, be quick-growing shrubs, and these three—the common Rhododendron, the Laurel, and the Portugal Laurel—are, we must admit, the most satisfactory. They must be planted in bold masses, not mixed, and thinned out in a few years by taking out alternate plants. Where this screening is not wanted, choicer shrubs should be planted, with knowledge, according to their growth, their requirements of aspect, their size, their colour, their time of flowering, their hardiness or delicacy, and so on ; all to be learnt from the ' English Flower Garden.' A good deal of what I have said on the planting of herbaceous borders applies here—namely, the necessity of grouping colour in masses, and not speckling the kinds about at random. The amateur must not be disappointed at finding that a good shrubbery, however well planted, will not make much effect under five or six years. This kind of planting is very much better understood by the landscape gardeners sent out by nurserymen now than it was some years ago.

If, instead of a new house, we buy a place that has been planted for some twenty or thirty years, the amount that has to be thinned out is incredible. People in England are so afraid of thinning out ; if they would only try it with greater boldness, they would soon realise how very quickly the gaps are filled up again by the improved strength of the plants. Short of destroying protection from winds, I should say it is hardly possible to do any harm if, where two plants are crowded together, the Laurel is always sacrificed. But remember that severe clearing of shrubs must be done in the summer, as when delicate shrubs that have always been surrounded by strong growers are exposed late in the year, they are apt to be killed if the winter is severe. Wherever Hollies or Yews have been crowded, they look very ugly, after clearing, for a year or so ; but if well cut back, they soon recover, and make better plants than young ones would do in many years. It is quite superfluous for me to give a catalogue of desirable shrubs, for there is an admirable list of all the hardy flowering trees and shrubs in the introductory part of the later editions of the eternally-mentioned ' English Flower Garden.' Their cultivation and propagation are all given in the body of the work. Where edging is necessary to keep the soil separate from the gravel road, I should advise, instead of the grass, flat pieces of stone, where it is possible to get them, or bricks put in edgeways, or drain-tiles, tiles, or flints. There are all sorts of low-growing things which may be planted behind this edge, according to situation and aspect, such as Periwinkles, St. John's Wort, London Pride, and other *Saxifrages, Heuchera, Tiarella cordifolia,* and the hybrid *Megaseas* (large-leafed *Saxifrage*) in many varieties. However many or few of these varieties are chosen, each sort must be planted together in groups, never dotted about. Beside the more picturesque effect produced by masses, there is a practical necessity for this : the stronger-growing plants crowd out the weaker. Some want replanting or dividing every year, others thrive best left alone.

What I have said above refers to moderate-sized places, but I think I can especially help people with regard to much smaller gardens, which I have so often seen ruined by coarse-growing shrubs, not one of which should be admitted. I should not allow anything coarser-growing than the green and variegated Box, the golden Privet, Bay-tree (which can be constantly cut back), *Daturas, Viburnum plicatum*, Irish Yews, *Cotoneaster* grown as a bush, *Choisya ternata*, Berberises, *Buddlea globosa*. If you have room, and can get the special soil, *Azaleas* and other of the smaller American plants are very desirable. I may mention now that for a very small garden no turf is advisable. Do not try to copy the Manor House garden, but rather take the cottage garden for a model, improving and beautifying it. Make the background of shrubs take the place of the background of cabbages of the cottager, and have only one paved path down the middle, and a narrow earth one round the outside. If you have a little spare space on one side or at the back, then turf that over and plant it with Apple-trees, spring and autumn bulbs, Columbines for summer, together with Snapdragons and Foxgloves—all of which grow well in grass. The grass must then only be mown once a year, in July.

Many of the houses built round the neighbourhood of London in the early part of the century were built close to the road, and have a ludicrous and pompous approach of a drive passing the front door, with two gates—one for entrance and one for exit. Surely this is a great waste of ground with no proportionate advantage. Most places of this kind would certainly be improved if the two gates were blocked up, the drive done away with, and a straight paved or bricked path made from the door to the road, with a shelter of wood, or even of corrugated iron, painted to match the house, and creepers planted along the posts that support it. The space on either side of this path could be planted with low-growing shrubs, or in some instances laid with turf.

In spite of all the charming things Mr. Robinson says about it, ' wild gardening ' is, I am sure, a delusion and a snare. I live near one of the most beautiful so-called wild gardens in England, but it requires endless care, and is always extending in all directions in search of fresh soil. What is possible is to have the appearance of a wild garden in consequence of the most judicious planting, with consummate knowledge and experience of the plants that will do well in the soil if they are just a little assisted at the time of planting. I saw the other day the most lovely Surrey garden I know, though it is without any peculiar natural advantages from the lie of the land—a flat piece of ground on the top of a hill, a copse wood of Spanish Chestnut, Birch, Holly, and Fir. Even in the original thinning of the wood the idea had been formulated that certain plants and trees had better be kept together as they grew, and broad open spaces had been cut, broken up with groups of Holly for protection. The paths were laid with that short turf that grows on Surrey commons, and only wants mowing three or four times a year. The planting had been done with the greatest skill, almost imperceptibly getting more and more cared for and refined as it got nearer the house. Here I saw, among many other things, the finest specimens of the smaller *Magnolias, Stellata* and *Conspicua*. This surprised me, as I thought they required heavy soil. The ground had been thoroughly well made, and they were well away from any trees that could rob them ; but in the lightest, dryest soil they were far finer plants than the specimen plants in the grass lawns at Kew. This whole garden was such a beautiful contrast from the usual planning and clearing-away of all the natural advantages that generally surround a place which is being built or altered. The land, as a rule, is dug over and made flat, and planted in the usual

horrible shrubbery style. I have seen such wonderful
natural advantages thrown away, a copse laid low to
extend a lawn, a lovely spring, which could have been
turned into a miniature river, made into a circular pond,
with Laurels, *Rhododendrons*, and other shrubs dotted
about, and twisted gravel paths made round it. Another
lovely natural pond I knew, into which the rains drained,
though nearly at the top of a hill, where water was
precious and scarce. Now it is cemented all round with
hard, cold cement, on which nothing can grow, and into
which, in the wettest of weather, the water can no longer
drain. The pond never fills, and nothing can grow
around it. I know few things more depressing than an
utter want of feeling for Nature's ways of playing the
artist, as she does at every turn. I cannot understand
anyone walking down a hilly road after rain without
admiring the action of the water on its surface, with the
beautiful curves and turns and sand islands that Nature
leaves in playful imitation of her grandest efforts—the
St. Lawrence, for instance, cutting its way to the sea
through its over two thousand miles of flat plains in
North America. It has long been said, ' God sends the
food, and the Devil sends the cook.' I am sure the
same might be said of the owners, the nurserymen, and
the landscape gardeners, who most carefully, as a rule,
throw away every single natural advantage of the piece
of ground they are laying out, and believe they are
' improving ' ! What would give me the greatest pleasure
would be to have the laying-out of a little place on the
side of a hill with a fine view to the south and west, and
the land sloping away and gently terraced till it reached
the plain at the bottom. But for this kind of garden
clever terracing and a good supply of water are absolutely
necessary.

September 20th.—Towards the end of this month we
take up the double Violets—old Neapolitan and Marie
Louise are the ones we grow—exchanging runners with

friends and neighbours in the spring, as it is not well always to go on growing from the same plants, especially in a light soil, as they deteriorate. In April the old plants are broken up and the runners planted in a good, well-made bed of loam and leaf mould, not much manure, under a wall facing north, to keep them cool and shaded all the summer ; they must be watered if the weather is very dry. At this time of year we make a deep hole in the full sun in the kitchen garden, fill this in with the ordinary stuff for making a hot-bed, putting the frame over this, with the sides a little sunk to keep out the cold, and fill up the frame with good mould. It is of supreme importance that the Violets should be planted quite close to the glass of the frame, touching at first, as the mould always sinks a little. If the winter is cold, it helps the Violets very much to put some rough boards a foot away from the outside of the frame, and fill up the space with leaves or manure. We find nitrate of soda useful for many things, and especially so for Violets. For Czars and other outdoor Violets it is useful to cut a ditch running north and south, and plant both banks with young runners of Violets in April. The position is more natural to the plants than on the flat ground, and they are shaded during part of each day ; this makes a great difference to so many plants. *Ophiopogon spicatus* is a small herbaceous plant which no one would grow merely for its unshowy little lilac flower, which appears late in the autumn, but it is well worth growing in every garden, because its pretty foliage is in its prime about December and January, and is most useful for mixing with small greenhouse flowers.

September 25th.—The plants moved from the reserve garden in July have done very well. The Michaelmas Daisies are unusually good. There are a great many dwarf kinds, very suitable for small gardens. Little shapely trees covered with starry white or lilac flowers are, I suppose, to be got anywhere now ; mine came from my neighbour, Mr. Barr, who has a grand collection. I can only repeat what I said before, how easily these plants can be divided and replanted in spring, and in large and roomy places a Michaelmas Daisy garden can be made for the late months. *Boltonia corymbosa* is a charming plant, more restrained than the Michaelmas Daisy, and better suited to small gardens. It is very pretty picked, but its fault is that it comes in rather early.

The wet weather has suited one of the handsomest of autumn flowers, the tall white *Pyrethrum*. Salvias do well here, but they like it dry and hot, and are not so good as usual this year, though flowering well now. *S. patens*, the dark-blue, and *S. splendens*, the beautiful scarlet one, are the two that no one should be without. They grow most easily from cuttings every year, though we keep the tuberous roots of *S. patens*, as we do Dahlias, from year to year. There are other *Salvias* quite worth growing, but none I know so good as these two. Things are keeping on well in the kitchen garden with the wet and the absence of frost. We have still some excellent late-sown French beans. As a rule gardeners stint the slightly uncertain crop of French Beans by not sowing them in succession, depending for the kitchen supply on the Scarlet Runners, which are not nearly so delicate, and have not half the flavour of the true French Beans. Late Peas completely beat us. We have never had them but once ; they damp off. This must be, I should think, from the western aspect of the garden. I will try sowing them the first week in June next year in an open field we have, exposed to the full sun and wind, to see if in that position they will do better.

September 30th.—We have tried for the first time just lately the baby chickens, which were a fashionable and expensive luxury last season in London. Roast them as you roast a quail, or they can be boiled and served cold with a covering of delicate white Mayonnaise sauce. They should be killed when five or six weeks old, cooked the same day, and each person should have one. This sounds very extravagant, but a chicken the day of its birth is not worth much more than the price of an egg, and feeding them six weeks is no great expense. I can strongly recommend anyone who keeps poultry to try them, as we found them very delicate and tender.

For those who keep pigeons and want to kill them off —which, of course, must be done—I do not advise you to roast them and place them on the *menu* as ' Bordeaux pigeons ' (which a friend of mine did, to the indignation of her sons), but to cook them as they do ptarmigan in Norway :—Stew them quite fresh in an earthenware stew-pan (with the livers, &c., chopped up, inside them) in good stock, with a lot of vegetables cut up, especially onion and a bunch of herbs, which is removed before serving. If more details are wanted, the receipt for jugged hare in ' Dainty Dishes ' will supply them. Serve with a hot compote of Cherries, dried or bottled, or Cranberries or Bilberries or Barberries, instead of the usual Red Currant jelly. If you have a great many pigeons, they could be boned and made into the French Pie, according to the receipt in ' April.'

We grow a great many Morella Cherries on the east and north side of the wall. These ripen enough to be used for compotes in July, but by covering up the trees they can be kept on till now, or even later, and this is the best time for making them into Brandy Cherries, as follows :—Cut the cherries off the trees, leaving a little stalk, and let them drop straight into the bottle. When the bottle is half-full, shake in some powdered white sugar. Fill up with more cherries and more sugar. When quite full, pour in brandy, and leave it till next day. Then fill up the bottle with brandy, and cork it down. Seal the cork as in receipt before given (*see* pp. 122, 123). The brandy cherries are better if kept for two years before eating.

All gardens at this time of the year are full of unripe green Tomatoes ; they are generally left hanging on the plants till the frost touches them, and then thrown away. If picked and stewed in a little butter in an earthenware dish, they are excellent. They have not quite the same flavour as the ripe ones, but still they are very good, and some people think them nicer than the red ones when cooked.

Carrots are a very neglected vegetable in England, and yet they are good in so many ways. The following is a Belgian receipt :—Cut the red part into thin Julienne strips, boil for fifteen minutes, drain, then put them into a stewpan with a nice piece of butter, a little sugar, and cover with light stock. Stew for about half an hour ; then set over the fire, and boil till they are nicely glazed. Young Carrots are good done in the same way, but only take about half an hour's boiling. Carrots are excellent purée'd like mashed Turnips. French Beans and Scarlet Runners are very much better boiled whole, if not too old, only partly drained, and butter added at the last ; they should be boiled enough to break up when the butter is stirred in. To be served very hot. For a second-course dish cream may be added as well as butter. When French Beans are old and the seed ripe, they cook as well as the real white Haricots.

Every year I grow Red Cabbages, and cook them as recommended in ' Dainty Dishes.' I also make large jars of pickled Red Cabbage, most useful in the winter. The following is a German receipt, and also good :— Cut the cabbage as for *choucroute*. For three or four large cabbage heads take ¼ lb. of butter, put it into an earthenware saucepan on a coal fire. When melted, add the cabbage, salt, pepper, and a little flour and a large cupful of good broth ; cover well, and let it cook for about an hour and a half, turning it from time to time. During the last half-hour add a glass of strong red wine.

Some years, and this has been one, the Siberian Crabs

ripen in great quantities. They look so lovely on the
tree, one hates to pick them ; but the moment they are
ripe the missel-thrush clears every one off, with the same
rapidity with which he leaves us without a single berry
on the Mountain Ash in the summer. So we harden our
hearts, and gather them to make into jam, according to
the following receipt (the fruit of the *Rosa rugosa* can be
utilised in the same way) :—

Remove the stalks and well wash the fruit, put this
into a preserving-pan with just enough water to cover
them ; boil until quite tender ; then rub through a brass
wire sieve, and for every 1 lb. of pulp add 1 lb. of
sugar. After bringing to the boil, simmer for three-
quarters of an hour and put into jars. It will become
firm as it cools. It is, although not so clear, almost as
good as Currant jelly.

An immense improvement to stewed Apples or Apple
tart—if the crust be baked apart, as recommended in
' March '—is to put in four or five Peach leaves, fresh
from the trees, and take them out before serving ; it
gives the Apples a most excellent flavour.

OCTOBER

October 1st.—Once more we are back in the month when the robin sings so much. The robins, I find, are the tamest of all the birds in a garden ; and as we fork over the beds, or dig new ones, they follow us all about, enjoying much the newly turned-up earth. Almost the prettiest lines in the ' Christian Year ' are about the Robin Redbreast, and were written by a friend of Keble's. I wonder if the ' Christian Year ' is read now, and is as well known as it used to be ? I will risk it, and recall the two favourite little verses :—

TO THE REDBREAST

Unheard in summer's flaring ray,
  Pour forth thy notes, sweet singer,
Wooing the stillness of the autumn day ;
  Bid it a moment linger,
          Nor fly
Too soon from winter's scowling eye.

The blackbird's song at eventide
  And hers who gay ascends,
Telling the heavens far and wide,
  Are sweet.   But none so blends
          As thine
With calm decay and peace divine.

The following four verses are, I think, very pretty, and not likely to be generally known (I do not know who wrote them) ; and how we do, all of us, ' love the sweet fall of the year ' !—far the most beautiful of all the seasons in England :—

> I wondered this year—for the autumn was in,
> The acacias were dark and the linden leaves thin,
> And the south wind in coming and going was loud,
> And odorous and moist, like the breath of a cloud—
>
> I wondered, and said, ' Then the autumn is here.
> God knows how I love the sweet fall of the year ;
> But the feeling of autumn is not in my brain ;
> My God, give me joy in Thine autumn again.'
>
> I woke in the morning, and out in the air
> I heard the sweet robin his ditty declare,
> And my passion of autumn came down from the skies,
> And I leapt from my bed with the tears in my eyes.
>
> Ah ! robin, sweet robin, dost thou know the power
> That comes on the heart with the fall of the flower,
> The odour of winds, and the shredding of trees,
> And the deepening of colour in skies and on seas ?

October 2nd.—How beautiful are these early autumn mornings ! Here, at any rate, they have qualities unequalled all through the long year. The flowers shine with colour out of the grey mists, as they do at twilight in the long summer evenings, and the gardens now are all filled with dewy gossamer.

Two new autumn Crocuses have lately been brought to my notice ; one, *C. speciosus*, is very pretty standing up straight and strong on a border or rockery. It is of a very blue colour, with a centre of lovely stamens and stigma forming a bright orange tassel. These species of Crocus are much more satisfactory to grow in borders than the pale *Colchicums* of the Swiss meadows, as they are true Crocuses, and only form in spring slight narrow leaves instead of the despairingly coarse growth of the *Colchicums*, which, dying down in the end of May, make such an eyesore in the borders ; it seems best therefore to plant the latter in grass. My double and single Italian Daturas are later this year than usual, owing to the wet weather ; but they are covered with blooms now, and very sweet. The double ones will last longer in water, scenting a room, than the single ones. We plant them out at the end of May ; and when they have been out three weeks or so, a spade is passed round them to cut the roots, and a ditch made, which is filled in with manure. This generous treatment makes the whole difference in their flowering well. I cannot say whether it would be necessary in a damper soil, but I think it would, as cutting their roots in spring stimulates them to flower earlier, before the frost comes. The old plants are taken up and put into pots, and housed for the winter. This is such a happy time of the year for a gardener. There is a sense of power about it ; all the planting and planning and changing are done now. One is loth to disturb beds till the frost comes and kills things down ; but it is most desirable not to put off planting, and to get everything done one can before any real cold comes.

I am gradually clearing away nearly all the Laurels I found on the place, only keeping those growing under trees, and others that form a protection against the north-east wind ; but even those few that are left want constantly cutting back, as they soon encroach and choke everything else. At the stores they sell a most excellent instrument for pruning, called the ' Myticuttah.' There are some with long handles and some with short ; they cut through quite big branches like butter, and are really indispensable. The work is not too tiring for any woman to do herself, and everyone should have a strong pair of French nippers as well, for cutting back smaller shrubs and plants. One is always seeing in catalogues that this plant or that will do for the borders of shrubberies. My experience is that no summer herbaceous plants do in the borders of shrubberies at all, though spring 'and autumn things may do fairly well ; and many of the smaller shrubs, like Lavender Cotton, Rosemary, and Brooms of sorts, will hold their own in front of larger shrubs.

October 4th.—The *Nerines* (*see* Johnson's ' Gardener's Dictionary ') have flowered well and been charming this year. *N. Fothergillii* is the finest colour, but all are most useful autumn bulbs, and last a long time in water. They are easy to manage, and, like many Cape bulbs, flower before the leaves are produced. During the growing of the leaves they must be carefully attended to and watered ; and even, now and then, a small dose of liquid manure does them good. They are best not re-potted, except very rarely ; and as the leaves die down they must be laid on their sides and dried and well baked in the sun, just like the Freezias, only not shaken out and re-potted, as recommended for them. The bulbs, too, should be planted, like *Vallotas* or Hyacinths, well on the top of the pot. I never can understand why these very ornamental bulbs are not grown in larger quantities especially as they increase and improve, instead of being almost useless, as is the case with the spring bulbs after forcing.

A Cape family of small, very sweet-smelling shrubs called *Diosma* (*see* Johnson's ' Gardener's Dictionary ') are well worth growing ; in fact, no greenhouse ought to be without some of them. Their charm is principally in their foliage and scent, as the flowers are insignificant. They are easily increased by cuttings in spring under a bell-glass. The growing of Cape plants is always interesting. Small Cape Aloes have charming pink flowers in spring, which last long in water, not unlike the *Lachenalias* (*see* catalogues), all of which are worth growing.

Leonotis leonurus has not flowered out of doors with me this year at all, either in large post or planted out

in a bed. The plants were covered with buds, and so
we lifted them at the end of September, and put them
into the heat, where they have flowered well. This
would be worth while for anyone with plenty of room,
as it is such a handsome unusual flower when picked.
Like the *Daturas*, they may be extra late from the ex-
cessive dryness of May and June, and the wet afterwards. It is a Cape plant ; there it forms large bushes
covered with bloom. Another African greenhouse plant
well worth growing is called *Sparmannia africana.* The
covering of the bud is white, and shows, when the flower
opens, between the four petals, forming an unusually
pretty star-shaped flower with a brush of yellow stamens
tipped with red.

We have a good many fine Sweet Chestnut trees, and
they ripen more or less well every year. We cook them
in a great many ways : boil them and shell them, and
warm them up in butter or with a little stock, as a
vegetable. They are very good made into a purée with
butter and cream, to eat with cutlets ; or boiled and
rubbed through a wire sieve, to serve round whipped
cream well flavoured with sugar and vanilla. Of course
the cheap Chestnuts sold in London can all be cooked in
the same way, but only the best Italian Chestnuts are
good for roasting.

October 8th.—I have been lately on the East Coast.
One cannot help being amused to find that gardening is
so like life, each one has his own difficulties. I was
suggesting to my friend to plant her Violets in leaf-
mould, when she said : ' Why, we have not a single leaf.
The few there are on the dwarf trees blow away into
space.' Oh ! what a fight the poor plants have with
the salt-laden winds ! But some things thrive and flourish
by the sea as they do nowhere else. I think the sunk
Dutch gardens, before described, will be found most
useful by the seaside.

October 14th.—It is a very good plan, when you want

192 POT-POURRI FROM A SURREY GARDEN.

to cut a new bed or alter the shape of an old one, to
shuffle along the wet dewy grass on an October morning
—and this leaves a mark which enables you very well to
judge of size, shape, and proportion—before you begin
to cut your beds out. I am taking up and replanting—
in the way before described of massing all the plants
of one colour together—my long herbaceous borders.
These borders run right across what was once a fair-
sized lawn, and the principle of the garden is to have
it all beds and low-growing shrubs, except the paths,
which are turf ; the main paths are left gravelled for
the sake of dryness in bad weather. I only replant the
herbaceous borders every four or five years, mulching
them well every winter ; and even then it is best only
to replant them partially, as certain fine plants are much
injured, if not killed, by moving at all, and these plants
remain as landmarks both as regards height and colour
for the replanting of the borders. Keeping colours together and some empty spaces for annuals or filling up
in spring or summer out of the reserve garden, makes it
much easier to prevent the borders looking dull and
shabby at any time during the summer months.
     The large square beds are planted now with all kinds
of spring-flowering things, not formally, but in broad
patches—Wallflowers, Forget-me-nots, Tulips, *Silene,
Limnanthes douglasii* (a Californian annual much loved
by the bees), sowing a large patch of Love-in-the-mist
and the annual *Gypsophila* (for early flowering, sown in
September), Spanish Iris, Pinks and Carnations, Madonna
Lilies, a large corner of Anemones, and another of
Scabiosa caucasica (*see* ' English Flower Garden '), both
these grown originally from seed. And as the spring
flowers pass away, their places are filled up from autumn-
sown plants, Snapdragons, &c., which are quite hardy
when young and in the seed bed, but which get killed
and injured by cold winds in the open. Let everyone
read what is said in the ' English Flower Garden ' on the

giant *Saxifrages, Megaseas.* There are several varieties, all worth growing, and they are most useful, satisfactory plants for all sorts of purposes, not nearly grown enough for covering the ground and making fine masses of low-growing foliage. To keep out weeds by planting low-growing and spreading plants is a great secret of gardens that are to have a picturesque appearance, and, in fact, be a cultivated wilderness rather than a tidy garden.

October 15th.—This is the great Apple time. All the windfalls that take place in September and October we collect, and either eat or stew down into Apple jelly. It is very useful through the winter in many ways, and injured Apples never keep.

Quince jam and jelly we also find good. This is an old-fashioned receipt :—First boil the Quinces till soft, for about half an hour ; take off the outer thin skin. Cut the Quinces in half, removing the core, and pulp them. To every pound of Quince pulp add half a pint of the water in which the Quinces were boiled. Peel carefully and cut up some Blenheim Apples ; add half a pound of Apples to every pound of Quince pulp, and three-quarters of a pound of sugar to every pound of fruit. Boil for three hours.

We find the ripe Beans of the Scarlet Runners very good if well boiled, and then served with a little of the water and a good bit of fresh butter stirred in just before dishing up. Many years ago Mr. Bright, in the ' Lancashire Garden,' wrote : ' One excellent vegetable I have generally grown I would recommend to anyone who has space to spare—the French White Haricot. It is not often seen with us, though it is so very common in France. It is a species of French Bean, of which you eat the white bean itself instead of slicing up the pod. I suspect that, taking England through, there are very few gardens where the White Haricot is found.' This was true nearly twenty years ago, but the astonishing thing is that it is true still. It is wonderful how rarely

7

the *Haricot blanc* is to be seen at English tables. Is this the fault of the gardener or the cook ? I suspect both. It is very disheartening to grow vegetables the cook does not know how to use. English housekeepers, so extravagant about many things, are often curiously economical on the subject of butter. To use that horrid, fatty, adulterated stuff called ' kitchen butter ' with vegetables is fatal ; it must be good fresh butter. There are only two economies that generally rather wasteful people try to practise—one is in coals, and the other is in butter. Neither makes much difference in the year, and many other things could be so well done without. Compared to the expense of wine and meat, they are really nothing at all. Vegetables should not be cooked in butter except when really fried ; they should be boiled, and drained, and warmed up, and cold butter stirred in just before serving. Vegetables should not look or taste greasy, or rice either.

In the autumn those who keep fowls always have some to get rid of that are better stewed than roasted. The following is an old family receipt I have not seen elsewhere :—

Poulet à la Turque.—Truss a chicken as for boiling, put it in a deep fricandeau-pan, spread it thickly with butter, and lay therein a dozen pieces of raw ham, some carrots, onions, parsley, and a little nutmeg, pepper, and salt ; cover with a buttered paper. Braize it for one hour. When it is dished, place round the chicken in groups stewed rice, sultanas, and prunes. Pour a lightly seasoned curry sauce over the chicken, and serve more sauce in a sauce-boat apart, if desirable—especially if there are two chickens.

People who have a good deal of game get rather tired of the eternally roast pheasant or partridge with bread sauce. The following is a good receipt to make a variety :—

Partridge or Pheasant à la Sierra Morena.—Take a

brace of partridges properly trussed. Cut into dice
I inch thick a little less than ½ lb. of bacon, put them
into the stew-pan ; cut 2 large onions in quarters, take
6 whole black peppers, a little salt, 1 bay-leaf, a ½ gill
of vinegar, 1 gill of port wine, 1 gill of water, 1 tablespoonful of salad oil. Put all these ingredients into the
stew-pan ; cover with half a sheet of kitchen paper ; stew
on a slow fire for 2 hours. Then take out the partridges
and dish them, and put round some of the quarters of
onions which have been stewed, pass the gravy through
a sieve, and send to table.

Just now the greengrocers' shops in town and country
are full of very cheap large melons brought from abroad.
I find they make a very good compote if the hard outside is taken off and the pulp cut into pieces the size of
a plum. Make a syrup of sugar flavoured with the melon-
peel, spice, bay-leaf, and a little powdered ginger ; boil
this up, and pour it over the pieces of melon.

Turnips are often strong and hard with us. This year
they are delicious, and we have had a very pretty dish—
much appreciated—of small round Turnips boiled tender,
and served with a white sauce made of milk boiled till
it thickens, into which has been stirred a little butter
and cream.

Carrots, too, are delicious done in this way with the
addition of a little parsley and sugar.

The following is a good cake :—The weight in flour
of four eggs ; beat to a cream, butter, sugar, rind of
lemon grated, a few Sultanas, and citron ; then add the
yelk of each egg, one by one ; then add the flour, and
beat the white of the eggs to a froth just before putting
it into the oven. Bake for half an hour in a flat tin dish.

October 18th.—I have at last succeeded in flowering
the *Schizostylis coccinea.* I am relieved to see that in
the new edition of the ' English Flower Garden ' this is
pronounced a great difficulty in a light dry soil. It is
probably owing to the very wet autumn we have had

that these little Cape bulbs have done so well. They were planted in fairly good garden soil, under the protection and shade of a wall facing east ; so they did not get much sun except early in the year, when at rest ; and when they began to grow, they were watered till the rain came. When the flower-spikes began to colour and nearly open, as the nights were very cold, I cut them and put them in water in a warm room, and they bloomed quite well. Two or three sticks as a support, and mats or newspaper thrown over them, help these late-flowering plants in prematurely cold weather, which often lasts only a day or two.

October 24th.—This is about the time we replant the Violas and *Saxifrages* in the sunny beds, taking them out of the shady border in the reserve garden. London Pride is better taken up and divided every two years. As Saxifrages do not mind the dry springs, it is well worth while to grow a quantity of London Pride, the bloom of which resembles in colour a faint pink evening cloud ; this is not only a satisfactory plant when picked, but it will travel well, and makes a lovely support for Iceland poppies and other flowers.

October 27th.—I have been taking up to-day the *Lobelia cardinalis* and *L. fulgens*. *Cardinalis* is the one with the dark leaves and the handsomer grower ; the other flowers rather the earlier.

October 28th.—With all the weeks and weeks of wet we have had this year we have waited long for our ' St. Luke's Summer ' ; and now it has come at last, it is not with its usual still, lovely warm days. It has come fine and lovely, yes ; but hand-in-hand with Jack Frost, and the garden is cleared for the present of nearly every bloom that was left.

A first foggy day ! How beautiful it is in the country, and what an endless pleasure when, at midday, the sun conquers the mist !—reminding one of Milton's simile at the end of his description of his hero, Satan :—

. . . As when the sun, new risen,
Looks through the horizontal misty air
Shorn of his beams.

And how useful are days like these in the country !
There is no such time for noticing the shapes of the
groups of shrubs and forms of plants, and what ought
to be cut away and what left as it is.   Some low-growing
plants luxuriate so in the wet autumn days, they make
us believe no winter is coming—such as the foliage of
Pinks and Carnations, Sweet Williams, Golden Feverfew,
and last, but not least, another of the treasure weeds of
a garden, the common Marigold.   Down the kitchen
garden I have a patch of border given up to the Marigolds, and they sow themselves over and over again, and
flower at all sorts of unexpected times.   As they proudly
defy early frosts, they become really precious with their
grand glowing orange faces.   As is so often the case, the
single ones, with their varieties of dark and light centres,
are prettier than the double ones, though both may be
grown to suit all tastes, the colour always being good.
No garden, however small, should be without this patch
devoted to Marigolds.   I do not dislike their pungent
smell, as many do.

The wet has kept the leaves long green and fresh on
the trees, but the cold of last night brought down at
once the great succulent leaves of some young Horse
Chestnuts not far from here.   Just about this garden
they will not grow, as they so dislike the sand.   As I
passed them to-day I noticed the leaves all lay in heaps,
freshly fallen round the slight stems, on the green grass,
fold on fold, in the low autumn sunshine.   Very beautiful, like Keats's description in ' St. Agnes' Eve ' of fair
Madeline unrobing :—

Of all its wreathèd pearls her hair she frees,
Unclasps her warmèd jewels one by one,
Loosens her fragrant bodice ; by degrees
Her rich attire creeps rustling to her knees,
Half hidden, like a mermaid in seaweed.

So the trees stood up this afternoon, with all their summer clothing round their feet.

I always long at this time of the year to have been to Japan to see one of their Chrysanthemum shows. I am told our individual flowers are far finer, but their method of arranging the shows is so superior to ours, and the effect produced is naturally much more lovely. They arrange them in bands and waves of colour, from the darkest red to the palest pink, fading into white ; and up again from pale lemon, yellow, and orange to the darkest brown. I am sure, even in small collections, picked and unpicked Chrysanthemums look far better if the colours are kept together in clumps, and not dotted about till the general effect becomes mud-colour, as English gardeners always arrange them, only considering their height or the size of their unnaturally disbudded blooms. They are, I admit, most beautiful and useful flowers. What should we do without them ? But owners of small places, and I think even large ones, should guard against too much time, attention, and room being given to them. For putting into vases, there is no doubt Chrysanthemums look better allowed to grow more naturally and not so disbudded. A huge Chrysanthemum that is nearly the size of a plate, though it may have won a prize at a local flower-show, looks almost vulgar when picked. Bunches of Chrysanthemums with their buds will go on blooming a long time in winter, and make in a room a natural and beautiful decoration, instead of painfully reminding one of the correctness of the flower's paper imitations.

A kind gardening friend living in Lancashire has written me out the following list of ornamental shrubs and flowering plants which, for one reason or another, look well in August, September, and October. I think, though I mention several of the plants elsewhere, it useful to give it in its entirety, as many are of opinion that in those three months it is necessary to be entirely dependent on bedded-out plants for colour and beauty.

Trees for autumn leaves and berries :—Ash (Mountain), Cherry, Siberian Crab, Buckthorn (sea), Elder (golden), Filbert (purple), Hawthorn, Hornbeam, Maple.

Creepers and shrubs for autumn :—*Aristolochia sipho*, Arbutus, *Azara microphylla, Berberis thunbergi*, Clematises of sorts, *Clerodendron, Colutea, Cotoneaster, Cydonia japonica*, Dog-wood, *Eccremocarpus scaber, Escalonia macrantha, Euonymus* (both European and *latifolius*), *Genista*, Heath, *Hibiscus*, Honeysuckle, *Hydrangea paniculata, Hypericum, Indigofera*, Jasmine, *Laurustinus*, Lavender, *Leycesteria formosa, Mahonia, Olearia haasti*, Pernettyas, *Lithospermum, Pyracantha, Prunus pissardii, Rhus laciniata, Rosa rugosa*, Roses (autumn), Rosemary, *Rubus* (Brambles), *Skimmia*, Snowberry, *Spartium junceum*, Tamarisk, Virginia Creeper, Vines of sorts.

Plants.—*Achillea ptarmica flore pleno, Aconitum* (Monkshood), *Adonis autumnalis, Anemone japonica* (most useful, three shades), Asters, Michaelmas Daisies of sorts, *Ageratum, Antirrhinum, Armeria cæspitosa* (Sea Pink), Bergamot, *Calendula*, Marigold, *Callistephus* (China Aster), Campanulas of sorts, Campion (Rose), *Cannæ, Centaurea*, Chrysanthemum, Colchicum (autumn Crocus), *Convolvulus tricolor, Coreopsis lanceolata, Cucurbita* (Gourd), *Cuphea zimpani* (good annual), Dahlias of sorts, *Datura, Dianthuses* of sorts, *Desmodium, Diplopappus, Echinops, Erigeron, Eryngiums* of sorts, *Exogonium purga* (Jalap plant), Fuchsia, *Funkias* of sorts, *Gaillardia, Gaultheria, Geum coccineum, Gladioli* of sorts, *Gypsophila paniculata, Harpalium rigidum*, Helenium, Helianthuses of sorts (Sunflowers), *Helichrysum* (Everlasting), Heliotrope, Hollyhock, *Hyacinthus candicans, Hypericums* of sorts, *Ipomæa* (Convolvulus), *Lathyrus* (Sweet Pea), *Lengogium autumnale, Lilium tigrinum, Linaria, Linum, Lobelia cardinalis* and *fulgens, Lunaria* (Honesty), *Mathiola* (Stocks of sorts), *Oxalis*, Pentstemons of sorts, *Physalis alkekengi* (Winter Cherry), *Phytolacca decandra*, *Plumbago carpentæ*, *Polygonums* of sorts, Poppies of sorts, *Pyrethrum uliginosum*, *Reseda* (Mignonette), *Rudbeckia neumani*, Scabious of sorts, *Statice latifolia Tagetes* (Marigold), Tansy, *Tritonia tropæolum*, Nasturtiums of sorts, *Vinca*, Periwinkle, Viola, Verbena, Yucca, Zinnia.

It seems hardly necessary to mention that many of these plants flower earlier further South than they do in Lancashire.

October 26th.—The French proverb, ' La variété c'est la vie,' always appeals to me in many things, especially domestic ones. I know nothing such a test of a good housekeeper as a periodic change of biscuits. Everybody tires of the best biscuits in the world, and the new shape and the old biscuits of better quality should ring the changes. All through the summer a slight surprise and pleasure comes at the end of a little dinner if a buttonhole of sweet-smelling flowers and leaves are carefully tied up (fine wire does them the least clumsily) and dropped into the water in the finger-bowls. Nothing should be used but what is really sweet—Lemon-scented Verbena and Geranium leaves being the principal foundation ; and in summer there ought always to be plenty of these two in the smallest gardens.

I think it may be a little amusement or help to some of you if I make a list of a few of my dinner-table decorations during the six months in the country :—

April.—White Allium with greenhouse Asparagus, red Geranium in low vases between, with no green. Various spring flowers and blossoms arranged, each separate, in small narrow-necked vases, having the effect of a miniature spring garden.

May.—A Japanese arrangement of *Clematis montana* and greenhouse Asparagus. Parrot Tulips in narrow glasses all about the table. Pink ivy-leaved Geranium,

called Souvenir of Charles Turner, in a large flat glass
in the middle, and a pretty pink *Pelargonium* all round.
Oriental Poppies, no green. In the middle an arrangement of German Iris of four or five different shades.
Perennial herbaceous Lupins, white and blue, with their
own lovely leaves ; they must never be allowed to
droop, but go at once into water. Lilies of the Valley
and *Narcissus poeticus*. *Narcissus poeticus* and *Stachys
lanata*.

June.—Iceland Poppies (three colours), Cornflowers,
and London Pride ; no green ; very pretty, like a
Frenchwoman's bonnet. Herbaceous Peonies, white and
pale pink. *Lilium thunbergianum* and green. *Gloire de
Dijon* Roses floating in water in flat vases, and greenhouse Maidenhair Fern. Mrs. Sinkins Pink and *Gypsophila elegans*. *Gypsophila* and pink Shirley Poppies.
Yellow Snapdragons and *Gypsophila;* this was pretty
and uncommon. Mixed Roses. White Madonna Lilies
with various white flowers, and pale green.

July.—Yellow French Daisy and *Gypsophila panicu-
lata*. Small vases with blue *Campanula turbinata*.
Calceolaria amplexicaule. *Gypsophila paniculata*, Nas-
turtiums, and leaves of variegated ground Ivy. *Clematis*
(Travellers' Joy) trained up a Bamboo in the middle,
wedged. Mixed Carnations and *Gypsophila paniculata*.
Carnation (Lady Agnes) with own green, or from Mrs.
Sinkins.

August.—White Sweet Pea and *Gypsophila paniculata*.
Branches of the Everlasting Pea laid on the tablecloth.
Salpiglossis and *Gypsophila paniculata*. Sweet Geranium
leaves and pink Ivy-leaved Geranium (Souvenir of
Charles Turner).

September.—Red Virginia Creeper leaves and Geranium
(Henry Jacoby). Single *Helianthemums* and Carrot
leaves of various shades. Red Virginia Creeper leaves,
Nasturtiums, and a large tray in the middle piled up
with fruit—apples, pears, peaches, grapes, &c.

October.—Single Dahlias and Venetian Sumach. Green-house Chrysanthemums.

October 30th.—It is an excellent plan, if you have a very sunny window that you are glad to have shaded in the summer and not in winter, to put two bars of wood like a bracket out from the wall as a support for one long bar ; or if your window is high, and so requires more width to shade it, have two, or even three, bars across the top. You plant on one side a Vine or a Wistaria, and train it over this kind of wooden eyebrow. If you have a Wistaria, the flowers hang through in spring ; if you have a Vine, the little bunches of grapes hang charmingly along the top of your window in autumn. In both cases the branches become quite bare at the first frost, and so your room is not shaded at a wrong time of year. I think this method of growing certain plants usually grown against walls will please many plant-loving people.

I have been so often asked about London gardens, and in two cases have taken real and active interest in them—one a small square piece of ground behind an old house in Westminster ; and another much larger, very near the Addison Road Station. In all cases in and near London I say, emphatically, ' Avoid evergreens.' They get black and miserable, and look horrid, even in winter ; though, if syringed and pruned, I think both Aucuba and Box, and especially the latter, might be kept clean and flourishing, and even prove useful for picking. Ivy, too, on a wall facing north is often prefer-able to the bare wall. I have said a great deal in August against growing Virginia Creeper and *Ampelopsis veitchii*, because of its spoiling and hiding beautiful old houses ; but in London, and where we want to hide, they are the most useful and, indeed, invaluable Creepers that can be planted. They have every merit, are quick growers in any soil, graceful if pruned and cared for, and yet doing well if left alone. Their growth in the spring and early summer is full of beauty, and in London they hasten to lose their leaves without colouring them.

On the back of a house my parents built in '41, in Rutland Gate, was planted, I think, the first Virginia Creeper I ever remember in London. In those days beyond this house it was all fields and nursery gardens. London was not then quite so black as it is now—not in that part, at any rate. I well remember the beauty and glory of this Virginia Creeper. It was never pruned, and hung from top to bottom of the house in lovely masses of falling foliage. Virginia Creepers, like many other things, vary a little in their growths; one that has its leaves out early in the spring is the best for London. The *Ampelopsis* is prettier for being very much starved, as the leaves keep smaller, and less like the redundant growth at Boston, which I so condemned before. But on the whole, even for London, I prefer the growth of the common Virginia Creeper.

Autumn effects need never be thought of in London at all. When people come back to the West End, after the holidays, it is nearly winter. The poor leaves, choked and smothered in soot, have fallen sadly and greyly to the ground, leaving all their autumn glory to their more fortunate country brethren; and all can be swept clean and tidy before anyone comes back. Amongst deciduous shrubs all the ordinary common ones do very well, and only want attention and pruning, and pulling-off of suckers, as the same plants require in the country. Privets, being half-deciduous, do very well also. Bamboos are useless, as they are never in full beauty, even in the country, till the autumn and winter. In all small gardens it is my advice to avoid turf, and especially in London. It never looks well, and is expensive and troublesome to maintain, which is one reason the day-gardener likes it. Have as wide a border all round the wall as you can afford, and some red gravel or a bricked or tiled square in the middle of the garden to sit on.

Have a sunk tub, in the sun, under a tap, from which to fill a watering-pot, to water more delicate things; and do not hose too much, especially if your soil is damp, except in very warm weather. On the walls have *Ribes sanguineum* and Forsythias, as they flower very early. Vines and Fig-trees, white Jasmine, and *Jasminum nudiflorum*, all do well in London. Wherever there is room on the walls facing south put the deciduous Magnolias (*see* ' English Flower Garden '). The *Magnolia grandiflora* has such polished and very shiny leaves; it grows very well near London. I remember some very fine plants of the same that used to grow in gardens at Walham Green and Fulham, where in my youth people gave what are now called garden-parties and used then to be called ' Breakfasts '—why, I do not know, as they never began till three o'clock in the afternoon. Perhaps the French refugees brought in the fashion of such entertainments, full of the recollections of the *déjeuné champêtre* of Louis XV. and Louis XVI. and their Courts.

I know a Magnolia in Addison Road—I think it must be a *M. conspicua*—that, though crowded up and apparently neglected, flowers most beautifully every spring, nearly as well as the famous one which is such a marked ornament every year in the Champs Elysées. A Forsythia at the corner of Marlborough House garden in the early spring has often excited my admiration. I quote these examples to show that plants will grow and flower in London still, if well chosen and cared for.

For the borders, I recommend no edging; it is expensive and useless. The gravel is enough; and it is, I think, prettier to disguise the fact of a line than to accentuate it. Plant what you have in bold clumps—the tall plants, of course, at the back; but rather in waves of height, with bays of the front low-growing things, running back towards and under the wall. Anything looks better than a row of plants all the same, or nearly the same, height. There are the line of the wall and the line of the path. Your object must be, not to repeat these, but to work into your border that which makes either beautiful form or beautiful colour, or both at the same time. Do not repeat your clumps over and over again. For instance, if you have a good number of German Irises (many of which grow admirably in London), put them into two large groups—one facing east or south (which is the best) and the other facing north or west. In this way you may hope for a succession, an object that anyone who plants for flowering reasons ought never to have out of their mind. Spanish Irises would, I believe, do very well in a London garden if planted every year in a sunny corner in October. They are not expensive (*see* catalogues). Buy no double or even single Dutch Hyacinths ; they are not worth it. They last a very short time, are often injured by the weather, and can be seen in the Parks in mournful and irritating regularity and perfection. Buy Snowdrops, Crocuses, Scillas (*see* ' English Flower Garden '), especially *S. hispanica*, blue, white and pink (though the pink one is rather the least pretty), *S. bifolia*, *S. sibirica*, *S. italica*, and our own common Blue-bells (Wood Hyacinths), *S. nutans*. I think the only real Hyacinth worth trying would be the early Roman. The only seed I would recommend sowing in place is Mignonette, and that would want watering. For all other annuals, and many other things that are not annuals, I would pocket my gardening pride and act in the following manner :—In April, and again in May, make out from the books a short or long list of plants, those common things that you would like to have, which flower early. Send or go to Covent Garden, taking a basket with you, and buy the seedlings there two or three inches high ; bring them back, plant them at once, and water them and watch them. Plants are just like children ; it is a keen, watchful, ever-attentive, thoughtful eye they require—not, figuratively speaking, pulling up by the roots to see how they are getting on. If you cannot go to Covent Garden, go to the nearest nurseryman, and try and get there what you want. I would buy Daisies, Forget-me-nots, Violas, Pansies, common Marigolds, Nasturtiums, blue Lobelias, Geraniums, Sweet Verbenas —in fact, nearly all the things you see. Only make notes year by year as to what does best, and try to learn for yourself what likes full sun and what likes half-shade, and what can be planted in April and what not till the end of May. I believe in this way a very bright London garden might be seen—during May, June, and July, at any rate—at a very small expense.

Sowing your own seeds takes too long, and is too uncertain without a hot-bed. Do not put off planting all the hardy plants too late. London is warmer than the country, and your great object ought to be to get things early. All Pinks, Saxifrages (especially London Pride), Ferns, and all the hardy perennials you like to try, ought to be planted in October, at the same time as the bulbs. The Campanulas named in June would do well in small London gardens ; the shade of the walls and the moisture would suit them excellently. Perhaps they might want water, if the weather was very dry, to help them to flower.

There are often a few cold nights at the end of May, when the icebergs are floating South—those wonderful, beautiful ice-mountains, once to have seen, never to be forgotten ; they have eight times their height below the water, and this keeps them straight as they float onwards, glittering in the sunshine. Beautiful as they are to those who see them, they are cruel destroyers of our poor un-certain spring weather. A very good plan on cold nights is to throw over your plants some newspapers, held down by stones ; or if you cover up some wicker or wire hen-

coops with muslin, they will keep out five or six degrees
of frost. These protections can be removed in the morning. All spring-watering should be done in the morning,
not in the evening ; and it is better to add a very little
warm water than to use very cold water out of pipes.
The handsomest, easiest-grown, hardiest, most useful
plant for London gardens is the *Polygonum cuspidatum*
(there is a lovely drawing of it, by Mr. Alfred Parsons, in
Mr. Robinson's ' Wild Garden ') ; but its whole beauty
and utility, as I have said before, depends on taking up
the suckers as they appear in early spring. Without
that, the plant is a useless weed ; but treated as I recommend, I am sure no one can be disappointed with
this strong-growing herbaceous plant. The larger-leaved
kind, *P. sacchalinensis*, is very good also, if you have
room for both, but it has not quite such a beautiful
up-standing and yet graceful growth.

I think the *Bocconia cordata* would also do in London
gardens, as it is a very handsome herbaceous plant, and
comes to perfection early, throwing up its feathery
blooms in July. None of the Primrose family are any
good in London ; the leaves are too woolly.

Do not allow the beds to be dug over or pulled about
in the autumn ; it is a very bad plan. Consciously or
unconsciously the man digs everything up, and I believe
many a gardener thinks it is good for trade !

No Roses are worth trying in or near London, though
a few are growing in Holland House Gardens that look
fairly healthy ; but that is a very large open space, and
they are old-established bushes, which have been there
a long time. I think that most beautiful shrub, *Hydrangea paniculata*, might do well ; it is best cut down
every March, and is such a beautiful thing. It likes a
strong soil, but flowers rather late for those who leave
London early. Lilies of the Valley do very well in
London if planted under a wall ; facing east is the best
position, and they should be left alone. Most of the

hardy Lilies would thrive if planted in October, especially the scarlet Lily, *Lilium chalcedonicum*, which flowers early. One reason why London gardens do so badly very often is that they are neglected in September and October. Wallflowers are best planted in September ; and I am afraid many beginners fail to realise what are annuals and what are not, and the greater the difficulties the greater the care necessary. I saw once in a review of an American book on gardening that the late springs and the early heat in parts of America made the growing of many of the larger annuals a great difficulty, as they could not be sown out of doors early enough. The reviewer quoted the author of the book's statement of how she ingeniously devised the following method :— Determined not to be beaten, she grew the single seeds in empty egg-shells stuck into boxes of sand ; when the time came for planting, and the little seed had grown, the shell was just broken and the whole thing dropped into the ground where it was to grow. In this way she got Poppies, &c., to flourish—plants that will not bear moving at all, as a general rule. I mention this as an example of the whole spirit of gardening, a patient conquering of difficulties. Riding on the crest of the wave that tries to submerge us is one of the phases of our existence that makes life most satisfactory and worth living, and it is the secret of all progress. If gardening were easy, even under favourable circumstances, we should none of us care to do it.

It must strike everyone when driving through the streets of London in the summer how elaborately ugly is the planting of many of the window-boxes. What seems to me to look best is to keep the flowers as distinct and as unmixed as possible. To set out plants that are not really hardy before the end of May is waste of money, and gives me a feeling of unloving ignorance of plants which is as the murdering of the innocents to those who are fond of them. A pretty mixture is the yellow French

Marguerite with two or three—according to the size of the box—little upright *Cryptomeria japonicas*, either in the middle or at each end of the box, according to the shape of the window. White French Daisies do just as well, if preferred. Calceolarias and white Daisies are also pretty. I have lived so little in London in the summer of late years that I am more prepared to criticise than to suggest. One day I saw outside a dining-room window some large, heavy, oblong Japanese flower-pots planted with single plants, and they looked very well, as one was able to see the growth of the plants. These Japanese pots are glazed, and much thicker than the ordinary flower-pot, and thus lessen evaporation and the risk of being blown over. No plants can possibly succeed on balconies or windows in ordinary English flower-pots unless they are sunk in boxes or other pots as a protection from the sun and wind.

NOVEMBER

November 2nd.—I recommend housekeepers to take
down about the end of October all muslin curtains, silk
blinds, &c., which shade the windows, only keeping
such curtains as are drawn at night for warmth. The
difference it makes in the appearance of the room is
very pleasant. In all manner of ways possible—in our
house and gardens, in our cooking and dress—the adapting ourselves as well as we can to the changing seasons
is sensible and desirable ; it gives point and variety to
existence, especially for those who live most of the year
in one place. In the case of the south windows in our
sitting-rooms the pouring-in of the low winter sun is
delightful—' le soleil de Saint Martin,' as the French
play had it, comparing it to the love of an old man,
' qui échauffe et ne brûle pas.' It is only just now we
enjoy this very low sun. It is a great delight to watch
the changing year, and how differently the sun affects
the house and garden. In summer he shines high above
our heads, beating and burning on the roof ; and in
winter he bows and smiles at us just above the tree-tops.

November 8th.—To-day we have had our first dish
of preserved French Beans out of the salt pan, before
described ; and they are really delicious, just as if they
had been freshly picked in August.

I suppose everybody knows that Jerusalem Artichokes

are much better if left in the ground and only dug up as
they are wanted, though before hard frost they must be
dug up and housed. This vegetable is amongst the most
useful ones we have in the winter, as it can be cooked in
such a great number of ways. It is one of the things
much improved by growing from fresh seed, and not
planting the old tubers over and over again. The Artichokes can be made into soup, can be purée'd like
Turnips, or fried in thin slices like Potato chips. ' Dainty
Dishes' has one receipt for cooking them. The only
way in which they are not very good is the ordinary
English way—plain boiled, with a floury butter sauce.
The best way of all is *au gratin*, like the Maccaroni-cheese
in ' Dainty Dishes'; only they require more sauce.
Everything *au gratin* is very much improved by using
half Parmesan, half Gruyère, and a very small piece of
shallot. I used to think this plant, from its name
' Jerusalem ' being derived from the Italian *Girasole*,
with its curious English amplification into ' Palestine
Soup,' was perhaps the only Sunflower (*Helianthus*) that
had not come from America, and might have been
brought here by the Crusaders; but all this is not the
fact. It does come from America; and a curious confirmation of the same is that the French name is *Topin-
ambour*, a corruption of Topinambout, a native tribe in
the Brazils, whence the plant comes.

November 6th.—The last few days there has been quite
a hard frost, and last night our garden thermometer
registered ten degrees. This means, of course, death to
everything not quite hardy; and even the hardiest hang
their heads, and flop their leaves and look dying, though
we know it is only affectation, and that a steady rain,
bearing in every drop heat from the tropics, will revive
many things again. I confess I like these sudden deaths
in Nature. When the time comes, it is better that things
should go, than linger on, as they do in very mild autumns.
Never since I have lived here have the berries of the

Pyracanthus and Holly been so fine ; the latter are covered with berries. In old days they used to say it meant a cold winter and a providential providing of food for the birds. Now we say it means a fine spring and a wet autumn, which is just what we have had this year ; but a wet autumn may mean a cold winter.

November 9th.—One or two hardy bamboos should be in all gardens, because of their appearance just now, apart from all other reasons. The ' English Flower Garden ' gives the best kinds, which must be selected according to the size of the garden and the situation in which they are to be placed. They by no means require to be planted in wet places—in fact, I imagine it is that which kills them in winter—but a few cans of water daily in dry weather, at their quick-growing time of May and June, helps them very much to throw off sooner that shabby appearance in spring which is one of their drawbacks. Another drawback is that they live such a short time in water after they are picked. The Japanese have many devices for preserving them ; the simplest of these is burning their ends in the fire before putting them into water. This answers with many flowers. In a small garden, Bamboos look much better for thinning out every year ; and the long canes make very useful, tidy sticks for pot-plants. At this time of year, when all else is dying or dead, they are healthfully and luxuriantly green. I have found by experience that, if Bamboos are really injured by frost, it is best to cut them down entirely the following spring. It requires some courage to cut out the tall, well-grown canes ; but, once nipped by frost, they do not recover, and they make better plants the following year if cut right back.

It is well worth while for anyone walking round the kitchen garden in November to pick the few remaining frost-bitten pods of the Scarlet Runners. When gathered and opened, what a treat of colour they display !—recalling wet shells on the seashore, mottled and marked,

and of a rich deep purple, and no two alike. I grow
Scarlet Runners singly, or two or three together, between the Apple-trees ; and it is a good plan, as they
bear much better than when planted in rows in the open,
and look much prettier. They creep up into the branches
of the Apple-trees ; the growth is so light it does no
harm, while it protects the late pods from frost.

The dear, bare branches of my favourite *Polygonum
cuspidatum*, here planted in a hole in the grass, look
lovely now at this time of the year, red in the sunshine
against a background of evergreens. I have now on the
table before me—cold and grey as it is out of doors—
Marigolds, Tea-rose buds (that are opening in the room,
and looking so pretty with a shoot of their own brown
leaves), Neapolitan Violets, some branches of small white
Michaelmas Daisies, and of course Chrysanthemums—
those autumn friends we are half tired of, and yet we
could so little do without. Another striking feature in
the garden just now are some small Beech-trees, quite
small, grown and cut back as shrubs are pruned. In a
soil where Beech-trees do not grow naturally, it is well
worth while to have them in this way, because of their
peculiarity of retaining on their branches the red dry
leaves more than half through the winter, causing a
distinct point of colour against the evergreen shrubs.

November 14th.—This is my last day in the country,
calm and warm. I eat my luncheon by the open window. All Nature is very, very still, the silence broken
now and then by the chirp of a bird and the distant crow
of a cock in some neighbour's yard ; the sky is pearly and
grey, and soft light-grey mists hang about, just enough
to show up the glory of some autumn bush or leaf. In
front of the window there are some little delicate leaves
of one of the shrubby Spiræas, planted on purpose to
shine, coral and gold, late in the year. It does not
matter about its being planted in a choice bed, as its
growth is not coarse ; if it looks a little dried up in

summer, it is not noticed when all the flowers are about. The dear little black and white pigeons—'Nuns,' they are called—with outspread wings, are flying down to feed. The flight of a pigeon is so beautiful ; no wonder Dante immortalised it in the famous lines in the Paolo and Francesca episode. That old cynic, Voltaire, used to say that Dante's fame would always grow, because he is so little read.

As I sit and watch, the low yellow winter sun bursts out, illuminating all things. To-morrow he will not shine for me, as I shall be in that horrid dark London.

One other morbid little poem, appropriate to this time of year, I think I must give you, for it used to be a great favourite of mine in past days, before the cheerfulness of old age came upon me. If I ever knew who was the author, I have forgotten it now :—

LA MÉLANCOLIE

Que me dis-tu, morne vent d'automne—
    Misérable vent ?
Toi dont la chanson douce et monotone
    Jadis charmait tant ?

Tu me dis, hélas ! qu'amour et jeunesse
    M'ont fait leurs adieux . . .
Et du fond de l'âme un flot de tristesse
    Me déborde aux yeux !

Tu me dis, trop bien, où le sentier mène
    Que l'espoir a fui . . .
Et ton chant piteux, traduisant ma peine,
    Triple mon ennui.

Ce mal qui courbait sur mon foyer vide
    Mon front désolé—
Ta complainte, O vent, et ton souffle humide
    Me l'ont révélé ;

C'est le mal des ans—c'est la nostalgie
    Des printemps perdus :
Et ton vieux refrain n'est qu'une élégie
    Sur ce qui n'est plus !

Modern Gardening Books.—In the month of March I

finished noticing the books in my possession up to the end of the last century. I begin again with this century, and shall carry them down to the present day.

1803. (An XI.) 'Le Jardin de la Malmaison.' By Ventenat. Illustrated by P. J. Redouté. In two folio volumes. This is one of my great possessions—a handsome book, sumptuously produced, as was likely to be at the time, dedicated as it is to Madame Bonaparte, just at the height of her power and influence. The implied flattery in the dedication to her is as large and magnificent as the paper is beautiful and the printing perfect. On the title-page is a little motto in Latin, saying that if the praises of the woods are to be sung, the woods should be worthy of the Consul. The book is an obvious imitation of Jacquin's 'Flora Schoenbrunnensis.' The illustrations are, I think, less artistic and certainly less strong than Jacquin's. They are not hand-coloured, like his, but are very fine examples of the best and most delicate (then newly discovered) method of colour-printing. The reason why Redouté's work is artistically inferior to Jacquin's is, that in his delicate rendering of the flowering branch he always puts it exactly in the centre of the page, without reference to its size or growth. The plates are at the end of each volume, and the descriptive text, which is in French, at the beginning. Poor Joséphine ! She was so fond of her gardens ; and I am told there is still an order preserved in our Admiralty that, when French ships were captured in the war, any plants or seeds that were on board for Madame Bonaparte were to be expedited. That was a gracious order ; and gardening in those days meant so much more than it does now. A flower blooming then was an interesting event all over Europe, and the gentle perfume of it rose and permeated through the smoke and din of the Napoleonic wars. Nevertheless, there always have been, and there always will be, those who would rather sing the old French rhyme :

Jardiner ne m'amuse guère,
Moi je voudrais faire la guerre.

Redouté, the artist, in this fine Napoleonic book plays only a secondary part to Ventenat. 1805. (An XIV.) ' La Botanique de J. J. Rousseau, ornée de soixante-cinq planches d'après les peintures de P. J. Redouté.' Apparently Redouté brought out this book to please himself, for it is a reprint of Rousseau's ' Elementary Letters on Botany to a Lady.' It has sixty-five such beautiful illustrative plates, exquisitely drawn and colour-printed like the last. Were ever such beautiful things done for those who wished to adapt natural flowers to chintzes, needlework, or wall-papers ? French artists, no matter of what school or of what period, always excel all others in the beauty of their actual draughtsmanship. Among these illustrations there is a very fine old-fashioned dark-red single Chrysanthemum called *Astre de Chine :* I have never seen anything in the least like it growing. The Daisy and the Dandelion, too—were they ever more beautifully or more sympathetically rendered ? Everything done is in honour of botany, nothing as a representation of a flower worth growing. The text is in French.

My other Redouté book is a very charming one, though my large octavo edition is, alas ! not the best, which is a folio in three volumes. The title-page states that the drawings have been reduced, re-engraved, and coloured under the eye of Monsieur Redouté, 1824. He had now become famous. The title is ' Les Roses, par P. J. Redouté, avec le texte par C. A. Thorry '—the order of the artist and author being just reversed from that in the work of his early days, ' Le Jardin de la Malmaison.' The book begins with the following charming sentence : —' Les poètes ont fondé dans l'opinion les seules monarchies héréditaires que le temps ait respectées : le lion est toujours le roi des animaux, l'aigle le monarque des airs, et la rose la reine des fleurs. Les droits des deux premiers établis sur la force et maintenus par elle avaient en eux-mêmes la raison suffisante de leur durée ; la souveraineté de la rose, moins violemment reconnue et plus librement consentie, a quelque chose de plus flatteur pour le trône et de plus honorable pour les fondateurs.'

Anyone who cares about Roses ought to try and see this book at the Botanical Library of the Natural History Museum at South Kensington, as it is very full of suggestions. Had I a soil·that suited Roses, and room to grow them in, I should try and make a collection of the wild Roses of the world and the roses figured by Redouté in 1824, many of which I have never seen. The Banksia Rose, which now covers the walls all along the Riviera, is here called *Le Rosier de Lady Banks* (wife of the botanist Sir Joseph Banks). There are Moss Roses and China Roses, and every form and kind of Eglantine ; but nothing larger or more double than the Cabbage Rose. The Malmaison Rose, though called after Josephine's garden, must have been a much later introduction. In fact, in 1824 there were no Roses and no Strawberries in our sense of the word. Even what is now called the Old Maiden's Blush is not in the book. The *R. lucida*, which I grow successfully in Surrey (for it is easy of cultivation, and has a lovely foliage), the York and Lancaster, and the Centifolia are all in this book. Even my small edition I look upon as one of my chief treasures ; it is bound in an old-fashioned bright-green leather. I suppose few people have seen this book, otherwise I cannot imagine how anyone has ever had the courage to publish the modern illustrated Rose books with pictures that look so coarse and vulgar in comparison with these delicate coloured prints.

1804. 'Exotic Botany, by James Edward Smith, President of the Linnean Society ; figures by James Sowerby. Two volumes in one.' This book is, of course, an English one, but on the title-page is the fol-

lowing quotation from Rousseau's seventh ' Promenade.'
I copy it, as it expresses the feeling of the times :—

'Il y a dans la botanique un charme qu'on ne sent
que dans le plein calme des passions, mais qui suffit seul
alors pour rendre la vie heureuse et douce : mais sitôt
qu'on y mêle un motif d'intérêt ou de vanité . . . . tout
ce doux charme s'évanouit. On ne voit plus dans les
plantes que des instruments de nos passions, on ne
trouve plus aucun vrai plaisir dans leur étude. . . . On
ne s'occupe que de systèmes et de méthodes ; matière
éternelle de dispute, qui ne fait pas connaître une plante
de plus . . . . de là les haines, les jalousies,' &c.

I wonder if it will strike anyone on reading this that
the sins of the botanist have been inherited in some
degree by the modern gardener ?

The book is dedicated to William Roscoe of Liverpool.
Rare and interesting plants from all parts of the world
are figured here, and many of them are uncommon to
this day. Some are familiar garden plants, such as
Rosemary-leaved Lavender Cotton, which, the author
tells us, ' Clusius says he met with on the sloping sides
of some hills near Narbonne, in the year 1552, when
travelling with his friend, the celebrated Rondeletius,
from Carcassonne to Montpellier. It is said to grow in
other parts of the South of France, as well as in Spain,
chiefly on open hills near the coast. It bears our climate
in the open border, flowering, though very rarely, in
August. We receive it from the Botanic Garden of
Liverpool by favour of Mr. John Shepherd.'

Such a passage, one of many, seems to stretch a hand
across the centuries, and explains the kind of charm
these old books have for those who like them. The
plates are carefully drawn and well coloured. This book
contains many plants from New Holland which must
then have been rare ; some are noted as grown in gardens
at Paddington, some as never having flowered in Europe
at all. It is certainly an interesting book.

1810. 'The Gardener's Kalendar,' by Walter Nicol.
This is the earliest of my gardening directories, and it
is not illustrated. It is an excellent little book, but one
learns nothing from it except that nearly all we know
now was known then.

1810. 'A Small Family Herbal,' by R. J. Thornton,
M.D., interesting as it claims to be illustrated by Thomas
Bewick. The little woodcuts of plants and flowers are
charming. The arrangement of the book is sensible and
clear, and has, at the end of the medical part, some
receipts for currant wine, elder wine, &c.

1812. 'A Family Herbal,' by Sir John Hill, M.D.
The illustrations are coarse, and not well drawn, though
hand-painted. It is a typical book of the day, when
there were so many of the same kind.

1812. 'The New Botanic Garden. Illustrated with
133 plants, engraved by Sansom from the original pictures, and coloured with the greatest exactness from
drawings by Sydenham Edwards.' There is considerable
boldness and character about these drawings of ordinary
garden plants and flowers, but the colour has changed
on several of them. Like other books of the period, the
flowers are illustrated and described in an absolutely
chance and desultory way ; the only exception is when
the authors confine themselves to one family, like
Andrews' 'Heathery,' or Jacquin's 'Oxalises.' What is
striking in all these books is the beautiful paper and printing. The drawing and painting are just beginning to
decline.

1814 (about). 'The Botanic Garden,' by B. Maund.
I think this the most useful, from a modern gardener's
point of view, of all the old books in my possession.
Nothing approaches it for instructiveness in herbaceous
plants till we get to Robinson's 'English Flower Garden.'
The complete set, consisting of sixteen volumes, is difficult to find, though odd volumes or broken sets are often
advertised. This lovely 'Botanic Garden ' is arranged

on an entirely new system. It is purely gardening and botany, no medicine at all. The volumes are quarto, and the illustrated page is divided into four. Each square is filled with an illustration from a flowering plant, every one of which—from the tallest Hollyhocks to the smallest Alpine—is drawn exactly the same size, to fill the space. This, to my mind, is a grave fault, continued to this day in flower illustration.

In some of the old Dutch books which I have seen, but, alas! do not possess, they had a plan of drawing the flowering branch, life size, in the middle of the page, with a small drawing in the corner representing the growth of the whole plant. This is a sensible and instructive method. I should like all flower illustration to be exactly the size of a fine specimen in Nature, quite regardless of filling or non-filling the page. To give a correct impression of the plant illustrated is very much more important than attempting to make uniform or even artistic pictures.

But to return to Maund. The letterpress follows the illustrations, one page to each plant, and the following characteristics are given above the drawing in every case :—(1) Name of country the plant comes from, (2) height, (3) when it flowers, (4) duration of plant, (5) when first cultivated. This gives, at a glance, a comprehensive idea of the plant. There are constant allusions through the book to Parkinson, Gerarde, and other old botanists. The earlier plates are far superior, better drawn, and more delicately coloured than those in the later volumes. In the twenty-five years which were covered by the serial issue of this publication the decline of flower-painting marched apace.

1814. ' Flore Médicale. Décrite par F. P. Chaumeton, Docteur en Médecine. Peinte par Madame E. P—— et par P. J. F. Turpin.' This is a lovely book in eight octavo volumes. The illustrations are most delicate and fine, and in the Redouté manner. He influenced all

flower-painting at that time in Paris, professional as well
as amateur. Flower-painting only ceased to be good
when it was no longer considered the handmaid of botany
and medicine, which necessitated quite a different order
of merit and precision from what was required for mere
flower illustration for gardening purposes. One of the
useful and uncommon idiosyncrasies of this book is that
at the top of each page describing the plate the name
of the plant is given in seven European languages. The
curative properties of various medicines are named, but
there are, alas! no cooking receipts. This is what is
said about Cardoons, the vegetable so little used in
England because the cooks do not know how to dress
it :—

'Le Cardon *Cynara cardunculus* dont les feuilles,
prodigieusement amples, deviennent, en blanchissant,
une de nos meilleures plantes potagères. La culture en
a fait des variétés et des sous-variétés, dont deux dé-
pouillées d'épines sont plus faciles à manier, cependant
on préfère au cardon d'Espagne, tout inerme qu'il est,
le cardon de Tours, armé d'épines longues et très aiguës.
Celui-ce est moins sujet à monter ; ses côtes sont plus
grosses, plus tendres, et beaucoup plus délicates. Le
professeur Gilibert a connu un médecin qui depuis dix
ans prenait tous les matins un verre de décoction des
feuilles vertes de cardon, avec la persuasion intime que
ce remède l'avait guéri d'un engorgement au foie, et en
prévenait le retour.' It is curious how, in these old
books, the faith seems always to have been in what was
put into the water, not in the good tumblerful of any
hot liquid—plain water being perhaps the best of all,
though no doubt in any decoction of vegetable there
would be small quantities of soda. The book is full of
all kinds of interesting information, and there are constant allusions to the use of vegetables in all sorts of
illnesses, especially gout and stone. There is an article
in the 'Edinburgh Review' of November 1810 on the

uses of vegetarianism for the cure of stone. It seems now as if we were once more tending towards the system of Abernethy, who lived in the early part of the century. The recommendation he gave to his patients was : ' Live on sixpence a day, and earn it.'

1824. ' The Universal Herbal,' by Thomas Greene. This is an ambitious book in two large fat volumes. It professes to contain an account of all the known plants in the world, adapted to the use of the farmer, the gardener, the husbandman, the botanist, the florist, and country housekeepers in general. Mine is the second edition, revised and improved. The frontispiece is coloured and very funny ; it is called ' Wisdom and Activity collecting the various treasures of the Vegetable Kingdom.' Wisdom is represented by an old woman in the background under a hedge. In the foreground on the left is a youthful Flora, and on the right Activity is represented by a middle-aged husbandman, who does not look active at all. On the title-page is an extraordinary collection of young women without too many clothes, which I should have thought represented the elements or the seasons, only there are five of them. Surrounding these is a wreath of vegetation and flowers, held up at the top by fat winged Loves. The book is alphabetically arranged, and every now and then there is a page with four coloured flowers on it, only moderately executed. Compared to those gone before, these are not worth noticing, but they are not so bad as those about to come. This book certainly contains an extraordinary amount of detailed information and instruction ; its comprehensiveness may be imagined when I note that sixty-seven Oxalises are described in separate paragraphs. It is exceptionally interesting for the botanical account it gives of garden plants and flowers. The medical properties of many plants which hitherto have been spoken of as certain panaceas are here alluded to in a comparatively doubtful tone. The treatise on gardening, at the end of the second volume, is very amusing ; and the prints enable me to realise the date and origin of our characteristic villa plantations, approaches, drives, &c. There is an illustrated page of ornamental flower-stands, which, ugly as they are, I think might be improved and adapted so as to be rather pretty and useful in some greenhouses and windows.

The lists of plants, bulbs, and seeds are useful even now, and would have been exceedingly so to me some years ago. The way these books fell out of knowledge and fashion is quite extraordinary. The botany they contain was constantly superseded by newer books ; faith in herbalism died out ; and the beautiful herbaceous plants were swept away from our gardens. I suppose I did not look out for these books, knowing nothing of them ; but I never saw one of them till I began to be interested in them and to collect them five or six years ago.

1825. 'The Manse Garden,' which has long been out of print, I have. Canon Ellacombe praises it most warmly and justly at the end of his 'Gloucestershire Garden,' published last year. It has no name and no date, but he says it was written by the Rev. N. Patterson, at that time—nearly seventy years ago—Minister of Galashiels and afterwards a leading member of the Scotch Free Kirk. 'It is altogether,' Canon Ellacombe adds, ' a delightful book, full of quaint sentences, shrewd good-sense, and quiet humour ; and the cultural directions are admirable.' This praise I entirely endorse. The chapter at the end, called 'The Minister's Boy,' is especially human, in the modern sense of the word. It is a modest, non-old-fashioned-looking little book, and is, I expect, to be found hidden away in many an old Scotch house.

1825-1830. 'Cistineæ: the Natural Order of Rock Rose,' by Robert Sweet. This, once more, is a book entirely confined to one family, the extent of which is such a surprise to most of us. Who would have expected that there are thirty-five Cistuses, seventy-eight Helianthemums, and about a hundred Rock Roses? The drawings are good ; but the colouring, though still by hand, compares very badly with Redouté's lovely Rose book. Cistuses are such charming plants, opening their papery blooms in the sunlight ; they do very well in the light Surrey soil, but very few of them are really hardy. *Cistus laurifolius* is hardy with me, and *C. florentinus* only dies in very severe winters. Mr. Robinson gives a list of them, and they are such pretty little shrubs that they are well worth any trouble. The mixed Helianthemums (Sun Roses) are best raised from seed, and it is very easy to keep any specially good ones from cuttings made in the summer, when they strike freely. I take potfuls of cuttings of the shrubby kinds every year as well, in case of accidents. There are several other books by Mr. Sweet, all of which must be well worth having.

1826. ' The Gardener's Magazine,' conducted by J. C. Loudon. This publication, of which I have seventeen volumes, was, according to his biographer, Mr. Loudon's own favourite, into which he put the best of his ideas and work. It is only illustrated with small wood-cuts in order to explain the text, but is crammed with interesting information, well-arranged lists of plants, and descriptions of country houses, the culture of fruit and flowers, green-houses, and stoves. I repeat, the especial use of these older books is to help us to the knowledge and cultivation of non-hardy exotics—a subject which the great authority of the day, Mr. Robinson, does not touch upon. They, however, require to be read with understanding, as in Mr. Loudon's day gardeners were much more afraid than they are now of treating plants as hardy—the risk of losing them being then too great, whereas now it is only considered as being good for trade. In nearly all private gardens of the present day it is almost forgotten that plants can be easily reproduced by layers, cuttings, and seeds. Modern gardening shares in the common fault of our generation, which is so prone to waste and to buy, rather than to produce.

Mr. Loudon seems to have been an upright, hardworking and educated man, who was rather forced by ill-health into the life which he took up. There is an interesting portrait and biography of him in a little book of his, published after his death, called 'Self-Instruction for Young Gardeners.' As is frequently the case with men whose whole mind is taken up with some absorbing intellectual occupation, he neglected his own money affairs, and at the time of his last illness he had to make an appeal to his many friends and admirers for funds to enable him to publish his great work, which has not yet been superseded, though it calls for re-editing, the 'Arboretum Botanicum,' of which more hereafter. Mr. Loudon died on December 14, 1843, before he heard of the kind way in which his friends had come forward and responded to the appeal. His wife states that he died on the anniversary of the death of Washington, thus linking us on by an allusion to older times, which seem to us so very long ago.

The story of Mrs. Loudon's marriage is rather interesting. As a girl (1825) she wrote what she herself describes as 'a strange, weird novel,' called ' The Mummy ' —perhaps the first of the prophetic stories that have been so common in my time, the scene being laid in the twenty-second century. Mr. Loudon was struck by a review of this book, and read it. It made so deep an impression on him that two or three years afterwards he expressed to a friend his great wish to know the author, whom he believed to be a man. An introduction was brought about, which in a short time resulted in their marriage. They lived in a charming house at Bayswater, which was then quite in the country, and ' The Gardener's Magazine ' alone brought him in 750*l.* a year. Soon after their marriage they saw at Chester, in 1831, the first number of Paxton's 'Horticultural Register,' the earliest rival to 'The Gardener's Magazine,' which gradually declined from that time, and was given up immediately after Mr. Loudon's death. The impetus given by Mr. Loudon's books and periodicals to landscape gardening and greenhouse cultivation, for pleasure and beauty alone, and for the ornamentation of the houses of the wealthy, must have been immense. But from that time the books assumed the deteriorated character from which they are only now beginning to emerge. Cheapness became a desirable object—necessary for the propagation of the instruction. This change greatly enhances the interest and value of the older books. The illustrations only served to elucidate the text, and in the case of coloured plates several plants were often crowded into one page for the sake of cheapness in reproduction. The gardener was no longer a botanist and an artist, but employed inferior draughtsmen to illustrate his instructions.

The original debt on the 'Arboretum,' published just after Mr. Loudon's death, was 10,000*l.*, which seems a very large sum, considering how poor the illustrations are. It is a book of immense study, great interest, and valuable instruction. The work is in eight volumes—four letterpress and four illustrations.

1842. 'Ladies' Magazine of Gardening,' by Mrs. Loudon, published just before Mr. Loudon's death, has some rather good illustrations of flowers, some certainly not commonly grown now. What she calls the Golden-haired Anemone is quite unknown to me. The illustrations for gardens and rockwork are elaborately descriptive of all which should be avoided ; but in every book of the period there is much for the student to learn. Failing income induced Mrs. Loudon, no doubt helped by her early efforts in literature, to publish books on gardening for the use of amateurs. When she and her little daughter were left very badly off, her efforts assumed a more ambitious line.

The first edition of ' The Lady's Companion,' which I have, was published by William Smith in 1841. It is a delightful little book, alphabetically arranged, with a few useful illustrations, light to hold, and beautifully printed. It always mentions the country from which the plant or flower comes, and it often suggests, most usefully, the soil or locality where the plants do best in England. This is a point too often omitted in modern gardening papers. The book was afterwards enlarged. It went through several editions, and had many imitators. Mrs. Loudon's earlier books are often to be picked up, very cheap, at secondhand shops, and I strongly recommend all ladies interested in gardening to buy them whenever they can lay their hands on them, either for themselves or to give away. It is not that they are really better for the advanced student than the modern books, but that they are more simple. They begin more from the beginning, they teach more what amateurs require, and they are not complicated with the immense variety which in modern books and catalogues drives unfortunate young gardeners to despair. A good deal of this applies as well to the many imitators and humble pupils of the Loudons' school who published between 1840 and 1850. One book I have is called ' Every Lady her own Flower Gardener,' by Louisa Johnson (seventh edition !), published by W. S. Orr, 1845. Any lady with a small villa garden would find most useful instruction in this little manual. The gardening matter in all the books of this time is excellent ; where they fail, like the Loudons themselves, is that they are permeated with that early Victorian taste now thought so execrable—baskets and vases, summer-houses and seats, are all tortured into frightful ' rustic ' shapes. The planting and laying-out of grounds are equally bad ; they constantly recommend both kinds of Laurels, which time has taught us are the most destructive of plants, killing all other shrubs in their neighbourhood with their insolent and devouring roots.

Those who have larger gardens would do well to try and get Mrs. Loudon's six quarto volumes, illustrated with coloured pictures. Though artistically bad as flower-paintings, and inferior to those published now in the weekly gardening papers, they resemble the flowers enough to be recognisable. They most usefully illustrate the text for the ignorant amateur, who learns far more quickly when pictures and letterpress are combined than by any written instruction alone, however good.

Mrs. Loudon's quarto volumes are now rather difficult to get complete. There are two volumes on perennials, one on annuals, one on bulbs ; this one is perhaps the most valuable of the lot, as it gives many of the best-known bulbs as they arrived from the Cape, before they were so over-cultivated and hybridised by the modern nurseryman. Perhaps the volume on greenhouse plants is the least interesting, as so many things are recommended for cultivation under glass which have since been proved to be hardy, or nearly so, and grow very well out of doors—at any rate, through the summer months. The volume on English wild flowers, which completes the set, is a little superficial, but helpful. It has rather good pictures of many of our native plants, some of which are now very rare. The best of these wild flowers can be cultivated from seed, even in small gardens, giving us most beautiful effects with very little trouble and expense.

1828. ' Mémoires du Musée d'Histoire naturelle.'

1834. ' Mémoires sur quelques Espèces de Cactées.'

These are portions of two books with most beautiful and curious illustrations of Cactuses, the only examples of old botanical drawings of Cactuses I have been able up to now to procure. They are not coloured, but delicate and precise in drawing to a high degree.

1829. ' A History of English Gardening—Chronological, Biographical, Literary, and Critical—Tracing the Progress of the Art in this Country from the Invasion of the Romans to the Present Time,' by George W. Johnson. This little book is so comprehensive in subject that it is rather dry reading, though Mr. Johnson's introductory chapter abounds in interesting information about the gardens and vegetable cultivation of the ancients. Cato's description of the cultivation of Asparagus is very much the same as what is now recommended. Gardening, at no time in the world's history, seems in any way to have been the especial property of the good and simple, in whose hands alone ' it is the purest of human pleasures.' To sit about gardens in summer sunshine, to listen to the birds, and to enjoy the scent of the flowers cultivated by others may be very enjoyable, but in no sense does it deserve to be called ' the purest of human pleasures.' No one who does not actually work in his own garden can ever really realise the pleasure of having one, and the enjoyment of a garden entirely worked by others is merely a form of idleness and luxury. The title does not accurately describe the book, as the gardens of the ancients are confined to the introduction, and the history of English gardening begins only from the accession of Edward III. The main part of it is a detailed account of all the books that have been written on the art of gardening. Mr. Johnson most critically describes the letterpress of gardening books, but very little notice indeed is taken of any illustrating, and when he reaches Curtis's beautiful ' Flora Londinensis ' he gives it no more praise than to any little short gardening essay that may have appeared at the time. Anyone going to the Museum Library with this comprehensive catalogue would have but a slight idea of what are the best books to ask for. Till the appearance of Miss Amherst's book in 1895, I believe this was the only existing book of reference on the history of English gardening.

1830. ' On the Portraits of English Authors on Gardening, with Biographical Notices,' by S. Felton. A curious and really valuable book of reference. Mr. Felton, in his preface, pays high tribute to the ' History of English Gardening,' just described, and says : ' Mr. Johnson's work is the result of original thought and of an ardent and extended scientific research. Mine is a compilation " made with a pair of scissors," to copy the words of Mr. Mathias, which he applies to a certain edition of Pope. I content myself, however, with the reflection of Mr. Walpole, that " they who cannot perform great things themselves may yet have a satisfaction in doing justice to those who can." ' This reminds me of the flippant newspaper critic who called Sir George Cornewall Lewis's ' Influence of Authority in Matters of Opinion ' ' a book to prove that, if you did not know a thing, you should ask some one who did.' There is a delightful wisdom in this remark.

1830 (about). ' The Florist's Journal and Gardening Record.' I have two volumes of this publication. The plates are well drawn and coloured, and are more delicate than those in Mrs. Loudon's books. One volume contains a fascinating picture of that rather rare flower, which I have failed as yet to bloom, called *Zauschneria californica.* The two volumes are good specimens of the books of the period.

1834. ' The Magazine of Botany,' by Joseph Paxton. In this year the intelligent gardener at Chatsworth started his ' Magazine of Botany,' which was finished in 1849. I have the complete set of sixteen volumes. The first volume contains a somewhat fulsome and yet touchingly hearty dedication to his master, the Duke of Devonshire. Each of the succeeding volumes are dedicated to more or less exalted members of the peerage—some men, some women. The ' Magazine ' to this day is interesting, useful, and full of instruction as regards the cultivation of desirable and uncommon greenhouse and stove plants.

The title-page is quite simple. Evidently the fashion for adornment, allegorical or otherwise, hitherto so much in use, seems to have entirely died away, and plainness rules the day. The page has nothing on it but the title and the famous Bacon quotation, which can never be too often repeated : ' God Almighty first planted a garden, and indeed it is the purest of human pleasures : it is the greatest refreshment to the spirit of man, without which buildings and palaces are but gross handiworks ; and a man shall ever see that, when ages grow to civility and elegance, men come to build stately sooner than to garden finely, as if gardening were the greater perfection.'

Bacon is delightfully solemn, but one cannot help remembering Adam found it so very dull till Eve came that he even sacrificed a rib for the sake of a companion.

There is a sad falling-off in the plates, both wood-cuts and coloured ones, though they are executed by different people, and some are much better than others. Paxton must have studied hard, as he constantly refers to the older books. What is of chief interest about him is that he was the greatest unconscious instrument in the movement he helped to develop, which altered the gardening of the whole of England, and consequently of the world. He used the old patterns of Italy and France for designs of beds, filling them, as had never been done before, with cuttings of tender exotics, which were kept under glass during the whole winter. Endless sums of money were at his disposal, and everything was done which could facilitate his efforts to make the terraces of Chatsworth a blaze of colour during the months of August and September, the months when his master came from town. From his point of view this was a most praiseworthy object, and no doubt gave great satisfaction. It was copied, for the same reasons, by most of the great houses in England. But what was really unfortunate, and can only recall the old fable of the ox and the frog, was the imitation of this system in all the gardens of England,

down to the half-acre surrounding a vicarage, or the plot
of ground in front of a suburban residence. The ox, as
we know, was big by nature ; and when the frog imitated him, it was flattering to the ox, but the frog came
to grief. So I think to this day, if bedding-out is ever
tolerable, it is on the broad terraces facing large stone
houses, with which we have nothing to do here. Where
it becomes intolerable, and perhaps it is hard to blame
Paxton for this, is in the miniature Chatsworths, with
their little lawns and their little beds, their Pelargoniums
—often only coloured leaves, like the Mrs. Pollock—their
dwarf Calceolarias, their purple Verbenas, and their blue
Lobelias ; where the lady is not allowed to pick, and
where the gardener, if he is masterful and gets his own
way, turns the old herbaceous border in front of the
house into that terrible abomination called ' carpet-
bedding.' Paxton was a very remarkable man in his
way. When taken up by the Queen and the Prince
Consort, he built in 1851 that wonderful and ever-to-be-
remembered glass case, in Hyde Park, the first general
International Exhibition, which enclosed two large elms.
Poor trees ! how they hated it ! Their drooping au-
tumnal appearance is my strongest childish remembrance
of that Exhibition. Paxton was knighted by the Queen,
and partly built the Crystal Palace at Sydenham with the
remains of the Hyde Park Exhibition.

1835. Culpepper's ' Complete Herbal.' A republica-
tion of his original ' Epistle to the Reader ' is dated from
' Spitalfields, next door to the Red Lion, September 5,
1653.' The frontispiece has Culpepper's portrait—a
sharp amiable face, with long hair, a white collar, and
a Puritan dress. Below is a little picture of the upright,
modern-looking London house, surrounded though it is
by fields, in which he lived and died.

The instructions for ' the right use of the book ' are
so curious that I may as well copy them : ' And herein
let me premise a word or two. The herbs, plants, &c.,

are now in the book appropriated to their proper planets. Therefore, first consider what planet causes disease ; that thou mayst find it in my aforesaid judgement of diseases. Secondly, consider what part of the body is afflicted by the disease, and whether it lies in the flesh, or blood, or bone, or ventricles.

'Thirdly, consider by what planet the afflicted part of the body is governed ; that my judgement of disease will inform you also.

'Fourthly, you may oppose diseases by Herbs of the planet opposite to the planet that causes them, as diseases of *Jupiter* by Herbs of *Mercury*, and the contrary ; diseases of the *Luminaries* by the Herbs of *Saturn*, and the contrary ; diseases of *Mars* by Herbs of *Venus*, and the contrary.

'Fifthly, there is a way to cure diseases sometimes by *Sympathy*, and so every planet cures his own disease ; as the *Sun* and *Moon* by their Herbs cure the Eyes, *Saturn* the Spleen, *Jupiter* the Liver, *Mars* the gall and diseases of choler, and *Venus* diseases in the instruments of Generation.

'(Signed) NICH. CULPEPPER.'

The whole book runs on the same lines. Of course it can only have been re-published as late as 1835 as a curiosity.

1835. 'The Language of Flowers, with Illustrative Poetry.' Inseparable from a collection of flower-books of this period is one example at least of the curious childish sentiment—or, rather, of the sentimentality which was the fashion of the day. The frontispiece is a little bouquet of flowers which means, being interpreted, 'Your beauty and modesty have forced from me a declaration of Love.' It is always the woman's fault, somehow, in all times. The little book is dedicated to the Duchess of Kent. The 'illustrative' flower-writing is curious, and the dictionary of the language of flowers

very arbitrary.   How utterly the whole thing has passed
away !   The outside of the little book, bound in stamped
green silk, is rather pretty.

1837. ' Amaryllidaceæ,' by the Honourable and Reverend William Herbert, and dedicated to Leopold, King
of the Belgians.   This book is very botanical, and dry
to the ordinary reader, though, I should think, comprehensively descriptive and interesting to the student.
The drawings are good and delicate, and very slightly
coloured.

1839. ' Pinetum Woburnensis, or a Catalogue of
Coniferous Plants in the Collection of the Duke of
Bedford, at Woburn Abbey, systematically arranged.'
This is a very handsome book, unfortunately not large
enough to show off the really fine plates to advantage,
as they are all folded in half in the middle.   I imagine
it is the only work of its kind, and seems, so far as I
can judge, to be very complete.   Considering how late
was the date of publication, the plates are very well
drawn and coloured by hand.   The introduction, dated
1839, is written by the Duke of Bedford.   In it he gives
such an amusing anecdote of his grandfather that I
cannot resist quoting it :—' In the year 1743 my grandfather planted the large plantation in Woburn Park
known by the name of the " Evergreens," to com-
memorate the birth of his daughter, afterwards Caroline,
Duchess of Marlborough ; it was something more than
one hundred acres, and was, before that time, a rabbit-
warren, producing nothing but a few blades of grass,
with the heath or ling indigenous to the soil, and without a single tree upon it.

' In the course of a few years the Duke perceived
that the plantation required thinning, in order to admit
a free circulation of air, and give health and vigour to
the young trees.   He accordingly gave instructions to
his gardener, and directed him as to the mode and
extent of the thinning required.   The gardener paused,

and hesitated, and at length said, "Your Grace must pardon me if I humbly remonstrate against your orders, but I cannot possibly do what you desire ; it would at once destroy the young plantation, and, moreover, it would be seriously injurious to my reputation as a planter."

'My grandfather, who was of an impetuous and decided character, but always just, instantly replied, "Do as I tell you, and I will take care of your reputation."

·'The plantation, which ran for nearly a mile along the road leading from the market town of Woburn to that of Ampthill, was, consequently, thinned according to the instructions of the Duke of Bedford, who caused a board to be fixed in the plantation, facing the road, on which was inscribed, "This plantation has been thinned by John, Duke of Bedford, contrary to the advice and opinion of his gardener." '

1843. 'Flora Odorata : a Characteristic Arrangement of the Sweet-scented Flowers and Shrubs cultivated in the Gardens of Great Britain,' by Frederick T. Mott. A useful, suggestive, little book, and the only one on the subject that was ever printed, I believe, till the appearance of a book in 1895, 'Sweet-scented Flowers and Fragrant Leaves,' by Donald McDonald. This last often gives the name of one scented variety in a perfectly scentless family, such as the Camellia. *C. drupifera* has scented flowers. I observe that the very faintest odour justifies the inclusion of some plants in both these books.

1846. 'Flowers and their Associations,' and 'The Field, Garden, and Woodland,' by Anne Pratt. I have none of Anne Pratt's books except this curious little one, given me off a Christmas-tree, by a serious old uncle, because I was fond of flowers, when I was a child. It is roughly illustrated, and contains much desultory information.

1848. 'The Rose Garden,' by William Paul. This is a most interesting publication as regards plant growth, increased variety, and the utter collapse and deterioration of the art of illustrating. Viewed by the light of Redouté's Rose book, it is like turning from a Greek goddess to the stoutest of matrons. The poor Rose !— it has swelled and amplified under cultivation to a despairing degree ; but the execution of the plates is answerable for much, no doubt. We have now the figure of the *Bourbon* Rose, called ' *Souvenir de la Malmaison.*' Roses have increased apace in the quarter of a century since Redouté painted them, but many of the Roses in this book are now called old-fashioned. The plans and instructions for Rose gardens are not what are now admired, and, one would say, are singularly unsuited to the spreading wild growth of healthy Roses.

1854. ' A History of British Ferns,' by Edward Newman. Enthusiastic gardeners in the 'Fifties gave a great deal of time and attention to Ferns. . Now, people wisely do not attempt them where they will not grow. My other Fern book, published in 1868, is ' Select Ferns and Lycopods, British and Exotic, by B. S. Williams. A useful book, as Fern-growing in stoves and greenhouses will always be well worth while.

(No date, but I imagine in the 'Fifties.) ' Profitable Gardening : a Practical Guide,' by Shirley Hibberd. A nice old book, full of clear instruction and practical hints. Books of this description are often to be picked up on old bookstalls, and are very helpful, as being the A B C to more advanced modern books.

1855. ' Flora of the Colosseum of Rome,' by Richard Deakin, M.D., with a print of the ruins of the Colosseum before the days of photography. I bought this book, I must confess, out of pure sentiment, as it is too strictly botanical to suit my ignorance. I spent a winter in Rome when I was a little girl, and the vegetation which grew all over the Colosseum, both plants and flowers, was deeply impressed on my mind. I never saw Rome again till about twelve years ago, when the scraped and tidy appearance of the Roman ruins, though no doubt necessary for their preservation for posterity, struck a cruel blow at my youthful recollections. This curious little book gives the botanical description of 420 plants growing spontaneously on the ruins of the Colosseum at Rome. The record of this absolutely vanished vegetation has, I think, a touch of poetry of its own which can better be felt than expressed. The book has some little architectural illustrations of no great merit.

1855. 'Beautiful-Leaved Plants,' by E. J. Stone. This is a book rather interesting to the collector, and illustrative of a peculiarly bad period. Its quotations and general appearance are rather those of a 'Lady Blessington Annual' than of a serious gardening book, but I should think it was a standard work on hothouse foliage plants. It has one great merit : the illustrations are in very bright colours, and the plant in full growth is printed in black and white on the opposite page ; this is a first-rate way of illustrating a book of the kind. The letterpress gives a detailed botanical story of the plant illustrated, and the method of its cultivation. A useful book, I should imagine, for head-gardeners whose employers are fond of beautiful-leaved plants.

1869. 'The Parks, Promenades, and Gardens of Paris,' by W. Robinson. This is the earliest of many most interesting books that I possess by Mr. Robinson ; a book full of information, branching into many directions. The third, and I believe last, edition, with the illustrations much improved, was published in 1883.

Next comes, in 1871, his 'Sub-tropical Garden, or Beauty of Form in the Flower Garden.' This second title refers to that which, to my mind, is the great value and interest of the book, and to be attained almost entirely as well by hardy plants as by sub-tropical ones. In 1871, however, the idea was new, and is even now but most indifferently carried out or understood in nine out of ten gardens that one sees, in spite of all Mr.

Robinson's invaluable teaching both in this and many other of his books.

'Alpine Flowers for English Gardens.' Mine is the third edition. The illustrations are popular, and inferior to those in most of Mr. Robinson's books. How much joy do the Alps recall to thousands of people! Even for those who do not enjoy mountain scenery, there are always the lakes and the flora.

> Avec leurs grands sommets, leurs glaces éternelles
> Par un soleil d'été que les Alpes sont belles !

Some of Mr. Ruskin's happiest lines, I think, are in the ' Mont Blanc revisited ' :

> O mount beloved, my eyes again
> Behold the twilight's sanguine stain
>   Along thy peaks expire ;
> O mount beloved, thy frontier waste
> I seek with a religious haste
>   And reverent desire.

And who can ever think of Switzerland apart from Matthew Arnold's two wonderful Obermann poems? Do not some spirits still exist who slip ' their chain ' with Matthew Arnold?

> And to thy mountain chalet come,
>   And lie beside its door,
> And hear the wild bees' Alpine hum,
>   And thy sad, tranquil lore.
>
> Again I feel the words inspire
>   Their mournful calm—serene,
> Yet tinged with infinite desire
>   For all that *might* have been.

De Senancour! how these poems 'To Obermann' have carried your melancholy eloquence from the early years of the century to its very end!

The first edition of the ' Wild Garden ' was published in 1881, and of all modern illustrated flower-books it is the only one I know that makes me feel really enthusiastic. The drawings in it, by Mr. Alfred Parsons, are exquisite and quite original. At the time of its publication the method was new, and, to my mind, it has not yet been surpassed. I have also the fourth edition, which came out in 1894, with much new matter and several new illustrations, especially landscapes ; but I prefer the first edition—perhaps because we get fond of the particular edition that originally gave pleasure.

I am afraid that the hopeful instructions on ' wild gardening ' so cheerfully laid down by Mr. Robinson must be taken with a great many grains of salt when it comes to putting them into practice, especially in dry soils. With care, labour, knowledge, and space, exquisite gardens may be laid out, suitable to the various soils of England ; but, in my experience, even the best planting goes off without renewal of the soil. This shows itself with the happy possessors of these so-called ' wild gardens ' by the constant desire to extend them into pastures new. Mr. Robinson's description of a garden at Weybridge ought to open the eyes of everybody as to what can be done in light soils. All I wish to point out is that merely buying the plants and sticking them in does not make a wild garden. No one can look at Mr. Parsons' beautiful drawings of the Evening Primrose and the Giant Cow Parsley without longing to grow such things. But the first essentials are space and isolation ; they are worth nothing if crowded up.

1875. ' The Vegetable Garden,' by M. M. Vilmorin-Andrieux. English edition published under the direction of W. Robinson. This is one of the books mentioned in January as indispensable to anyone who wishes to be up-to-date or to grow special vegetables in the kitchen garden. The illustrations are from the French edition, and though not artistic, are admirably drawn, and give one quickly an intimate knowledge of the shape and growth of vegetables, whether they be roots or plants.

The first edition of the now far-famed ' English Flower Garden' came out in 1883, and the one published this year (1896) is the sixth edition. It has been immensely added to, and the present illustrations are among the most beautiful modern wood-cuts I know. It is said that books are now written to be read and understood by the village idiot. If this be so, I must own that the first and second editions, with their quantity of small, gardener's catalogue illustrations of the plants and flowers, are more helpful to the ignorant amateur than is this beautiful illustrating of, let us say, a branch of Hawthorn or a full-blown Tea-rose. This seems a cruel criticism of a beautiful book ; and it should never be forgotten that the fault lies with the ignorant amateur, not with the new edition.

' God's Acre Beautiful, or The Cemeteries of the Future ' is a strong plea for cremation. My edition is the third, published in 1883. Everyone interested in the subject ought to read it. The picture, at the end of the book, of a section of a pauper corner in a London cemetery is, I think, enough to convert anybody ; but it does not seem to me that the practice of cremation is gaining much ground. The recent sweeping-away of West End London cemeteries contrasts badly, even from the point of view of sentiment, with the tombs at Pompeii used for urns ; the chapter referring to these is headed ' Permanent, Unpolluted, Inviolate.' That is certainly not the modern cemetery !

In 1892 Mr. Robinson published two lectures of considerable severity, called ' Garden Design ' and ' Architects' Gardens.' These lectures were mainly directed against two books ; one, that seemed to contradict all Mr. Robinson's work, was ' The Formal Garden in England,' by Reginald Blomfield and T. Inigo Thomas. The fact is, that near large and stately houses there must be some kind of formal laying-out of the ground, even if ever so informally planted (Mr. Robinson himself would be the first to recognise this), unless everything is sacrificed to stateliness, and turf alone is admitted. The whole discussion is full of interest to those who possess large places. The next book on which Mr. Robinson pours the vials of his wrath (I love righteous indignation on one's pet subject) is ' Garden Craft, Old and New,' by John D. Sedding. Of all Mr. Robinson's books, the ' English Flower Garden ' will always remain his masterpiece ; and I repeat here, what I said in January, that no modern gardener can get on without it. Every village club should have it, as well as his first-rate little halfpenny paper, ' Cottage Gardening,' which has many useful things in it besides gardening.

Anyone who can remember the gardening of the last thirty years will have no difficulty in recognising all that we owe to Mr. Robinson. His untiring energy, the pains he has taken to bring his books up to the highest and most complete standard of useful knowledge and reference, his newspapers (the coloured illustrations of which come nearer the excellence of the old coloured engravings than those in any other modern periodical), and, above all, the true taste and knowledge he has brought to bear on English gardening are influencing the whole of Europe, America, and our colonies ; for he has headed the movement in the right direction, teaching the true principles of the laying-out of gardens and the preservation and cultivation of plants and flowers.

I have (bound) a great many years' numbers of ' The Garden ' newspaper. To look over them is endlessly interesting and suggestive, though it is apt to be discouraging, as so many plants are mentioned that we have not got and would like to have.

1872. ' Flowers and Gardens,' by Forbes Watson.

This is the only break I make in my resolve to mention no book not in my possession. My reasons for doing so are that it has long been out of print, and that I want to make a short extract from it. So far as I know, this was the first of a long series of books—not so much practical gardening books, as books about the garden as a whole and the way in which the grouping and growing of plants affect the individual writer. An attractive, suggestive, and pathetic little book, written by a sick man to beguile days he knew to be his last. Mr. Watson was perhaps the last of the men who combined the three callings of doctor, botanist, and gardener. What he writes is much in advance of the feeling of the day, and it is full of what we now think quite the right tone about gardening. In the following quotation he expresses better than I can do it what I want to say. He begins : ' Solon declared that to be the best of Governments in which an injury done to the meanest subject is an insult to the whole community.

' This is pretty much the law of a garden.

' Nothing is more objectionable than the manner in which the common plants are often treated to make way for the grandees. Bulbs taken up before they are ready, and dwarfed for next season in consequence ; small trees or shrubs transplanted carelessly, and thrust in wherever they will do no harm, because a little too good to throw away, and not quite good enough to deserve just treatment ; and many other plants neglected, overshadowed, or in some way stinted of their due, as not being worth much trouble. At times, even worse than this, we see murderous digging and slashing amongst plants in their period of growth. This is not a healthy process for the mind. Whatever is unfairly treated is better altogether away, since we can view it with no hearty relish. And this injustice to the least is felt inevitably in a measure by all, for it affects the spirit of the place. Half the charm of the old-fashioned garden lies in that look of happy rest among the plants, each of which seems to say : " All plant life is sacred when admitted, my own repose has never been disturbed, and I am confident it never will be." You feel this to be a sort of heaven of plant life, preserved by some hidden charm from the intrusion of noxious weeds. The modern garden, on the contrary, is too apt to assume a look of stir and change ; here to-day, gone to-morrow. The very tidiness of the beds and the neat propriety of the plants contribute to this impression. We feel the omnipresence of a severity which cannot tolerate straggling. None have been admitted but polished gentlemen, who will never break the rules ; and we feel that the most cherished offender would be instantly punished.

' I have been referring here to the herbaceous plants and evergreens of the ordinary beds—Thujas, Junipers, Rhododendrons, &c.—rather than to the larger trees and shrubs. To run down the glorious Rhododendrons in themselves would be preposterous ; but they always have, however large they may grow, an air of gentlemanly restraint—a drawing-room manner, as it were —which must produce the effect we have described wherever they are very numerous. But the old garden impresses us always by that loving tenderness for the plants. " That wallflower ought not to have come up in the Box edging—but never mind, we must manage to get on without hurting the wallflower ; " and it is this spirit of compromise—this happy, genial, kindly character, as contrasted with the sterner and less loving spirit, which you feel is ready to descend upon any transgressor in a moment, that makes the difference of which we speak.'

Mr. Watson is very severe in his condemnation of double flowers, and in a way which, I think, indicates the same nature that could not admire Rubens or the Venetian painters. Surely many people with a sensuous temperament are no more to be blamed therefor than are people who blush to be reprimanded by those who do not. In their power of giving pleasure the strong-scented double garden flowers are superior to the beautiful single ones, and the Neapolitan Violet, the warm, exquisitely scented Tuberose, the tender but full-odoured garden Rose, and the Carnation, give great delight in a harmless way to people of certain temperaments. Why should this be condemned, when that which pleases the eye in the beautiful forms of the single flower is praised? Mr. Watson says, 'Above all, scorn nothing'; yet he himself utterly condemns the cultivator who prefers the double sweet-scented flowers. It is the old story; as Samuel Butler puts it, the damning of the sins we are not inclined to. We all do it more or less. To me some few flowers seem vulgar, partly from association and partly from the unsympathetic harshness of their tint. But surely in gardening, as in all else in life, the broadest view is best, and the wisest attempt is to please as many as we can. The taste of the ignorant and the critical taste of the cultivated never can be the same on any subject, but both are better than indifference and no taste at all. I know one man who dislikes any flowers, and only has stunted Portugal Laurels growing in green square boxes on his lawn. I know another who will not plant anything that does not flower or fruit in the autumn months, because that is the only time he intends to live at his country place. All tastes are respectable, though we may each of us find it difficult to admire the taste of the other.

1872. 'My Garden: Its Plan and Culture,' by Alfred Smee. Second edition, revised and corrected. This book is one I can really recommend to beginners. It is modern in illustration, and yet it retains some of the characteristics of the older books. It really teaches you what to do, and gives a very fair idea of all that a good-sized garden requires; it names and illustrates hardly any plants not worth growing; it includes kitchen garden, flower garden, Alpine garden, greenhouse, stove, and water plants ; and it winds up with garden insects, animals, and birds. The illustrations are much above the average. Those who want to buy one single book likely to help them, especially at first, could not do better than get this one, which is often to be seen mentioned in catalogues of second-hand books.

1874. ' Alpine Plants,' edited by David Wooster. This work, which is in two volumes, contains a great many colour-printed illustrations of Alpine plants—not, however, as they grow in the fissures of their mountain slopes, but as they may be seen in Mr. Backhouse's most interesting gardens in Yorkshire. The drawings are rather exaggerated in size and harsh in colour, but the book is distinctly instructive as portraying, among what are called ' Alpines,' the most showy and the best worth cultivating in English gardens.

1879. ' A Year in a Lancashire Garden,' by Henry A. Bright. This little book is the one I alluded to in March, and to which I consider I owe so much. It often gives me pleasure to read it over now. It has qualities like the garden itself. The same flowers come up each year, the same associations link themselves on to the returning flowers, and the verses of the great poets are unchanged ; so this little book will always be to me like poor Ophelia's Rosemary, ' that's remembrance.'

The quotations throughout the book are quite unusually original and appropriate.

(No date.) ' Gleanings from Old Garden Literature,' by W. Carew Hazlitt. Of all the recent little books referring in some way directly or indirectly to gardens, this one, I think, gives me the most pleasure. It has all the charm of a conversation with a clever and sympathetic man on subjects that are dear to him and to oneself. Mr. Hazlitt quotes, from Cowley's preface to his poem of ' The Garden,' the delightful wish which comes home to so many when the strife and toil of

life are more or less over and evening is drawing near :
—' I never had any other desire so strong and so like
covetousness as that one which I have had always, that
I might be master at last of a small house and large
garden, with very moderate conveniences joined to
them, and there dedicate the remainder of my life to
the culture of them and the study of Nature.' To anyone who has found any interest in my book-notes, I
would say, ' Get this little book ; you will find pleasure
in it.'

1881. ' Notes and Thoughts on Gardens and Wood-
lands,' by the late Frances Jane Hope. This is a most
excellent and helpful work to the true amateur gardener.
Though without the unique literary flavour of that book,
it belongs in a way to what I would call the ' Lancashire Garden ' series, and is not only useful by reason of
its suggestive and instructive qualities, but is full of
individuality and information. Miss Hope strikes the
true note, and one, it seems, of the real difficulties of left-
alone half-wild gardens, when she says, ' These two
winters and one summer have spoilt our spring beds and
borders, and a thorough upturn and change of plan will
be requisite. It was impossible to use a fork or hoe in
1879 in our soil ; the result of the leave-alone system
is a carpet of *Marchantia* and *Hypnum sericeum.* To
scrape these pests off does no real good, for the earth is
caked below and impervious to air, sun, or rain. So we
are longing for our bulb treasures to be up, and to get
on to our alterations, do away with rings and surfacings,
and whatever prevents us loosening the earth between
each plant. Looking at our border, the only real advantage of what is called bedding-out struck me forcibly,
being the thorough working and justice done to the soil.'
The whole book is simply about gardening, but of the
most intelligent and suggestive kind.

1884. ' Hardy Perennials,' by John Wood. An excellent, cheap, instructive little book. Mr. Wood, of

Kirkstall, Yorkshire, has a very fine collection of herbaceous plants for sale.

1884. 'Days and Hours in a Garden,' by E. V. B. This is a garden book rather breathing the sweet luxury and joy of a garden than one very full of instruction or practical experience. E. V. B. herself owns one of the most beautiful gardens I know; and the book has, I think, that power which is one of the highest qualities of art, of making one feel beauty. The little pen-and-ink drawings are full of charm; and on the expanse of an inch—for these little headings to chapters are scarcely more—one breathes the pure air of Heaven. As she herself quotes, ' To the wise a fact is true poetry and the most beautiful of Fables.' In 1895 E. V. B. published a second book, called ' A Garden of Pleasure.' It has the same qualities, but is not perhaps quite as good. We are apt to think this of second books on the same subject—perhaps we are prejudiced in favour of our first friend.

1890. ' The Garden's Story, or Pleasures and Trials of an Amateur Gardener,' by George H. Ellwanger. I suppose nearly all readers of garden books have seen this charming, clever, tasteful, little contribution from the other shore; I do not mean the next world, but America. In spite of the constant interchange of books between the two countries, it required an introduction from so well-known a gardener as Mr. Wolley Dod to make the book known here. Let us thank Mr. Wolley Dod cordially, and thoroughly agree that an international exchange of information on so all-absorbing a subject as gardening is most interesting. The climate of America, with its hot summers and long cold winters, makes gardening a much more serious undertaking than it is in our own damp, equable little island. Mr. Ellwanger gives us a most luxurious and opulent receipt for the old favourite mixture called, all the world over, *Pot-pourri* :—' The roses used should be just blown, of the sweetest-smelling

kinds, gathered in as dry a state as possible. After
each gathering, spread out the petals on a sheet of paper
and leave until free from all moisture ; then place a
layer of petals in the jar, sprinkling with coarse salt ;
then another layer and salt, alternating, until the jar
is full. Leave for a few days, or until a broth is formed ;
then incorporate thoroughly, and add more petals and
salt, mixing daily for a week, when fragrant gums and
spices should be added, such as benzoin, storax, cassia
buds, cinnamon, cloves, cardamom, and vanilla bean.
Mix again and leave for a few days, when add essential
oil of jasmine, violet, tuberose, and attar of roses, together with a hint of ambergris, or musk, in mixture
with the flower ottos to fix the odour. Spices, such as
cloves, should be sparingly used. A rose *Pot-pourri*
thus combined, without parsimony in supplying the
flower ottos, will be found in the fullest sense a joy for
ever.'

1890. ' History of Botany,' by Julius von Sachs, translated by Henry E. F. Garnsey. This book will commend itself to those gardeners, and to amateurs generally, who love knowledge not hard to acquire. The
history of the long evolution of botany through so many
clever, patient, and painstaking hands, is even more
interesting than a smattering of botany itself, now that
we take its simple laws unquestioningly as we take the
great fact that the earth revolves on its own axis, though
we each day repeat the old expressions that the sun
rises and the sun sets.

1891. ' The Miniature Fruit Garden,' by Thomas
Rivers and T. Francis Rivers. The twentieth edition.
This fact proclaims more eloquently than any words
of mine can do the excellence and usefulness of this
little book. Of all the many changes to be noticed in
my life-time, I know none more remarkable than the
immense increase that has taken place within my memory
in fruit cultivation and fruit consumption.

1892. ' The Garden of Japan,' by F. T. Piggott. A charming little book, the fascinating subject of which is described by the title. The illustrations are very nicely drawn ; among them are two or three interesting Japanese flower arrangements. In March Mr. Piggott, writing from Japan, says : ' Every garden is full of the small shrubs [Daphnes], and every shrub is full of flowers.'

1893. ' A Book about the Garden and the Gardener,' by S. Reynolds Hole. This book is well worth having for a modern gardener. It gives a lot of instruction, and is written in a cheerful, parochial, kindly tone, most helpful to those who live rural lives in and near villages. He rejoices, as one would think everyone must, in the allotment system. He suggests in his preface that politicians should send horticultural teachers into our villages. This has now been done, and I am told the lectures given this winter in our own village at home have been most helpful and instructive. I myself should much like to see flower and vegetable shows managed on some other system. I think that prizes should be given for healthy quantity grown in a small space, and for the general clean and healthy appearance of well-stocked gardens. Such things are a great deal more important, for food-producing purposes, than that there should be a few giant Onions, Carrots, or Cabbages ; for size rarely adds to the excellence of vegetables. Dean Hole truly remarks that the allotment system will always have two opponents : there will always be idle men who will not have gardens, and ignorant men who will not know how to use them.

1894. ' Italian Gardens,' by Charles A. Platt. This is a book published in New York ; it is very pretty, and full of excellent reproductions of artistically taken photographs. The letterpress describes the gardens. Of Villa Lante, at Bagni near Viterbo, there are four illustrations. The book was given to me by two kind American ladies, a mother and daughter, who came to spend a summer's day with me in my garden. They had been all round Europe, studying gardens large and small, and the daughter hoped to lay out some original and typical gardens in America that would be suitable to the soil and the climate ; also to try and preserve the beautiful flora of that country, which is in danger of dying away. I thought the idea interesting. In their time and way, under their blue skies and in their lovely situations, nothing, I imagine, will ever come near the beautiful Medician gardens of Italy, which, even in their decay, are never forgotten by those who once have had the joy of wandering in them.

1894. 'The Natural History of Plants,' from the German of Anton Kerner von Marilaun, Professor of Botany in the University of Vienna, by F. W. Oliver Quain, Professor of Botany in University College, London. For the modern botanist this book is deeply interesting. I am, alas ! no botanist, and have no scientific knowledge ; but to take up the book, and to read a page or two anywhere, opens one's eyes wide with wonder. It refers principally to microscopic botany. The coloured plates are saddening to a degree ; they seem to me all that botanical plates ought not to be, and somehow appear to have been affected by Miss North's system of flower-painting. How valuable would have been her untiring energy, if the drawings so generously given to Kew had been either artistic, like Mr. Parsons', or, still better, from the scientific point of view, botanical and delicately true, like Jacquin's or Redouté's, or the drawings in Curtis's books ! In the chromo-lithographs of these four volumes we have attempts at the impossible— large plants in the foreground, with skies, distances, and middle-distance all out of tone. The wood-cuts are much better ; some are very good and delicate, especially the representations of strongly magnified subjects. I bought the book as bringing illustrated plant-lore down to the latest date. The account, in the third

volume, of the distribution of pollen is thrillingly interesting, and is within the comprehension of the aforenamed
' village idiot ' ; many of our ordinary garden flowers are
figured as examples. The saddest attempt at a picture
is a Brobdingnagian representation of an Alpine Rhododendron, with pines and snow-clad mountains in the
distance. I may be wrong, but to me it seems waste
of talent and time and money to illustrate books in
this way. These illustrations are printed in Germany ;
let us hope that the artists were also Germans.

1895. ' In a Gloucestershire Garden,' by Henry Ellacombe. I think most people who are personally interested in their gardens will enjoy this book ; there is
much to be learnt from it, and the second part is especially instructive. It breathes the true spirit of a garden,
independently of the human element or of book-making.
Canon Ellacombe names many of the old Roses, now
gone out of fashion, but I rather doubt if he has ever seen
Redouté's wonderful Rose book. He ends his book with
a warning to the clergy against gardening, as being too
interesting and too absorbing an occupation for them. I
can thoroughly echo this sentiment as a warning to all
young people. It can only be perfectly indulged in by
the lonely or the old, and by those who do not mind
neglecting their other duties, and who say, bravely and
honestly, ' I am quite selfish and quite happy.' But
of course this is the danger of all absorbing pursuits.
I agree with many of Canon Ellacombe's remarks ; one
especially can never be too often repeated :—' In nothing
is the gardener's skill more shown than in the judicious
use of the pruning-knife.' His experience of the American
Bramble is exactly mine—as far as the fruit goes ; it is
not worth growing, as the fruit is less in quantity and
inferior in quality to our own wild Brambles. But the
cut leaf is prettier, and at any rate makes a variety.

1895. ' The Story of the Plants,' by Grant Allen, is a
humble, little popular book ; but I am sure its perusal

252 POT-POURRI FROM A SURREY GARDEN.

will bring pleasure and increased understanding to many who read it. One of his sayings is ' that plants are the only things that know how to manufacture living material. Roughly speaking, plants are the producers and animals the consumers.'

1896. ' The Bamboo Garden,' by A. B. Freeman Mitford, C.B. Mr. Mitford tells us in his preface that his book is simply an attempt to give a descriptive list— what the French call a *catalogue raisonné*—of the hardy Bamboos in cultivation in this country. We ought to be grateful that he has brought within the reach of everybody all that is to be said on this most beautiful family.

1895. ' A History of Gardening in England,' by the Hon. Alicia Amherst. This is by far the most interesting and remarkable book that, I believe, has ever been written on the subject, and far surpasses in every way Mr. Johnson's ' History of Gardening,' before alluded to. The book is full of information, drawn from patient and most diligent research, and will be of real utility to students of the literature and history of gardening and to the owners of large places. It contains little that will practically help people who live in cottages and small villas. It alludes only very indirectly to the beautiful illustrated flower books, especially the foreign ones, which so far exceed our own in artistic beauty and skill. It is rather sad that when the Society of Gardeners wished to illustrate their plants in 1736 they had to engage the services of Jacob van Huysum, brother of the Dutch flower-painter ; and to this day the best periodical coloured flower-printing, though painted by Englishmen, is printed in Belgium (*vide* ' The Garden '). Miss Amherst's book is one for constant reference ; and the greater one's knowledge, the greater will be one's appreciation of it. I cannot but regret, however, that it has been printed on the disagreeable modern shiny paper, which also makes the book most inconveniently heavy.

This paper, I am told, facilitates the reproduction of the illustrations ; but these, also, are very hard and ugly, and quite unworthy of the book.

It is almost impossible to keep pace with the modern books about gardens, they are so numerous. Just to complete my list I will mention several in my possession, for, as the motto of one of them says, ' It is a natural consequence that those who cannot taste the actual fruition of a gadren should take the greater delight in reading about one.'

' Voyage autour de mon Jardin,' by Alphonse Karr, is charming, and has been translated into English.

' The Praise of Gardens,' by Albert F. Sieveking, is a collection of quotations of all that has been written about gardens. The selection is very complete. Unfortunately the book is out of print.

I need hardly mention ' The Garden that I Love,' by Alfred Austin, as it has been such a favourite with the public. It is, of course, a book written less to instruct about gardening than to show what a beautiful and enchanting place a garden is for conversation, especially when the right people come together.

In the ' Edinburgh Review ' for July 1896, there is an article called ' Gardens and Garden Craft,' with a long heading of gardening books, which many people will find interesting, as I did.

In the November (1896) number of ' The Journal of the Royal Horticultural Society ' is an excellent lecture by Mr. F. W. Burbidge, the Curator of the Botanical Garden in Dublin. In the ' Journal ' the lecture is divided into three parts—called ' Garden Literature,' ' Reference Books on English Gardening Literature,' and ' Garden Libraries.' It is interesting, besides other reasons, as being a somewhat new departure in the lectures delivered before the Horticultural Society. I strongly recommend those who care about the subject to read this lecture, as they will get a great deal of most useful information in a very condensed form. Mr. Burbidge strongly recommends garden libraries, in which I entirely agree with him. No large place should be without a room where gardening books and weekly gardening papers are within easy access of all the gardeners on the place, and no village club in England could not afford to take in Mr. Robinson's excellent little weekly paper called 'Cottage Gardening,' which I mentioned before. It costs one halfpenny, and is full of all sorts of useful information. Surely at village shows no better prize could be given than the back numbers (bound) of this most useful publication. Mr. Burbidge says : 'In America and in Germany the library seems to be thought as essential to good gardening and profitable land culture as here with us the seed room or the tool shed ; and in England we are beginning to perceive the value of technical education, and to recognise the vital importance of the most recent scientific discoveries relating to our crops and their diseases, and the soil in which they grow. Private garden libraries, while most desirable, really form part of a much larger and wider question. If libraries are essential for the garden, surely they are even more so on the farm.' Mr. Burbidge winds up : ' But to form libraries we must have good and useful books, and I shall give a short list of those I believe to be the best of their kind ; and one of the best ways I know of getting the best gardening books into the best hands is to award them as prizes to the cultivators and exhibitors of garden produce at allotment-garden and village flower shows.' With this I most cordially agree. Then follows a list of thirty-eight books.

Another paper of great interest is on the importance of British fruit-growing, from a food point of view, by Mr. Edmund J. Baillie.

DECEMBER

December 5th.—For anyone with a small stove I can
thoroughly advise growing some of the more easily
cultivated Orchids. For many years all Orchids seemed
to me to smell of money, and to represent great expenditure ; but this is not the case at all. They only want
the treatment suited to them, and the same care and
attention required by other plants that are grown in
heat. Cypripediums come in most usefully at this time
of year ; they last well in water, and continue to flower
at times all through the winter. There are endless
varieties of them to be bought, and some of the least
expensive plants are often as good as the costly ones ;
it is only the new varieties that are dear. Some that I
have—green, spotted with brown, and with clear white
tips—are lovely. They have looked well lately on the
dinner-table, arranged with little branches of a shrubby
Veronica, called, I believe, *V. speciosum.* It is a plant
well worth growing for the charming light green of its
leaves out of doors at this time of year, when fresh
green is so rare. Unlike most of the shrubby Veronicas,
it lasts well in water. It has a long white flower in July,
which is not especially pretty. We also grow very successfully *Dendrobium nobile, Oncidium sphacelatum,* and
several other Orchids that flower in the early part of the
year.

To-day there have come up from the country—not from my own home, which is too dry, but from near Salisbury—some branches cut from an old Thorn or Apple tree, and covered with long hoary-grey moss. I have put them into an old ginger-jar without water, and in this way they will last through the winter. They stand now against a red wall, where they look exceedingly well.

December 10*th.*—There has been in this year's ' Guardian ' a succession of monthly papers on a Surrey garden, written by Miss Jekyll of Munstead Wood, Godalming. I give her address, as she now sells her surplus plants, all more or less suited to light soils, to the management of which she has for many years past given special attention. These papers have much illuminating matter in them, and are called ' Notes from Garden and Woodland.' All the plants and flowers about which Miss Jekyll writes she actually grows on the top of her Surrey hill. Her garden is a most instructive one, and encouraging too. She has gone through the stage, so common to all ambitious and enthusiastic amateurs, of trying to grow everything, and of often wasting much precious room in growing inferior plants, or plants which, even though they may be worth growing in themselves, are yet not worth the care and feeding which a light soil necessitates if they are to be successful.

. This, to me, rather delightful characteristic of amateurs in every art was severely condemned by Mr. Ruskin in my youth, when he said that the amateur sketcher always attempted to draw the panorama of Rome on his thumb-nail, instead of humbly trying to reproduce what was at his own door. The practice is just as common in gardening as in music and painting.

Every plant that Miss Jekyll names is worth getting and growing in gardens that are of considerable size, and which more or less share her Surrey soil and climate.

I trust that before long these articles will be republished in book form, for every word in them deserves attention and consideration.

December 12th.—One of the every-day English dishes that is often so bad, and can be so excellent, is the old, much-abused hashed mutton. What I am going to say about it applies equally well to every kind of meat that is warmed up. Make the sauce early in the day with stock, gravy, onions, and other vegetables, or, failing this, a few drops of two or three of the bought sauces, and one or two drops of essence of garlic. Garlic, which is excellent as a flavouring to most sauces, is such a dangerous thing to use in a kitchen that the way I manage it is this :—Put five or six cloves of garlic into a wide-necked bottle and cover them with good spirits of wine. When wanted, stick a skewer or fork into the spirit and use a drop or two. The spirit evaporates and the flavour of the garlic remains. But even in this way it must be used carefully for English palates. To return to the sauce for the hash : avoid flour, or, if it must be a little thickened, let it only be with what is called 'brown *roux*' in 'Dainty Dishes.' The really essential point is to make your sauce first and let it get cold, and then warm up the meat and the sauce together. If you throw meat of any kind into hot sauce, you are certain to make it hard ; it contracts the fibre of the meat, and spoils it.

One of the very few ways in which wild duck can be warmed up is to mince it fine and then curry it with some well-cooked curry sauce. This is made on the same principle as the curry mentioned before ; that is to say the onion and apple (if you cannot get apples, gooseberries, or rhubarb, or any fruit will do) must be fried together, and the stock and curry powder added, well cooked, and rubbed through a fine sieve, allowed to get cool, and the mince and sauce just warmed up together before serving. For currying fish or vegetables a little milk or cream softens the sauce.

9

Stewed meats are seldom really good in England. The following is a good way of cooking haricot of mutton : Set a stew-pan on the fire (an earthenware one is the best) with a little butter in it ; put in some pieces of raw mutton, neatly jointed and cut up small ; fry till a nice brown colour. Take out the meat, place it on a dish, add some carrots, turnips, onions, celery, and a very little sugar, and fry in the butter. When brown, replace the meat, and pour in some cold water or weak stock—enough to cover all the ingredients. Stew gently for three hours. The stewing can be done in the oven or on the hot-plate. If cooked in an earthenware pot, this stew, as well as many others done in the same way, can be sent to table in the pot with a clean napkin pinned round it.

When vegetables are scarce in winter, and you have cooked carrots, turnips, onions, celery, &c., strained from the soup the night before, it is a good plan to chop them up and warm them in a little butter with a small lump of sugar, some pepper and salt, and serve them for luncheon. If the quantity is insufficient, you can easily add some cold potatoes and cabbage.

Potatoes, now so often forbidden by doctors, seem to me excellent, wholesome food for people who do not eat meat. They can be cooked in such an endless variety of ways, though most English cooks confine themselves, as a rule, to only two or three. The secret of good mashed potatoes is to boil them dry, and beat them up with boiling milk, adding a little butter or cream. Cold milk makes them heavy, and spoils them. Another way is to put in a stew-pan some potatoes and two or three sliced onions, to boil, with only enough water to cover them. When they are done, beat them well with a fork, have ready some boiling milk and a piece of butter, stir these in by degrees as you beat, till the potatoes are like a thick purée. ' Dainty Dishes ' has several receipts for cooking potatoes.

A seaweed called Laver is a delicious, wholesome, and uncommon vegetable in London in November and December. It is to be bought at any of the really good grocers', not greengrocers'. The London supply, I believe, comes from Devonshire, prepared and cooked, and requires nothing beyond a little stock and butter to moisten it when it is warmed up. It should be served in a small copper saucepan with a lamp under it, as it is not good unless very hot indeed. For helping it a small wooden spoon is better than a silver one ; at least, so it used to be served in old days in the North, when I remember it as a child. Half a lemon is sent up with it. A good many people do not like it, I am bound to confess ; but those who do, find it a treat they look forward to—and it is good either by itself or with any roast meat, especially mutton.

The same little copper saucepan is useful for a wild duck sauce which I always make on the table. The saucepan, on a spirit-lamp, comes up with some gravy in it ; I then squeeze in half or all of a lemon, according to quantity required, and add a little red wine—Port is the best—and some Cayenne pepper. When warm, I pour it over the slices of wild duck on each plate. Wild duck should be very lightly roasted.

Rice plays a large part in our cooking all the year round ; Patna is nearly always the best. Risotto à la Milanese is an original Italian receipt :—Cut up four onions very fine, and fry a nice brown. Throw into the stew-pan 1 lb. of rice, and let it slightly colour ; then moisten with good stock, and cook it for 35 minutes. Season with pepper and salt, a little nutmeg, and Parmesan cheese. Serve very hot. Chopped truffles or mushrooms may be added.

An excellent winter salad for serving with wild duck and many other birds is watercress, carefully picked and washed, pieces of orange (cut as described below for the compote), all the juice of the oranges, and a few drops of good salad oil added just before serving.

Orange compote depends almost entirely on the goodness of the oranges, and on the way they are cut. The best plan is to stick them on a fork, and with a sharp-pointed kitchen knife remove, at one cutting, all the peel and all the white. Then, with the sharp point of a knife, cut out all the pieces of orange between the white lines, leaving the white in the middle. Save all the juice, and cut small shreds of the peel without any white, put them into some water with sugar and the juice, and, if the oranges are very sweet, add a little lemon juice. Boil up this syrup, pour it over the pieces of orange, and allow it to cool. This is a good foundation for any winter compote. Apricots, bananas, or pineapple, all can be added, separately or together ; and a few dried cherries stewed improve the appearance. Another excellent winter compote is made by cutting up a ripe pineapple (often so cheap), stewing the peel in a syrup, to which is added the juice that runs out of the pineapple, and a little ginger. Strain, and pour it boiling over the pieces of pineapple. A few bananas cut up and added to the pineapple improve it.

Two excellent ways of serving cold chicken for small parties or suppers are the following :—Order the day before from a good baker some extra small dinner-rolls, cut off the tops, and take out the crumb. Mince a little chicken and ham or tongue ; it takes a very small quantity of either. Mix with well-made Mayonnaise sauce, a little chopped parsley, and a very little onion. Put this into the rolls, and replace the small round top on each. Finger rolls, cut in half and the crumb taken out, can be done in the same way.

The other way is to make some little open sandwiches—we call them Barrington sandwiches—in the following manner :—Butter some moderately thick slices of a good tin loaf, and cut them into medium-sized rounds. Lay across them, in pieces cut quite narrow, some breast of cold chicken, a quarter of an anchovy, and a thin shred of green gherkin. These form narrow bars of green, white, and red across the slices of bread. Trim the edges, and serve on a plate one laid partly over the other, like cutlets.

I particularly want to say a last word to housekeepers who are anxious to indulge in hospitality. Hospitality should mean, to my mind, not altering our whole way of living, but giving the best of our habitual food. For this nothing is so telling, whether the dinner be large or small, as the procuring of some special seasonable luxury. It is well worth taking the trouble to get any such luxuries, not from the usual shop in your neighbourhood, but from the very best shop you know of for each speciality, whether fish, game, vegetable, Italian goods more especially, fruit (fresh or bottled), dessert, biscuits, or cake. The really good housekeeper is alert to learn where the best things come from, and to take hints wherever she goes. One should never through idleness give up getting the best things. If you go to the expense of entertaining at all, it makes little difference in the way of money whether you deal at a specially good shop or a second-rate one, and the results at your table are very different indeed.

London shops are now full of sun-dried American fruits, principally apples and apricots. These appear to me to be safer and wholesomer, particularly for children, than tinned or bottled fruit. If carefully carried out, the following receipt makes them excellent :—Select the fruit you intend to use, and rinse it thoroughly in clear, fresh water ; then place it in a dish with sufficient water to cover it, and allow it to soak for ten or fifteen hours before it is required for use. After this, put it in the vessel in which it is to be cooked (which ought, of course, to be earthenware), simmer it slowly, letting it come just once in a way to the boil, until it is thoroughly cooked. If the water in which the fruit was soaked is thrown away, and fresh water substituted, much of the flavour and nutriment of the fruit will be lost. Sufficient sugar should be added, when the fruit is nearly done, to make it palatable. Dried fruit cooked in this way can be served either hot or cold, as may be desired. As a rule, when allowed to cool, it will be fully as palatable as if eaten warm. By cooking dried fruit according to this method, there will be secured a wholesome and palatable dish, full flavoured, and resembling as near as possible, in appearance, size, and taste, the original fresh product.

This also is good :—Bavarois of fruit, bottled or fresh. Warm the fruit and rub it through a hair sieve, and add just enough isinglass, previously melted in a little water, to set the fruit when cold. Add some cream, and pour into a mould, keeping back a little fruit to make a syrup, which should be poured round before serving. Icing improves the dish.

SONS

Boys and girls—The health question—Early independence—Public schools—Influence of parents—The management of money—Family life and its difficulties—Sir Henry Taylor—'Mothers and Sons'—The feeding of children—The abuse of athletics—Success in life—Spartan upbringing—Youth and age.

I FEEL sure you all, as my nieces, care enough for my views on most things to wish for a few remarks on the great question of how to bring up boys and girls. The opinion of anybody who has thought at all and who has lived a long life is worth having as the personal experience of one individual. Age is to life what distance is to landscape, it makes all things assume fairer proportions and embrace a larger horizon. We see more plainly the good and the bad in all systems, any convictions we may still have we hold conditionally, and we lose the confidence with which we stepped out when we knew less and felt more.

I had better begin first with the boys, and speak of the girls later on, which is certainly dealing with the matter in the old, conventional way.

It is a well-known fact that more boys are born into the world than girls, but they are more difficult to rear, which accounts for the greater preponderance of women in the end. I suppose I ought to have more to say about boys than girls, for, as you know, I have had only boys of my own. My mother used to say it was a merciful interposition of Providence that I had no girls, as I was totally unfit to bring them up. Naturally I do not agree with this, and should have liked immensely to have had three girls as well as three boys.

The health question from the very beginning is one of the greatest importance. In the case of boys, at any rate, it cannot come naturally to any young mother. Her knowledge and intelligence, however, should at least be sufficient to let her know when things are not going right. As a rule, children grow up as ' Topsy ' did : ' 'Specs I growed.' But every now and then terrible things happen which, with a little sense and knowledge of when to call in a specialist, are quite preventable. I pity the parent who has to say : ' Alas ! I knew too late.'

One of the great difficulties in the emancipating of the children of the well-to-do—by which I mean helping them to learn independence, and to take care of themselves in early childhood—is the nervousness of mothers and nurses. If parents would only consider how sharp are the children of the London poor in looking after themselves, I think they would gain courage, and their children would profit. I know a child, the youngest of a family, a fine, plucky little fellow, whose whole nature was altered by being put out of frocks into knickerbockers and his hair cut short when very young. One day this child was taken by his father, at the age of four and a half, to the City, and sent back alone on the top of a 'bus that set him down at the end of the street in which he lived. He had been given sixpence to pay his fare, and, arriving at home safely, he proudly and triumphantly handed the change to his mother. This same child, at twelve years old, after leaving his private school, and before going to a public school, was sent to Paris to learn French. With a guide-book in one pocket and a map in the other, he found his way about alone all over the town. To my mind, precocity that comes from development of character and independence, or from the stimulus of ambition, is as desirable as that resulting from over-excitement or over-bookwork is the contrary.

As soon as children are no longer babies, it is very unwise to leave them much with servants. Little boys have no natural employments at home, especially in towns, when once they go to school. I should recommend parents who live in London to give up dining out during the winter holidays. It is only for four weeks, and the evenings at home with parents out are certainly dull for boys ; this applies doubly where there are no sisters. I used to think the perfect education for boys was the foreign way, to live at home and attend a day school : but the universal condemnation of this system by young Englishmen has shaken me, and certainly we have hardly any machinery prepared for carrying it out. The public school system, therefore, seems to be the only one here. At any rate, boys are brought up at school in the mythologies of their time and country, as Huxley used to recommend ; and on the whole that seems to answer best. The thing most to be avoided, it appears to me as I look back on life, is bringing up children on any sort of fad, however genuine the conviction of the parents that they are right and other people wrong. There is no mistaking the bitterness with which young men talk if they have been brought up in any way that alienates them from their generation. This applies equally to great and little things—from the training of the strict Anglican clergyman, or in the Agnostic's morality, to affectations in dress or peculiarities of diet.

It is important that parents should not be unduly elated by good school reports, for they mean but little. The typical top-of-the-class boy, a good plodding fellow who gives no trouble, is always a favourite with the master, but he hardly ever does anything in after-life. An idle, naughty boy sometimes reaches the top out of sheer talent ; but that is quite a different matter. These things always depend a good deal on temperament. If you are stupid, it is easier to become good than to become clever ; and you must never forget that, for the tortoises to win the race, the hares must go to sleep—and that is just what does not happen in these days. The world of school is an immense experience in itself, but a world represented by one sex alone is apt to give only a narrow and one-sided training. The necessary discipline, too, by which a school is regulated gives but little scope for boys to learn how to take care of themselves in the every-day world outside of it. It is only in the holidays that they can gain any experience as to the management of their lives, or—and above all—the employment of their time independently of rule. I once asked a boy how he made up his mind at school about what was right and what was wrong. He looked up, and said without hesitation, ' I always try and think what father would say about it.' At school, morality and public opinion can be as little decided by hard-and-fast rules as in the world. There, as in after-life, always speaking the truth without reserve, especially when it concerns others, may resolve itself into being only a form of self-indulgence. A great many mothers recognise this when it is brought home to them that their boy has refused to speak the truth in a way that would implicate others. At the same time parents seldom put it plainly before a boy that there may be occasions when it is a far higher standard of morality to bear personal blame than to implicate others by speaking the truth. He ought not to have the addi-tional pain of fearing he is doing that which would displease his parents, and is contrary to the principle of simple and direct truthfulness which has been incul-cated at home. I hope nobody, on reading this, will imagine that I am advocating want of truthfulness as a principle, or that I doubt for a moment that the fact of speaking truth intentionally, even to the injury of self, is one of the most essential strengtheners of man's moral nature. It does not always come naturally, however, as many imaginative children lie, and weaklings are sure to lie, hate it as they may, for it is the certain fruit of fear. Jean Paul Richter speaks of it in the following terms :—' Lying, that devouring cancer of the inner man, is more severely judged and defined by the feeling of nations than by philosophers. The Greeks, who suffered their gods to commit as many crimes with impunity as their present representatives, the gods of the earth, do yet condemn them for perjury—that root and quintessence of a lie—to pass a year of lifelessness under the ground in Tartarus, and then to endure nine years of torments. The ancient Persian taught his child nothing in the whole circle of morality but truthfulness.'

Truthfulness is so essential to moral superiority that any young man who consistently acts a part in life for ambitious or other reasons is very apt to become morally degenerate, and hardly able to distinguish between truth and falsehood. It is one of the things which, when discovered, is perhaps almost unduly punished by the contempt showered on it by contemporaries. It has been finely said, ' Principle is a passion for truth.'

While boys are still at school, is it not distinctly wrong for both parents to be away and out of easy reach at the same time ? Accidents so often happen, and school authorities, more especially school doctors and surgeons, are not to be depended upon, as they cannot give the time and attention which a boy naturally receives at home. If the eyes of love could be bought with money, love would not mean very much in the world ; and it does mean a good deal, in spite of what many think, and still more, of what many say.

The common attitude of mind of intelligent boys who have recently gone to school, is that they know everything about life, and that their mother understands nothing. The boy thinks his mother good, and that no good women know anything of life ; and that settles the question. As he gets older, the mother must explain to him what she thinks proper. These matters, however, depend so much upon the character of the mother and son that it is impossible to generalise upon them. Mothers will, I think, rarely get much help from the fathers on the subject of school life. Most men have a wonderful knack of forgetting the difficulties of their own boyhood. The influence and example of the father in the home is immense. What he does, the boys will probably wish to do. Direct help in the difficulties of boy-life comes much more from the mother than from the father. For this reason I should say that the mother must take every pains to educate herself, and learn to understand as much about human nature as she possibly can. A course of French novel-reading—and, after all, a great many French novels are magnificent literature—is not otherwise than a harmless and yet useful way of eating of the tree of knowledge for a mother of five-and-thirty. The French have an extraordinarily honest way of facing the facts of life and the results of conduct, and they are far less sentimental than the English. This advice, of course, applies doubly to the woman who has not read French novels for her amusement in her youth. From the time a boy first goes to school, and still more, I think, when he is sixteen or seventeen, the mother should put a strong guard on herself not to worry him about his comings and goings, or in any way restrict his independence, as the sooner he learns to take care of himself the better. As regards the really serious things of life, you should not ' nag,' but up to a certain age you can forbid.

For a boy of seventeen, I believe it to be a very wise thing, as an introduction to life, that he should be given a latch-key. He is then proud of the privilege and much less likely to abuse it than if only given to him when he is much older. To deny it altogether to young men who are living at home seems to me both irritating and ridiculous. So many of the serious sorrows and troubles of life come from ignorance, rather than from wickedness, that it is advisable to send the boy of about this age to some friendly, worldly-wise, intelligent doctor, asking him beforehand to give the boy as much advice and instruction as a man of twenty-four might have learnt from bitter experience.

One of the most useful things a boy can be taught at home is the value of money. With a well-trained, sensible boy a half-allowance for clothes should be begun at twelve years old (by a half-allowance I mean an allowance that includes pocket-money and is sufficient to buy every article of dress except cloth clothes), and at fourteen the allowance should cover all clothes and pocket-money. When allowances are first given, be sure that the boy starts fair with a sufficient stock of clothes so that he should not be handicapped from the beginning. The best way to manage the allowance, having fixed the sum, is for the father or mother to be the banker. The amount of the yearly sum should be clearly made known to the boy, and he should draw the money himself when he requires it, as he would, later in life, from a real banker. This gives the parent a certain control over disproportionate expenditure. Accounts should not be insisted upon, nor even, I think, strongly urged, and, above all, never looked at. What *is* desirable is constantly to recommend the purchasing of useful things first, and to watch a little that everything is paid for with ready money, and the bills kept. So long as the world lasts, the prodigal by nature—not from mere want of training—and those who spend rather more money than they have, will always be more fascinating than the careful ones. The rash, the impetuous, and the thoughtlessly generous, must ever prove the heart-winners ; and yet those who abet them are the first to turn on them when they are at the bottom of the hill or in a ditch by the roadside. Because of this, parents should force themselves to be more willing to kill the fatted calf for the saving child than for the prodigal. This should be impressed upon the sons from their earliest years. In the case of a parent really wishing to pay an extravagant son's bills, the hardship of it will be brought home to the son if the parent obliges himself to give an equal sum to the other children who have not got into debt. I am told that giving allowances to young boys is extremely rare. I consider it of fundamental importance in their education. Where it fails, it is an indication of character that is full of anxiety for the future, a serious evil to be faced, like hip-disease or a crooked spine. As a rule, everything is provided for boys till the most dangerous time in their lives and then people are surprised that young men don't know how to proportion their expenditure to their means, which practice is the only wise one for rich or poor. Everyone is rich who has a margin, and everyone is poor who spends more than he has. To many people what I have just said will appear as giving a very undue preponderance to the management of money. Admitting the wisdom of what was said of old, ' The love of money is a root of all kinds of evil,' it is equally true that the discreet management of money is the root of all kinds of good, especially with young people. Nothing is so selfish as extravagance. No one can doubt the truth, as put by the modern writer who says : ' Never treat money affairs with levity— money is character.' If you can say of your children, when they are twenty-one, that they have never been in debt and have never asked you for money, you have attained a satisfactory platform, which will enormously help the dignity of the situation. Such children's minds have not been pauperised, and the parent has not been put into the difficult and painful position of having to refuse or yield to a beggar. Children, on the other hand, should be helped to remember that, however free they may be left as regards the expenditure of their own allowances, no man, woman, or child is free while entirely dependent on money which they neither earn nor possess by inheritance. How often does a son, fresh from leaving school, who is dying to go for a visit or a holiday, or to buy a gun or a dog, go first to his mother, of whom he is not afraid, to plead his cause with his father for the money he wants! This is a distinctly wrong system, whether the father is rich or poor, an extravagant man himself, or the contrary. If the boy gets what he wants at once, he accepts it as a right, and is quite ready at Christmas to ask for more. If it is denied or grudgingly given, he resents it with irritation as a want of generosity and a needless check on his pleasures. Whereas, if the amount of the allowance is from the first proportioned to the income of the parents, it is brought home to their minds what the children are likely to cost them; while the boy is made to realise that, be the allowance large or small, his expenses must be proportioned to it. In the case of really poor parents it is especially necessary to impress upon the whole family that, with regard to pleasures, education, or even necessities, everything is subservient to the fact that money can only go as far as it will. Of course, if it were necessary, or even desirable, each member of a family might contribute what he or she can afford to the advantage of one member of it. Not a bad illustration of what I mean is touchingly told in the Life of Sir James Simpson, the famous Edinburgh doctor. All his elder brothers contributed to educate the clever youth, above their station in life, for a profession of which he became so distinguished an ornament.

Once more I ask you to consider how common it seems in human nature that people will give what they are asked for and bothered about, rather than what they can afford. However much this weakness may be taken advantage of in the charitable world, it is most desirable that it should be kept out of family life. Some people even put forward the objection that allowances check the growth of generosity. As a matter of fact, the very essence of generosity is to give what is your own, and, in the highest sense, there is no generosity without self-denial. Often no one appears so generous as the worldly spendthrift, who gives with a free hand what in fact he owes to his tradespeople. Another idea is that the independence resulting from freedom in money matters increases the difficulty of home life. This is markedly more the case in England than in other European countries. Nations are so unconsciously steeped in the atmosphere of their literature that I have often wondered whether ' King Lear ' has helped to bring about the state of mind in parents who, though most anxious to leave money to their children after death, yet so grudgingly deal it out to them, either in allowance or capital, during their lifetime. One of the amusing anomalies of the new succession duties is that they have induced many parents, who have never thought of it before, to pay over while they are still alive a portion of their capital to their children. This gives a young man an experience in money management which he could not have gained while only receiving an allowance.

A frequent mistake of parents, even when they think a great deal about their children, is the conviction that they know them so well. After a child grows up and his nature develops, his one idea is to go forth and make his own friends and start his own life ; and when he comes back to the home, however much his heart warms to it when he is away, he re-enters it with different eyes, and often with a critical spirit. This seems very hard to the parents, who have changed but little. The best way of making their love appreciated is not to exact more than they get. The real time of trial to parents is when their children are between seventeen and twenty-one. They would do well to realise how little they know of the change that is going on in their sons. They can only cultivate them, humour them, and, if possible, win them. Till this has been done, it is absolutely useless to expect their confidence or to resent the fact that it is withheld. The more openly a child has been brought up and encouraged to speak his mind, the more odious and critical his language will appear at this age to outsiders who do not realise how far better it is that he should express his views without reserve at home than that he should disguise his feelings there and speak openly abroad. It should only be impressed upon children that it is in better taste and more according to the rules of society to keep their criticisms for the privacy of family life.

The judicious management of parents by good sons and daughters often makes a home seem happy for a time ; but I think a few open and even angry discussions are wholesomer for the characters of the young than a trained duplicity implying peace where there is no peace. In our present civilisation, no one being can rule the destiny of another by force, not even in the case of a father and his children. I think it well to remember in our homes Swift's saying that ' Government without the consent of the governed is the very definition of slavery, though eleven men well armed will certainly subdue one single man in his shirt.' A father cannot get the eleven men, so he had better not try to govern in this spirit. His only power, if he loses the affection and respect of his children, is that base and ignoble one given by money, which—in the case of men, at any rate—is powerless against the noblest and best. All people, both young and old, should remember the wise saying that we never feel so much at ease with our consciences as when we are dwelling complacently on the faults of others.

There will always be men and women, but perhaps more men than women, who all through life believe in luck—those who think when things go wrong that they have been cheated and frustrated by others, whereas nothing has happened but what was bound to happen. Men of this stamp often endure life heroically and are clever, inventive, interesting human beings ; but they are ruled by circumstances, instead of ruling them : they submit to life, instead of making it.

I must not omit to mention a book, called ' Notes from Life,' by Sir Henry Taylor. It is out of fashion and forgotten now, but it made a very great impression upon me in my youth. Sir Henry Taylor, as everyone knows, was the author of ' Philip Van Artevelde : a Dramatic Romance.' This work made him famous at the time of its publication ; it is still read by students of English literature, and there is no grander subject for a dramatist than the moulding of tough natures. I believe it was never put on the stage ; and, after all, an unactable play must always remain a kind of literary mule. Sir Henry Taylor bound himself to us most tenderly by writing a poem in memory of my father, who died at Nice in 1843. It was reprinted in Sir Henry's autobiography a few years ago. One of the most distinguished of our Lord Chancellors described it to me as the finest memorial poem in the English language. What little worldly philosophy I acquired in my youth I learnt from Sir Henry. The ' Notes from Life ' are on Money, Humility, and Independence, Choice in Marriage, Wisdom, Children, The Life Poetic, and The Ways of the Rich and Great. In spite of all that has been written on such subjects since, I still think the book well worth reading. The tone of the articles is more religious than would be the case now if written by a man who held the same broad and elastic views that he did. He belonged essentially to that large band of good and wise men who never tell their religion, but his language in these essays is that of the fashion of his time. The essays called ' Money,' ' Marriage,' and ' Children ' seem to me now as interesting and suggestive as when I first read them.

In 1892 a little book was published called ' Mothers and Sons.' It made some impression on a good many mothers, and this is not surprising, as it was written by the successful headmaster of a public school. I cannot but differ widely from a book which, while it professes to teach a mother's duty to her son, ignores all reference to the husband and father. The tact of mothers is disputed in the introduction, and it cannot be denied that women vary very much in their successful management of children and servants, and these two go pretty much together. But, however much a father may leave the training and management of his sons to their mother, his blood runs in their veins, his example is daily before them, and what he is they will be, more or less. Heredity, I admit, sometimes plays us strange pranks ; but I think, if people will honestly look round on the circle of their acquaintances, they will find, in nine cases out of ten, that the stamp of the children belongs to the name they bear—to the family of the father, not of the mother. The tone of a child's mind, especially a boy's, is very much what was represented in one of ' Punch's ' pictures some years ago—a manly young monkey standing up before his mother and saying : ' What a happy day it was for you, mother, when you married into our family ! '

I should not have alluded to the headmaster's book at all but for the very cordial way I agree with Chapter IV., called ' Food.' The following passage seems to me entirely true :—' Pendulums have a way of swinging ; and if starvation or under-feeding was a danger to boys thirty years ago, it is luxury and over-feeding with which the sons of nearly all classes are threatened in 1892.' No one advocates more strongly than I do that young children should be wholesomely and sufficiently fed (the size of the body depends on this with all animals), even to the point of occasional stomach attacks. The moment, however, that a child is not well, parents should realise that what weakens it is—not the want of food which it refuses to swallow, but the fever brought on by internal derangement from overloading the stomach.

Nearly all sick children like fruit, and I think, if fruit
and bread *alone* were given them for a day or two, they
would generally get well without any doctor or medicines. Of course, if the nurse insists on giving just a
little magnesia as well, the whole thing is spoilt. Fruit
does not do with any form of alkaline drug. It is most
important to keep to one treatment or the other—the
acid or the alkaline ; if not, the poor child's inside is
turned into a saline draught. The author points out,
with great severity and truth, the absurdity of the fact
that boys are fed in the most stimulating way on meat,
wine, and beer. If, as is sometimes the case, the wine
and beer are knocked off, they are doubly allowed and
encouraged to eat as much as they like, which, in order
to live healthily, they have to work off by playing for
hours at football and cricket. Inconsistently enough,
they seem to acknowledge that, for rowing, heavy eating
is bad. The athlete and the Alpine climber know it
well. It is proverbial that the navvy, who is said to eat
enormously with a view to keeping up his strength, is
worth nothing at all in the way of work by the time he
is forty. Nowhere are gout and rheumatism so prevalent,
in spite of the beauty of the climate, as in Australia,
where meat is cheap, and people live principally upon it.
I maintain that if more, and more decided, abstinence
were enjoined, there would be no necessity for the
number of hours that are now wasted in exercise. Mr.
John Morley, in a recent speech to some schools, refers
to this point. He says : ‘ Is there not a little too much
addiction to pleasure nowadays ? Do not young men
attend rather more to their athletics and sports than is
wholly good ? This was what had been said :—In Germany, young men who were going into the family business travelled and acquired languages, and learnt to
know the tastes and habits of the natives. In England
the sons of the house devoted themselves to pleasure—to
billiards, the theatre, sport, and so on. In Germany the

father said, " Thank God I have a son ! " In England
the son said, " Thank God I have a father ! " ' Mr.
Morley wound up, after saying that those who worked
hard ought to have pleasure, as follows :—' There was no
doubt, taking the country as a whole, that pleasure and
sport were now absorbing an amount of time and mental
occupation which must block out some other objects to
which it would be well if men and women paid attention.' The way to diminish exercise without loss of
health is by the very economical method of diminishing
food,' especially food of that kind which is well known to
increase muscle. From the little I know of French
schools it seems to me that the exercise there is very
inadequate. We are told that Germany is our successful
rival in many forms of physical prowess and staying
power, in spite of education being more complete and
universal in that country. Is it not possible that they
adjust the balance better between study and muscular
development ?

I am often accused by my friends of being too ambitious—indeed, worldly-minded—from caring too much
for the success in life of those whom I know well and
am fond of. The justification to myself of this accusation, the truth of which I admit, is that the youth of
life is a time of preparation, and if we get no results—
no outward demonstration—that when a man has done
his best he has done well, it seems to me like going up
for an examination and then not caring if you pass, like
acting to empty houses, writing books which no one
reads, painting pictures which no one buys, or losing
money instead of making it. Every now and then a
genius is passed over by his generation and acknowledged later on, but this is the exception. Broadly
speaking, the average get very much what they deserve,
and, in vaguely generalising, one can only speak of the
average. I do think that, having travelled half the
road of life, we have a right to expect moderate success,

and to feel disappointed if we do not get it. I am sure
to be asked, perhaps a little scoffingly, ' What do you
mean by success ? Happiness ? ' No, certainly not.
What I mean is easy to understand, though difficult to
define. It is the generally-accepted meaning of success,
perhaps in its lowest sense, the contrary of failure ; and
I mean the same as Mr. Morley does when he speaks of
success in the following words :—' It is the bitterest
element in the vast irony of human life that the time-
worn eyes to which a son's success would have brought
the purest gladness are so often closed for ever before
success has come.'

If the fashion grows of parents handing over to children some of the money which would otherwise come
to them only after their parents' death, the habit of
early saving when expenses are increased on first leaving home might enable young people to live much more
economically than they have done in the luxurious
houses where they have been brought up. Anybody who
remembers the accounts of the childhoods of our grand-
fathers and grandmothers will realise what a garret life
the children of rich people led at the beginning of the
century. The following anecdote is a small instance in
point :—My grandparents were very rich, and spent
60,000*l.* on the Parliamentary election of their eldest
son. My mother, who came in the middle of a large
family, has often described to me how underfed she was
as a child, and how she would gladly pick up and eat
the sucked crusts dropped by the babies on the nursery
floor. Another of the terrors of her childhood was that
during the cold Northern winters the nurserymaid used
to be sent down to break the ice on a fountain in the
yard, where the children were habitually bathed, as a
means of strengthening them. She also remembered the
keen delight with which they welcomed the news that
the ice was unbreakable. When they grew up, after
seventeen their life was merged into that of their parents,

and my mother used to wonder what they would think of her—she had seen so little of them during her childhood.

This bringing-up may certainly have had the effect of enabling the children of the rich to make poorer marriages than they are willing to do now after being nursed in the lap of luxury from their infancy. Poor marriages can be very happy if both parties realise what they undertake, and if the husband belongs to a profession where an increase of income is possible, and where his professional expenditure and the position he has to maintain are not out of all proportion to his income as a married man. Members of society who marry poor make a great mistake in thinking that by living even as many as eighteen years in retirement they will lose all their friends in a way that would prove disadvantageous either to themselves or their children. The friends of our youth are our contemporaries, and we never can forget or meet on terms of formality the men and women with whom we once were intimate. The first word that drops from the lips, on meeting after years of separation, is, as often as not, the old familiar Christian name.

More than thirty years ago the following little poem was given to me as having been written in fun by James Spedding, the distinguished author of the Life of Bacon. I thrilled with excitement when I first read it, which will not surprise anyone who remembers the position between youth and age fifty years ago. The young were supposed to be foolish, the old to be all wisdom and experience. Now this is so changed that the old are having rather a bad time ; and the truth contained in this poem still appeals to me, though from an entirely different point of view. Whether we are so fortunate as to have children, or so unfortunate as not to have them, it makes, in my opinion, no difference. Once we have reached a certain age, the sensible thing is to acknowledge that our lives are more or less over. The best way we can then serve our country, or give dignity and happiness to our old age, is to lend all the help in our power to the young—in fact, always to be ready to open the door to those who are knocking.

THE ANTIQUITY OF MAN

When I was a freshman, old age did appear
A reverend and beautiful thing ;
For knowledge must gather as year follows year,
And wisdom from knowledge should spring.

But I found the same years that supplied me with
knowledge
Took the power to digest it away,
And let out all the store I had gathered at college
Through leaks that increased every day.

So I said—and think not I said it in jest
(You will find it is true to the letter)—
That the only thing old people ought to know best
Is that young people ought to know better.

FURNISHING

I MUST give you a few of my views about furnishing, especially as I cannot say to you, ' Get such-and-
such a book, and you will know all I know.' I can
name no book that seems to me at all satisfactory on
modern furnishing. One published in 1887 and called
' From Kitchen to Garret,' by J. E. Panton, has gone
through many editions, and contains useful and practical hints, but I do not at all agree with a good deal
that it says. It recommends what I call upholstering
far too much, and the overcrowding and decorating of
rooms, and is not nearly simple enough. I should say
to any young housekeeper, ' Get the book and learn
what you can from it, but reserve to yourself a very
keen judgment about many things that it advises.' As
an example, I will mention that the author grudges a
man, as a matter of expense (!), his cigarette and cigar.
I know no one single thing that gives a woman half the
pleasure that smoking gives a man ; so, as an economy,
many things in a house might be given up first. If
smoking is supposed to be bad for a man, persuade him
to smoke less ; and I believe there is no better way of
inducing him to do this than to allow him to smoke in
every room in the house—drawing-room, dining-room,
mother's bedroom, nursery. There is no greater proof

282 POT-POURRI FROM A SURREY GARDEN.

that a house is kept sweet and aired, and therefore
healthy, than the fact that no room ever smells of
tobacco. After many years' experience in all sorts of
houses, small and large, country and town, I can vouch
for it that no house ever does smell of smoke, if cigarettes,
cigars, and pipes are allowed everywhere, provided only
that a thorough draught can be got through the rooms.
I well know how sensitive some people are about tobacco,
but it is wonderful how much this dislike can be overcome by custom and a desire to do so. A smoking-room
otherwise than as a man's general room, where he can
read and write, is, I think, a very objectionable thing,
and conducive to a great waste of time. Let a man
smoke during his employments, and not look upon
smoking as an occupation in itself. People should guard
against the sentiment of the cheerful country hostess
who received her guest with ' This is Liberty Hall ; you
can smoke in the garden.'

Another book, called ' How to be Happy though
Married ' (Fisher Unwin), has had an immense sale, and
is a much cleverer, better-written book than its rather
flippant title might lead one to suppose. I strongly
recommend it to young housewives. It has a short
chapter on furnishing, with which I cordially agree, and
much in the book is well worth reading and remembering.

Mr. William Morris's ' Lectures on Art,' published in
1881, helped me more than any other book I know ; it
cultivated my ideas and refined my taste. The first
time I went to Mr. Morris's old shop in Queen's Square,
quite as a girl, it was indeed a revelation. It had the
effect of a sudden opening of a window in a dark room.
All was revealed—the beauty of simplicity, the usefulness of form, the fascination of design, and the charm
of delicate colour. Added to this, came the appreciation of the things that had gone before, and which in
my time had been hidden away. I came back to the
various houses to which I had been accustomed with a

sigh of despair ; but the first step towards progress must always be discontent with what one has and with one's own ignorance. It has sometimes been a sorrow to me to see, in the Oxford Street shop, that even Mr. Morris did not keep up entirely the high and simple standard of his early years. He has some golden rules in the lecture called ' The Beauty of Life,' perhaps the truest and most concise of which is one that none of us really act up to : ' Have nothing in your houses that you do not know to be useful or believe to be beautiful.' What would happen to the great mass of modern wedding-presents if we really carried out this rule ? Mr. Morris preaches the sternest simplicity, and I must say, as a mental effort, I think we ought to try and agree with him ; though rooms, to my mind, should look warm and comfortable, and simplicity had better consist in an absence of rubbish than in a diminution of comfort. Mr. Morris goes on to explain what he means by a simple sitting-room : ' First, a bookcase with a great many books in it ; next, a table that will keep steady when you write or work at it ; then several chairs that you can move, and a bench that you can sit or lie upon ; next, a cupboard with drawers ; next, unless the book-case or the cupboard be very beautiful with painting or carving, you will want pictures or engravings such as you can afford—only not stop-gaps, but real works of art—on the wall ; or else the wall itself must be orna-mented with some beautiful and restful pattern. We shall also want a vase or two to put flowers in, which latter you must have sometimes, especially if you live in a town. Then there will be the fireplace, of course, which in our climate is bound to be the chief object in the room.

' That is all we shall want, especially if the floor be good ; if it is not—as, by the way, in a modern house it is pretty well certain not to be—I admit that a small carpet which can be bundled out of the room in two minutes will be useful : and we must also take care that it is beautiful, or it will annoy us terribly. Now, unless we are musical and need a piano, in which case, as far as beauty is concerned, we are in a bad way, that is quite all we want, and we can add very little to these necessaries without troubling ourselves and hindering our work, our thought, and our rest.' After this description, think how very rare it is to see a room on these lines at all. One of the most disfiguring and vulgar forms of modern ornamentation is sticking about quantities of photographs—masses of men and women of our acquaintance, or royalties and celebrities. I do not mean that we should not have one or two framed photographs, of dear friends or relations ; for certainly, in a small degree, photographs of those we love do fulfil Dr. Johnson's description of portrait-painting : ' That art which is employed in diffusing friendship, in reviving tenderness, in quickening the affections of the absent and continuing the presence of the dead.'

Mr. Morris spoke of the fireplace as such an important thing in our climate ; it is so indeed. One of the first essentials is that it should not smoke or be ugly, and another is that it should give out much heat with little consumption of coal. I consider the greatest increase of delight possible in any kind of fireplace, no matter of what size or make, is to have a very broad hearth of tiles, or bricks, or stone, or marble, or anything of that sort that is hard and fireproof, and then do away with every form of fender or raised rim round the hearth. People have an idea that this is not safe ; but that is an entire mistake. To be able to stand easily on the hot tiles is an immense joy added to life, and one much appreciated by men. Even for children, instead of tumbling over the low fender, which is a real danger, they soon feel the heat, and that warns them to keep away from the hearth. But it is essential that the hearth should be wider than is usual, both for appearance and safety; and if a finish is thought desirable between the tiles and the floor, a flat band, three or four inches wide, of brass or iron, looks very well—but it is not necessary. The fire-irons should be on a stand apart, or put against the chimneypiece on hooks, or in a hoop of iron or brass. Nothing, of course, supersedes the high wire fender for safety in nurseries and schoolrooms. White tiles as a lining for the sides, grates, and hearths of fireplaces are not often used, but to my mind they are far prettier than dark tiles, if the chimneypiece is made of light-coloured marble or white wood, as is so common. The adapting and improving of what we find in builders' houses is one of our modern difficulties.

Mr. Morris is severe on pianos, and it must be admitted they are very ugly, but great attention is now being given to improving them. One simple inexpensive way of doing so is to have the case very plain; the music desk plain bars, instead of ornamental fret-work; and the whole left absolutely without varnish or polish. The housemaid's rubbing only improves the marking on the grain of the wood.

In London everything ought to be sacrificed to sweetness and light. Let no one put on their walls or their floors that which they cannot afford constantly to renew. In an ordinary London house, merely keeping things clean one year with another, inside and out, adds a considerable sum yearly to the rent.

I have found it very clean and useful to wash the corners and sides of the window-panes with Sanitas, especially in the country in spring. It destroys the eggs of flies and insects of all kinds, and in no way injures the paint. It saves waste to lay on the Sanitas with a brush.

In London nowadays the houses of the young are freshly done up and clean and healthy. Where I find the greatest sanitary neglect is in the homes of the middle-aged, especially those who have lived long in one place. Even in the houses of rich and well-to-do people, in London, the dirt in the upstairs rooms and passages is inconceivable. The mistress of the house is lazy or indifferent ; and as we get older, the years run on so quickly it is impossible to realise how long it is since the last cleaning ; nothing is ever looked over, replaced, or renewed. A favourite economy, and one to which the best of housekeepers have a tendency, is to put old carpets out of dining-rooms or drawing-rooms into bed-rooms of boys and girls, often without even going to the expense of having them cleaned. The painted floor and a small piece of new drugget, clean and sweet, would be infinitely more healthy and more appropriate. Another constantly neglected corner is what is called the house-maid's closet. In houses where servants are not much looked after, and even where they are, this is often the glory-hole of dirt. I recommend the use of the white enamel slop-pails, which are so infinitely easier to keep clean than the old painted tin ones, though they, too, are quite clean if they are only repainted often enough. The whole system of living and housekeeping in England is still sacrificed far too much to show—large sitting-rooms, small bed-rooms, and unclean attics. However, things are infinitely better than they used to be. In the last century one or two footmen used to sleep on mattresses in the front hall of the crowded little houses in Mayfair · and even in my childhood the custom of putting three or four men or women into one room was quite a usual thing.

To those about to furnish I would say, ' Never buy new things when you can get them second-hand.' Pro-cure an ordinary illustrated price list from one of the large furnishing shops, and with that, by which to test prices, go to second-hand shops and sales. If you get a well-made second-hand piece of furniture that you really want for the same price as, or cheaper than, you could buy painted or varnished deal—well, you know you have not done badly. If you buy an old bookcase, or table, or sofa, for even a little more than you would give for the inferior modern ones, you may still congratulate yourself.

The only marked difference that I can see between my house and most others, both in the country and in London, is that I never have a roller blind. They are expensive to put up, expensive to maintain, and very difficult to keep clean in London. I never have them in my own rooms, in bed-rooms or servants' rooms, in the stable or gardener's cottage. What I do have is an inner curtain hung from a small rod on the window. It can be made of any variety of material, to suit the different windows and the requirements of the room— thin silk (the effects of light through silk—orange, red, yellow, or green—are very pretty), chintz, muslin, or the thickest dark blue or green twill lined with calico, to keep out light in the bedrooms in the country (in London I think light blue or green twill unlined is sufficient) ; and the most useful of all is the common red Turkey twill, lined or unlined, which washes year after year, and always looks fresh, clean, and bright, and practically never wears out. In many modern windows these inner curtains enable you to dispense with heavy outside curtains altogether—to my mind an advantage, as drawn curtains almost always make a room stuffy and nearly as airless as did the shutters of our forefathers. All the same, thick curtains are, of course, required in the country in winter for warmth. For an outside effect in London, it is very pretty if the wood of the window is painted dark or light green, red, or blue, and if the silk curtains inside are of the same colour to match the paint.

On first doing up a house, keep as many rooms as you can plainly whitewashed (' white distemper ' it is called), but see that it is white, and not mixed with black, blue, or yellow, such as painters delight in using. I think everything looks well against a white wall. Covering a wall with coarse canvas and then distempering it gives a variety to the surface. Some people think white walls unbecoming. I cannot agree with this. What suits the rose and the tulip as a background ought to suit a pretty woman in her pretty clothes. In a white room dark furniture never looks heavy (not even the darkest oak), and light furniture never looks poor. But white rooms must be kept clean, as ceilings are. This necessity is a great merit, and renewing is not expensive. [If staircases or passages are white-washed, a dado, about a yard deep up the side of the staircase and along the passage, of frilled cretonne, twilled red calico, or anything cheap, is an excellent way of protecting the wall from all the many injuries that happen to it. If you like, you can have one such dado for winter and one for summer, and they can be washed or cleaned. They look best frilled on to a thin lath of wood which pulls out. Rings are sewn on the back for hanging the curtain on to nails or hooks screwed into the wall at intervals. If the wall is soft, another thin lath of wood must be nailed to it to hold the screws.

In a white room a small piece of good drapery or old leather hung on the wall looks well, or even a few yards of very superior paper may be put in one place—between windows, over a chimney-piece, behind a picture, above a table, or under a bookcase. This form of decoration was the common one in the fifteenth and sixteenth centuries, and was, in fact, the way in which tapestry came to be used. In the old French *châteaux* of Touraine the hooks that held these draperies, silks from Italy, and no doubt many other things, are still to be seen in the walls. As the French Court moved from *château* to *château*, all this material moved with them.

If bookcases can be made to order, they are much better raised a certain height on the wall. This is more convenient, as grubbing on the floor for the book one wants is very tiresome. Besides, in this way you can have the large books at the top, with a wide shelf above them, and the small ones below, the shelves gradually diminishing both in height and depth from the wall. Mr. Morris advocates, in his lectures, the painting of deal ; the only other way of treating it is simply to oil it. Mr. Morris, I think, says nothing about painting the floors. But that seems to me the best solution; at any rate, for three feet round the room—red, green, black, and above all white as often as you like, especially for bedrooms. Nothing is so clean, the paint wants no scrubbing and no soda ; tepid water and a cloth make everything as clean as new. Staining, though a little cheaper, wears less well, will not wash, and looks common. Indian matting and felt look well in the country, but are not so clean in London. Both collect the black dust, and the former cannot be taken up. You want to be really rich to have polished floors of oak or teak. English housemaids cannot clean them, abroad it is always done by men. In London it has to be done by an upholsterer two or three times a year.

If economy is an object in furnishing, one of the best ways of reducing the outlay in bed-rooms is by dispensing with the modern washing-stands. The old-fashioned ones are often too small for comfort ; our ancestors cleaned themselves with little room and less water. A large unvarnished deal table with the legs painted to suit the room is what I recommend. For cheapness it can be covered with white oil-cloth, nailed down ; though I prefer a thick white dimity cloth, which can be washed as often as necessary. For a luxurious washing-table, plain coloured square tiles, sunk into a bed of cement and held firm by a metal band, make a delightful surface. A great addition both to comfort and tidiness in all bed-rooms is to have a small or large cupboard, or curtained shelves (for bottles, &c.) above the washing-stand. A couple of shelves at the head of the bed is the best place for a bookshelf in a bed-room. It is such a pleasure, morning or night,

to be able to reach, without having to get out of bed,
the book that suits one's mood.

Modern London builders have a most irritating way of
repeating, in house after house, the most obvious defects.
One of the worst of these is the bath : a large tin surface
indifferently painted, which is quickly injured by the hot
water, surrounded by a mahogany rim, the varnish of
which is spotted and marked by every accessory necessary to the bath. One can hardly imagine anything
more inappropriate. Doulton has invented a glazed
earthenware bath which obviates all these objections,
and would be more luxurious if the floor of the bath-room
were raised nearly to the height of its rim ; the steps
to reach this raised floor could be outside the room, or
inside, according to the hanging of the door. One of the
minor luxuries of life, often not found in the largest
houses, is to have really hot water when you expect it.
I have found that large cosies—the shape of tea-cosies
—to go over the hot-water cans (one for the little can
and one for the big), easily bring this luxury within the
reach of everybody. They are made of chintz, or of any
stuff that comes handy and suits the room, lined with
sateen to tone with or contrast with the outside, and
thickly wadded. If the water is put in really hot, and
the cosies are thick and large enough to cover the can
entirely, the water will keep hot till the morning. This,
of course, is doubly useful when there are no fires.

With all my recommendations about buying second-
hand furniture, of course I do not mean to include
bedding. I am old-fashioned enough to think that
mattresses had always better come, though more expensive, from the best shops. If my general advice is
to furnish simply, this applies doubly to nurseries and
bed-rooms. In fact, these rooms should be of such a
kind that if the surgeon or nurse entered them with a
view to an operation, they would wish nothing altered
—distempered walls, white or coloured, grave or gay,

as suits the taste; no carpets going into the corners,
but broad margins of painted wood, white is the best.
'Oh, it shows the dirt so!' says the upholsterer or
builder. 'So much the better,' should the owner of the
house answer; 'the dirt shown on white is harmless
and clean compared to the dirt hidden by dark colours.'
The curtains should be of the smallest and simplest kind,
hung on a brass or iron rod, merely to keep out light or
to make warmth; they should never reach to the
ground, unless the window does.

It is a serviceable and clean plan to sew strips of
holland or chintz, which can be removed and washed, on
to the edge of the mattresses; this prevents the house-
maid's hands from dirtying them. I remember the day
when all beds were covered with what are called counter-
panes, which were even left on at night. But these now
are universally acknowledged to be unwholesome, and,
for the daytime, they have been superseded by some
coloured coverlid. I like this coverlid, which keeps the
blankets clean by day, and is folded up by night, to be
the handsomest feature in the room, though its material
may vary from the cheapest twill or cretonne to the
richest needle-work or damask-silk, old or modern. The
walls can always be covered gradually by framed pictures, photographs, or prints of all kinds. In a nursery,
the choice of these photographs may make an impression
for life, artistic or the contrary. A young man once
said to me that in travelling in Italy one of the chief
joys he felt in visiting the famous galleries was the
recognition of a picture that had been an old familiar
friend as a framed photograph at home. He added that,
if ever he had children, he thought one of the best
decorations for a nursery would be a dado made of
photographs, of various sizes, of some of the master-
pieces of the world. The difficulty of this would be
that nurseries must be easily cleaned and renewed,
and I think the photographs to form the dado would

have to be stuck on to thick pasteboard or thin wood.

I would allow all young people, both boys and girls, as much as possible to do the decorating and furnishing of their own rooms, limiting them, of course, to the sum intended to be spent. Taste in decorating, as in all else, is a constant cause of difference, and what every person objects to most is what is to them old-fashioned —that is, what has immediately preceded their own day.

A detail of family life, but not at all an unimportant one in my estimation, is the providing of a large, firm, folding table in the general sitting-room. It can be kept outside or in a corner of the room, and should never remain open during the day, but be brought out nightly when the lamps are lit and the curtains are drawn. This plan enables every member of the family to have room for separate employment. Everyone knows how crowded the permanent tables become in an habitually used sitting-room. The use of an empty table was first suggested to my mind by some remarks made by Goethe to Eckermann in the 'Conversations.' He strongly recommends bringing out any good books or pictures that you may happen to have to show your guests. It is impossible to do this with any comfort without a good roomy table on which to spread them. Showing books to children of different ages often provides an excellent topic for conversation, and even, I might say, for instruction; only this, I am afraid, sounds so very priggish.

A distressing feature of modern civilisation is the utter waste, both in town and country, of the precious rain-water that runs off our houses. It will be argued that in London it would be black; but it is not very difficult to remedy this—sufficiently, at any rate, for use in washing. In the country it is priceless. No well-cared-for baby ought ever to be washed in anything but rain-water; and yet, rather than make tanks, rich people, who will buy every luxury, get their water (which in nine cases out of ten is as hard and full of chalk as it can be) from the nearest water company. Rain-water is even more essential for the plants than for the baby. I was told last year by a good gardener, who had been peculiarly successful in growing the rare and beautiful Table Mountain Orchid, *Disa grandiflora,* that he attributed his success entirely to keeping it very moist, but never allowing one drop of water to go near it that was not rain-water. This is the case, in a minor degree, with many other greenhouse and stove plants.

A DAY IN LONDON

Advantages of suburbs—London life—Picture exhibitions.

PEOPLE who live in London, and those who live in the depths of the country, are both equally inclined, for different reasons, to laugh a little, and even sneer, over the obvious disadvantages of suburban residences. By suburban I mean more the character of the surroundings than the actual distance from London or any other large town. The more favoured a place is as regards soil and climate, the more thickly populated it becomes. But the near neighbourhood of London has certainly immense advantages under many conditions. For young couples, if a man is strong and well, and has work to do in town, it is the very poetry of life compared to London itself, and is a phase of existence which a woman, if once she has had it, always looks back upon with pleasure. She has her children and her duties all day, and in the evening the man throws off his bothers and worries and comes back to peace and happiness, rest and pure air at home. When children get big, and have tastes and talents of their own which must be developed and educated, there is certainly much to be said in favour of moving the home for some years to London. When the parents are no longer young, and when, however friendly they may be and proud of each other, they have to pursue individually their own lives, and carry out that partnership which is the only perfect form of middle-aged married life, for the good of the children and the general well-being of the establishment, then the oneness of married life cannot possibly be carried on without a certain sacrifice of what is best for the growing-up children. But, again, in the evening of life, when friends gradually fall away, and we become rather a duty and perhaps even a slight burden to our children and relations, who have their own lives to attend to, I consider that residing in the suburbs solves, once more, a great many of the difficulties of our complicated family existence. Our children can easily visit us, and, if we are not too old, we can so well go to London for duty or pleasure, and in this way see, and hear, and learn all that is going on. If all this is true, as I think it is, we are saved, without actually living in London, from the reproach that, being buried in the country, we let ourselves go, and grow old prematurely. To be an easy distance from town, though saying this may seem rather a drop from the sublime to the ridiculous, certainly helps us to cultivate the enjoyment of Nature, and, at the same time, gives us the opportunity, if we have the power in however slight a degree, of acquiring knowledge for its own sake without regard to its practical application. Surely these are the only two perfect sources of human happiness ? I do not say this thoughtlessly. Love, in all its forms, gives a far intenser happiness, but even in its purest form—parental love—it is accompanied by anxiety and doubt. It begins with a kind of animal enjoyment, and ends in the practising of continual self-denial.

Much as I dislike leaving my garden, yesterday I obeyed the summons of my oldest friend to spend the day in London with her ; and certainly it turned out an example of what I have been saying—so much so, that I yield to the temptation of giving a slight account of it. We spent our time in visiting Burlington House, and I will tell you what struck us most as we wandered through

the rooms there, in the way we used to do at the old
Academy in Trafalgar Square, when we were young and
enthusiastic. First, I took my friend to the work that I
admired most, which, I believe, will no more die in the
generations to come than that of either Raphael or
Benvenuto Cellini has died, though it will be more or
less admired according to the fashion of the day. Mr.
Gilbert, the sculptor, is in my opinion one of the greatest
geniuses we have amongst us just now, and his exhibited
work in 1896 shows with peculiar force the comprehensiveness of his talent. Is not the stretch between the
massive, splendid portrait-bust of Professor Owen, and
the exquisitely finished, subtle, little full-length figure
of St. George, all that the Colossus of Rhodes could
boast—a foot on either shore ? With the assertiveness
of the true artist he must have insisted on the hiding
of the hideous colour on the walls, and hung a piece of
yellow-brown drapery, which harmonises splendidly with
his plaster cast. We crossed the room to look at the
least remarkable work of the three, perhaps, artistically
speaking ; and yet how the bust of Sir George Grove
stands out and lives, and almost breathes, compared with
the cold dead heads that surround it ! It has not the
colour of life nor the vulgar realism of waxwork, but the
plain chalk cast is a man of flesh and blood, rugged and
strong. Then we went back to the St. George, and
enjoyed it for ten minutes. Perhaps we shall never see
again its exquisite beauty—the little hands that express
so much feeling ; the sad, gentle face, almost mourning
over the worthlessness of human greatness, though the
dead dragon lies coiled about his feet, and the princess is
to be his bride ! Look at the cross-handled sword, and
the helmet, and the armour, and think of all it means, in
these days of cheap work, to put all that is here into one
small figure, which is, after all, only a portion of a railing
round a dead young prince's effigy, to be hidden away
for ever in a cool, dim chapel. We who studied the

little statuette are not likely to forget it, for, as a poet
said of his friend :—

> . . . Some, in whom such images are strong,
> Have hoarded the impression in their heart,
> Fancy's fond dreams and memory's joys among,
> Like some loved relic of romantic song,
> Or cherished masterpiece of ancient art.

As we passed back into the picture rooms we were
pleased to see that Lord Leighton's last work apparently
gains so immensely by being unfinished ; and it is in the
manner of his youth rather than of his age, rich and
harmonious in colour, passionate in sentiment—to be
looked at by those who knew him, this ideal President
of our Academy of Painting, with ' thoughts which only
upon tears can rise.' Far the most striking portraits in
the Academy are, alas ! by non-Englishmen—Mr. Sargent, who is an American, and M. Benjamin Constant,
who is a Frenchman. Mr. Sargent's ' Portrait of a
Lady ' is surely consummate : the painting of the pearls,
the smart, bright-coloured cape, are not to be beaten by
Vandyck at his best ; and oh ! how far beyond any
effort even of the old masters is the sad pathos of that
interesting nineteenth-century face ! Can we look at it
and not say with Balzac, ' Les drames de la vie ne sont
pas dans les circonstances, ils sont dans le cœur ' ? It
seems rather the fashion not to admire Mr. Chamberlain's
portrait, and it is not quite so finished, especially the
hands, as one would wish—doubtless for want of time
being given for the sittings ; all the same, it is a grand
portrait of a history-making Late Victorian statesman,
and will be looked at with reverent curiosity by the
student of the future.

And now we pass on through two or three rooms,
avoiding what we do not like when not able to fix our
eyes on what we do, which is the acquired knack of the
habitual haunter of galleries and exhibitions, and sit

down quietly to study Mr. Abbey's most remarkable picture of Richard, Duke of Gloucester, and the Lady Anne.

Was ever woman in this humour woo'd ?
Was ever woman in this humour won ?

And the more we looked, the more we studied, the more remarkable the picture appeared to us. The young, angry, and yet wicked face under the strange headdress, the nervous clasp of the left hand, while the right seizes the black veil, true to the instinct of some women, who, in the moment of their greatest joy or deepest grief, never forget their clothes ! Richard, with his winning courtesy and the bow which conceals the defects of his figure, in his red clothes, is a strange contrast to that other figure which we know, rather than see, lies stiff and cold behind the guards. Historically, perhaps, Richard looks a little old, as he was but thirty-five when killed on Bosworth field. The guards, the crowd, the varied expressions fading actually away into the canvas, are very fine. The painting reminds one of the old Germans, and yet is entirely original. Is it not indeed in Art what ' Esmond ' is in literature—an old story told in an old manner, and yet without absolute mimicry of anything ?

And so the two old friends of forty years wandered on and began to get tired, when we met an acquaintance, and she said, ' Have you seen the picture that Mr. Watts in his generosity says is better painted than anything he ever did ? ' ' No, where is it ? What is it ? ' ' " The Leper's Wife," by George Harcourt, in the eleventh room.' And so on we went with renewed strength into this honoured eleventh room, and stood before one of the most dramatic and moving of modern pictures. A splendid young woman, of five-and-twenty or so, clothed in bright red, rushes with her face towards you through a wood, with outstretched arms, her face

glowing with love and devotion, and her lips parted ;
behind her are great banks of cumuli, sanguine-stained
from the setting sun, and the stems of the trees glow
with the same light. Pure, small, white wood-flowers
grow about her feet. All this to represent the joy and
the pride of life, which she willingly leaves to join her
leper husband, who stands in the dark shadow of his
humble hut, clothed from head to foot in grey leper
draperies, slightly recalling Mr. Watts's own beautiful
figure of ' Love and Death '—the head turned away,
and the hand upheld forbidding her approach, unable
to appreciate the love she brings him, or loving her too
well to allow of any risk for her sake, though she cries :
' Kiss me, in the name of the everlasting God ! I will
live and die with you ! ' The sacrifice could bring him
no joy ; and so it will ever be, not only to the leper—
for the love of men is not as the love of women.

It seems impossible anyone should share our ignorance, so I will merely state that as the two old friends,
who had led such different lives, stood entranced before
the picture, we neither of us knew it was the illustration
of a poem called ' Happy, or The Leper's Bride,' in
Tennyson's last volume, ' Demeter and Other Poems.'
He gives in a note an interesting account of the decision
of the Church, in the twelfth century, that marriage was
indissoluble, and that the lepers' wives might rejoin their
husbands if they liked.

Once more overcome with fatigue, we sat down on
a bench, to rest before leaving, when a wonderful little
maiden passed, cleanly but very poorly dressed for these
days, with beautifully and yet fashionably dressed hair,
and far-away dreamy eyes. ' That, no doubt, is a young
artist treading the Asphodel meadows of her youth.'
My friend answered, ' I daresay it is true. Let us tell
her of the picture we have enjoyed so much ; ' and
running after her she brought her back, all smiles,
saying to me, ' This lady is not an artist, as we thought,

but the next thing to it, a model, enjoying the pictures she has helped to make.' Seeing she had no catalogue, we presented her with ours, and left her in that undying Elysian world of Art, while we slowly went down the steps with the strong conviction upon us that age had not yet robbed us of the power of spending a happy grey summer morning in London.

HEALTH

OUR home-coming this September was an agitating and
painful one. We had been warned by telegraph that we
should find grave sickness in the house, and so indeed it
was. Doctors, nurses, everything provided before we
were able to get back. How little can the young of the
present day understand the complete revolution that
has come over family life in the last half-century, and
how changed are our relations towards the sick, though
the invalid may be our nearest and dearest ! Thirty
years ago, even in the houses of the comparatively rich,
it was exceedingly difficult to get help in illness ; an
old char-woman, a coachman's wife, or a servant out
of place, was considered all that was necessary. Even
a partially trained nurse was a very rare thing, and
never sought for except in cases of severe operation or
dangerous fevers. It seems almost impossible to believe
that chloroform was not used till the middle of the
'Forties, and that Liston's first great operation with the
patient unconscious from ether was in 1846. Now, in
spite of the many blessings nurses generally bring to
the patients, I think the fact that they are usually good
and very easily obtained is one cause of the deterioration
in home-life clearly perceptible to all of us who are of
a certain age. Sickness does not now strain every nerve,
nor bring the same occupation, the same real work,

mental and physical, that it used to do. The feeling of responsibility, of constant anxiety, is taken off our shoulders and laid on the nurse. Loving members of a family have just to continue their ordinary lives, for mere occupation's sake, and to avoid the reproach of giving way to useless grief, however anxious they may be. Ministering to those we love is too often denied us, and the patient's gentle gratitude, which used to tighten for life the bonds of affection, either does not now exist, or is given to a hard-worked, perhaps overworked, woman who does not want it, and who is here to-day and gone to-morrow. Her services, however excellent and efficient, are given for money, and are and ought to be perfectly different from the tender and devoted services prompted by love. All sensible doctors recognise this.

George Eliot, whose large-minded philosophy did so much to form the youth of my generation, is not, I am told, much read—or, at any rate, not much appreciated —now by the young. There is a splendid passage in ' Janet's Repentance ' which brings home to us the lesson of the sick-room as no words of mine could do. This lesson is sadly missed under the modern condition of things, and the want of it has perhaps caused that rebellion against sorrow and sickness which we so often see nowadays. It is a lesson which those who learnt it young never forget, for it colours the whole of their lives :—

' Day after day, with only short intervals of rest, Janet kept her place in that sad chamber. No wonder the sick-room and the lazaretto have so often been a refuge from the tossings of intellectual doubt—a place of repose for the worn and wounded spirit. Here is a duty about which all creeds and all philosophers are at one ; here, at least, the conscience will not be dogged by doubt, the benign impulse will not be checked by adverse theory ; here you may begin to act without settling one preliminary question. To moisten the sufferer's parched lips through the long night-watches, to bear up the drooping head, to lift the helpless limbs, to divine the want that can find no utterance beyond the feeble motion of the hand, the beseeching glance of the eye—these are offices that demand no self-questioning, no casuistry, no assent to propositions, no weighing of consequences. Within the four walls where the stir and glare of the world are shut out, and every voice is subdued—where a human being lies prostrate, thrown on the tender mercies of his fellow—the moral relation of man to man is reduced to its utmost clearness and simplicity ; bigotry cannot confuse it, theory cannot pervert it, passion awed into quiescence can neither pollute nor perturb it.   As we bend over the sick-bed, all the forces of our nature rush towards the channels of pity, of patience, and of love, and sweep down the miserable choking drift of our quarrels, our debates, our would-be wisdom, and our clamorous, selfish desires.'

If this picture is true, and every word of it comes home to me as a truth, then surely life as it is now is in some respects a poorer, weaker thing in consequence of the modern idea which, under the power of the medical profession, sends our husbands to a private hospital for an operation, and hands over our sick in our own homes, let us say to the very best of women, but to women who never saw them before, and who, we hope, will never see them again.   These excellent women, though paid by you, are virtually the servants of the doctor, to do his bidding, and even, if necessary, to cover and veil his mistakes or screen his faults.   The professional reputation of the nurse is not in any way affected by the life or death of her patient ; so long as she does her duty, death is an incident in the course of business.   But her very livelihood depends on her saying that the operation was well performed, and on pleasing the doctor who attends after the operation is over.   I do not say this

as a reproach to anyone, or even as a condemnation of
a system which, if logically carried out, as fortunately
it seldom is, comes very near to being the greatest of
modern tyrannies. My reason for noticing it is that,
though under these conditions the responsibility of the
mother or wife becomes different and much less simple,
it is by no means entirely over, as many young people
seem to me to imagine. We none of us wish for one
moment to return to the nurses of the type described
by Dickens, but I do think we ought all of us, in our
homes and with any influence we may have on our
generation, to guard against throwing ourselves entirely
into the hands of the doctors and nurses, with an absolute submission of our intelligence—a submission which
we should think ridiculous and impossible in any of the
other conditions of life. It is bad for them and bad for
us. Such power is too much. Such a neglect of our
duties and such complete dependence on others may
have most disastrous consequences on ourselves, and,
still worse, may seriously injure the lives of those we
love. Nothing matters so much, be it old style or new,
as that sickness in the house, end it ever so favourably,
should hurt or lessen family love ; for, as Thackeray
says in one of his letters, ' *Aimons nous bien.* It seems
to me that is the only thing we can carry away, and
when we go let us have some who love us wherever we
are.'

Nurses have a very hard life, and almost all women
who work are apt to belong to the overworked portion
of the community. That they should combine in any
way that is possible, for their own advantage and for the
maintenance of their old age, is very much to be desired.
But the public should never for one moment forget that
nursing, which began in devotion and forgetfulness of
self, as a vocation, has now become, in the most acknowledged sense of the word, a profession and an employment for women, depriving them of the leisure and

pleasure belonging to their youth—that leisure and pleasure which justified Scott's description of woman as ' uncertain, coy, and hard to please,' and the want of which certainly also takes from them the right to consider themselves, or even the power to be, ' ministering angels.' What is done for duty and money can never be the same offering as what is done for love and devotion. The public only are to blame if they think a strong young woman ceases to be a human being because she works hard and wears a nurse's dress. It is of distinct importance that in the case of choosing a nurse for a husband, brother, or son, a woman should feel the responsibility of the situation, and not take the first nurse that turns up at an institution. The selecting of a nurse should most certainly not be left to chance. The nurse should be suitable for the case from the point of view of the family as well as that of the doctor. Why should we expose two human beings under our charge to temptations which we should not sanction under any of the other circumstances of life ? Convalescence ought to be a time of rest both for mind and body, not a time that is needlessly prolonged for the sake of foolish and unworthy flirtation, which is no more sanctioned by the higher members of the profession than is flirtation between a doctor and his patient. The accusations that just lately have been showered on the nurses, they deserve, it seems to me, no more than any other class of young women who share our common human nature. The blame rests with those who select the nurse—first the matron of the hospital or institution, and then the person who chooses her for the individual case.

The commonest of our national faults, and one which affects all our health regulations, is surely that we sanction the obvious causes of a situation, and then are surprised and grumble at their inevitable consequences. It is not so much a question of morality as of mere worldly common-sense and expediency. The laws which

should regulate such a new departure are not yet formed
—nursing, according to our modern ideas, being scarcely
a quarter of a century old. As long as the world lasts
and women are women, give them certain circumstances
and a sufficient temptation, and nothing will keep them
straight. Some women, too, take to nursing because
early trouble has made other openings difficult for them.
Under those circumstances we meet the most dangerous
type of woman that exists ; the world has turned against
her, and thereby caused her to become hard and bad,
and the enemy of society—the type that crushes, by
all the means in her power, any other woman who consciously or unconsciously crosses the path of her con-
quest. Few people seem to consider that the training
of a nurse is more hardening, and more likely to unsex
a woman, than the training of an actress. At any rate,
it is impossible to go through it without becoming very
much better or very much worse than the ordinary
woman. In France they understand human nature
better than we do, and would never dream of allowing
our system of nursing. Nurses in Paris are, I believe,
most difficult to get. We want more regulations and
more judicious assistance from public opinion. The
French want an increased staff of nurses who are well
conducted and not too young, to supplement the devoted,
high-minded, deeply religious class of women who can
alone join the Sisterhoods, as they apparently are insufficient in number. Time, the greatest adjuster of
all human difficulties, will settle these matters. What
concerns us is that no turn of fortune's wheel should
crush and injure ourselves or those belonging to us ;
and what matters now is that ordinary knowledge and
common-sense on the subject of health should be brought
to bear by every woman responsible in any way for the
well-being of others, and especially of the young. Public
opinion, I am glad to say, does not forgive a mother's
neglect of her children's physical condition ; and the

condemnation is severe when a boy, after all his work
and passing his hard examinations, is plucked in the
medical examination for some slight physical defect—
it may be nothing worse than neglected corns or a
crooked toe—which with ordinary care in childhood
or a slight operation might have been entirely cured.
Is it stinginess, or is it idleness, or is it ignorance, or is
it mere selfishness and a dislike to acknowledge delicacy
in their own children, or a half-conscientious repudiation
of responsibility and a blind trust in Providence, that
makes so many parents allow life-long misery and suffering to come upon their children just for the want of a
little care and study of the ordinary rules of health,
and of the watchful eye which is given by every hunting
man to his horse ?

One word more I must add about convalescence.
With the young and the healthy it is a time of hope and
even happiness, in spite of mourning over the lost muscles
and strength, and the irritating tyrannies of the sick-
room. But in long, chronic, hopeless illness modern
nursing, with all its real advantages, becomes an active
daily trial, only to be borne patiently from the same
feeling that makes all work and all trials bearable—
namely, for the time being, doing the disagreeable for
the sake of the ultimate good. It is our only method
of earning our daily bread by the sweat of our brow,
the old golden rule of life, which in all the forms it takes
is still the one that convinces us that life is worth living,
if not for ourselves, at any rate to continue our presence
here for the sake of those who dearly wish to keep us.
And so all the trials and fatigues of the three hours'
nurse's rule in the sick-room in the morning have to
be gone through as patiently and cheerfully as is possible.
But he or she can afterwards sink exhausted on the sofa
or bed, and can indeed say with the pride that belongs
to each one of us in our tiny sphere, ' I, too, have not
been idle—I, too, have done my best for those who are

dear to me.' But it is weary work, and for the very weak they can only feel how very much happier it would be to be left alone and lie still and unbothered, instead of feeling more tired than after a hard day's hunting.

For those who wish to learn, or those who are going abroad or to live in out-of-the-way places, and for those who do not care to have a doctor always in their house, I will name a few books written for the public by medical men and women of distinction and of great experience, and who are in no sense of the word quacks. The great difference, so far as I can see, between the books of medical men and those of so-called quacks, is that the latter have absolute faith in their remedies, and use almost the identical old miraculous words, ' Wash and be clean '—and this really often answers—while the books written by doctors employ a much more cautious language. To an immense number of human beings the narrow and forcible phraseology has great attractions, and goes a long way in affecting the nerves and mind, which are undoubted and powerful factors in all cures. Where disease is advanced and real, is it not admitted by all systems that alleviation, not cure, is all that is possible ? The simulation of disease is often merely the result of shattered or over-stimulated nerves. I fancy the medical books come near the truth when they suggest that an immense number of remedies and different treatments may all do good under different circumstances. In my opinion the cause of a vast amount of the bad health of the present day is owing to the number of drugs that people take—partly, at first, by order of the doctor and continued afterwards, and still more from the taking of quack medicines. When a doctor comes to the house, he should be given every chance, and obeyed in all he says ; but when he is dismissed, his medicines should go with him, and all amateur doctoring should be of the simplest kind— abstinence first and foremost, and various applications of hot and cold water. One of our great physicians two or three years ago, in his opening address to his hospital pupils, said that seventy per cent. of the patients in a great London hospital (think what that means !) would not be there if they were teetotalers and vegetarians ; and this statement passed unnoticed in all the daily papers in which the address was reported. If doctors could convince their patients of this, I fear their profession would be a less lucrative one, and that the health of the community would be far better—at any rate, fewer of the leisured moneyed classes would have to go to German watering-places, homœopathists, and quacks.

It is quite a latter-day thing for doctors to talk in this way about abstinence in health, but I shall never forget what I owe to an old-fashioned country doctor, who told me, whenever my children were ailing, to knock off at once all animal food—meat, soup, and even milk. Later in my life, I remember it was a favourite saying of Sir William Gull's : 'First get your patient hungry, and then keep him so.'

The first book I recommend is called 'On Slight Ailments and on Treating Disease,' by Lionel Beale. This is a collection of lectures delivered at King's College, London, on the principles and practice of medicine. If the book has a fault, it is that it is too comprehensive and medical to suit the palate of the ordinary amateur. The next contains the wisdom of the serpent and the simplicity of the dove, and has the attractive title of 'A Plea for a Simpler Life,' by George S. Keith, a well-known Edinburgh doctor. This little book is short, clear, and wise.

'Food and Feeding,' by Sir Henry Thompson. This is a much-to-be-commended and really instructive book. It goes into first principles, both of health and of the chemical properties of food, and would be far more useful to take to wild places or distant lands than any ordinary cookery book. The commonplace of living is taken up and handled for our benefit by a man of great talent and learning. Everybody who has not got it, ought to buy it—and study it, too.

The next is what, I suppose, would be called a quack-book, and its name is ' Power through Repose,' by Annie Payson Call. It is an admirable, healthy, and useful little book particularly suited to the straining, and striving, and overworking of the age. It will be found most helpful to the sleepless and the nervous, if they· will study it and give attention to its directions.

Last, but by no means least in its great utility, comes ' A Handbook of Nursing for the Home and the Hospital,' by Catherine Jane Wood. Miss Wood was for years lady-superintendent of the Great Ormond Street Hospital for Children, so she speaks with great authority. Though it has reached the eleventh edition, it is astonishing how many people have never heard of this first-rate little handbook. It is condensed and yet detailed, it is medical and yet simple and intelligible to a degree which brings it within the comprehension of anyone. In fact, I believe it to be the best book on nursing ever written.

This little poem of Mr. Lionel Tennyson's has, I believe, never been published ; a friend gave it to me some years ago. I think it will appeal to many people as it does to me :—

SYMPATHY.

In this sad world, where mortals must
    Be almost strangers,
Should we not turn to those we trust
    To save us from our dangers ?
Then whisper in my ear again,
    And this believe—
That aught which gives thy dear heart pain
    Makes my heart grieve.

God wills that we have sorrow here,
    And we will share it ;
Whisper thy sorrow in my ear,
    That I may also bear it.
If anywhere our trouble seems
    To find an end,
'Tis in the fairyland of dreams
    Or with a friend.

AMATEUR ARTISTS

DRAWING and gardening are so intimately connected, and
being able to draw is such a preparation to the study of
gardening, that I have thought it worth while to bring
in here part of an article I wrote last year (1896) in the
' National Review.' In it I tried to set down some
observations on the subject of amateur art, having myself had a life-long experience of it, of its great joys and
its many heart-burning disappointments and difficulties.
The increased taste for art and many other causes have
tended during the last twenty years to diminish the
number of those who draw for pleasure alone ; whereas
public opinion and family pride, which once thought
starvation and beggary more honourable than work, now
no longer prevent our sons and daughters from earning
their bread as professional artists, musicians, or actors.
But it is not to these that I wish to allude. They have
found their vocation ; their course is clear. I am speaking of the amateur proper, common enough a generation
ago. Nine-tenths of the amateurs are women, and it is
upon amateur art as an occupation for women that I
wish to insist. I am more and more convinced of the
importance to a girl of having an interest in life over
and above her affections and the trifling domestic duties
that may come in her way. If not, the time will come
when, either as a young married woman whose husband's

duties keep him absent during most of the day, or as one whom accident or choice has withheld from marriage, she will feel that *désœuvrement* which drives so many women into frivolity and folly, and sinks many more into ill-health and fretful misery.

Tennyson bade Lady Clara Vere de Vere employ, in what is now called philanthropy, the hours which might drag wearily with her if she desisted from playing with hearts. He recognised the fact that women who—through no fault of their own, be it remembered—are born to no very distinct duties, must have some occupation to fill their minds and lives, or they will infallibly take to some form of mischief. No doubt it is a gain that so much should now be almost universally acknowledged. The question of finding wise and fruitful work for the many women, married or single, who have time and heart and brain insufficiently occupied, still remains, whether we like it or not, one of the burning questions of the day. But the experience of the last twenty years has shown—I think, beyond dispute—that the late Laureate's solution of the difficulty is not a satisfactory one. Far be it from me to cast discredit on the noble work which has been done, and is still being done, among the poor of London and other great cities ; but in the opinion of all who have thought on the subject, and, still more, of those who have had practical experience of it, there is no channel from which the activity of amateurs should be more carefully diverted. The long apprenticeship, the severe application, the entire self-devotion, to the exclusion of other occupations, which distinguish the professional from the amateur, should be required before people are allowed to deal with burning social questions, to tamper with the lives of others, to risk pauperising individuals by indiscriminate charity, or, as is continually the case with visiting in hospitals, to stir up unintentionally class hatred by injudicious interference. It is a growing opinion that almost all such work requires, not zeal and intelligence alone, but the whole time and individual energies of those who devote themselves to it. Not all who can give these are endowed by Nature and education with the qualities which render them capable of being useful in that line.

Five-and-twenty or thirty years ago, serious education for women of the leisured class was hardly thought of. The teaching of domestic economy, as well as all real mental training, was neglected in favour of superficial accomplishments. It was then far more common to meet with the young lady whose æsthetic impulses found vent in flower-painting and landscape art than it is in the present day. Mr. Ruskin's teaching, the constant reading of art criticism—above all, the more thorough grounding now insisted upon in every branch of education—has opened girls' minds and increased their diffidence. They have a far more widespread and intelligent interest in art, but the actual number of amateur workers has greatly diminished. These influences, by educating the taste and increasing the knowledge of a large section of the public, have combined to deter those who in former days would have been only too ready to dabble in watercolours. They are now withheld by an exaggerated sense of the difficulties of the undertaking, or by a consciousness that they lack time or opportunity to learn to any purpose. Unfortunately this diffidence principally affects the more sensitive and poetical of the young people. For the sake of these, and just because encouragement is needed, I wish to point some of the reasons why their courage should not fail. It seems to me that there is much profit and enjoyment to be derived from an occupation which brings into the home none of the irritation so often produced by the piano or violin. Music, no doubt, not merely in cases of real talent, but also when only ordinary proficiency is attained, is the most sociable of hobbies. It brings other musical people to the house, and gives far more pleasure to those among non-performers who like it, if more annoyance to those who do not, than drawing. Many natures, however, have the temperament of genius without its creative power, and I doubt very much whether music gives the same vent and the same satisfaction to these which even a slight taste for drawing affords when cultivated. There is a rare delight in the exercise of creative power, however limited ; and this pleasure is given by drawing, even at its most elementary stage. What was a piece of white paper has something on it, and you have put it there. It has also the great advantage that it can be practised at all times and in all places—when travelling, at the dull seaside lodging, in town, or at the empty or sad backwater times of life that everyone experiences. Its danger to each individual is the same as that of all other pleasures and occupations to which we give our hearts, it encourages selfish absorption. But everything has its reverse side ; and I am sure that, to the person with no ear for music and no taste for independent study in science or literature, drawing may prove a lasting delight, a source of peace and content, a stimulus to moral and intellectual growth. The occupation, to those who have learnt to love it, causes time to fly on the wings of pleasure ; it adds new interest and zest to life, opening the eyes to a whole world of beauty which has hitherto lain unknown or unnoticed. Balzac said : ' The genius of observation is almost the whole of human genius.' If this aphorism is not comprehensively true, it serves at least to prove how life is enriched, even for the stupid, by cultivating observation ; and yet how many go through life without it ! As one branch of ' the genius of observation,' the artistic pursuit educates the taste in the highest sense of that much-abused word. It increases immensely the appreciation of works of art, both ancient and modern. It often leads to a reasoned study of the history of art, its interesting evolution, and its biographical and critical literature. Besides these, to come to more homely matters and the most feminine side of a woman's life—namely, the management of her dress and the decoration of her house—the knowledge of colour and the study of form will make both these more beautiful and less commonplace. They will also give her assurance to free herself from the often tasteless tyrannies of the dressmaker and the upholsterer.

Granting the wish, how is an ambitious girl to set about learning to draw? She may do a great deal by herself; but in the initial stage, help is very desirable—not in childhood, but after seventeen. Much waste of time and energy is prevented by a few timely lessons, even though solitary effort with the aid of books, especially such a book as Ruskin's ' Elements of Drawing,' might in the end conquer the difficulties. The old accusation against amateur work, of showiness and superficiality, was certainly well deserved in the days when the one idea was to send for a fashionable drawing-master, who taught his pupils to make feeble copies of his own drawings—which copies he most unfairly touched up, to make the results more satisfactory to parents or guardians. Of course, this system was deplorable; but those evils have disappeared to give place to their exact contraries in modern art teaching. The dryness of the grounding, the difficulties of getting through the earlier stages of an art school, often discourage the student who cannot give up all her time and energies to conquering these initial difficulties, which are made so great. The modern girl who works in a studio now spends months, even years, drawing rough charcoal studies of the nude. This, of course, is essential for a genius who is seriously going in for figure-painting. But to the ordinary amateur it brings about the desired results no more than the knowledge of the alphabet would give the mental development to be derived from literature. The upshot of all this serious study is that, as the girl's life gets fuller, her drawing can no longer be the accompaniment to her life, and she gives it up in despair.

It may be thought well that these half-hearted workers should be turned back at the outset. This would be right, if the drawing of amateurs were to be measured only by its results. But the least of its many advantages to them is the production of a mere drawing, especially as this is always so inferior to what they hoped to produce. The really important ends in view are the influence on character, the employment of time, and the attainment of innocent happiness, which are all of much greater importance than mere technical skill. I do not deny the usefulness of schools, nor the impetus they may have given to our national art. But their system has its faults, even as regards the training of professionals or of those amateurs whose great talent may carry them quickly through the drudgery these schools impose. It seems to me that there is room now for well-qualified teachers of water-colour sketching, without any revival of the old-fashioned and very superficial system of years gone by. A teacher should himself have been grounded in freehand, design, and perspective. He should be able to guide the pupil through these early stages into the happier plains of still-life or landscape painting from Nature more quickly and with less tedium than could be done in the school or the studio. I know that with patient work a girl may do all this alone. I do not want anything to be expected of the instruction I recommend beyond the smoothing of the path. It will avail nothing unless it teaches her to depend in the long run on herself, her own industry, and her own exertions. A certain amount of technical skill in the use of pencil and colours, certain rules of composition, the knowledge of how to stretch paper, prepare materials, and set about a drawing, may be imparted by a teacher. This saves all the time and vexation it would cost to learn these things alone. But though we may learn from another to some extent how to think, no one in the world can tell us what to think. The faculty and the will must be supplied by the learner. No teacher can instil them, though he may remove obstacles and help to quicken the growth of the powers within. Unless a girl have it in her to feel, in however small a degree, the beauty of the light summer cirrus which floats above her head, or to know how to look with joy into the glowing heart of a flower, no books and no teaching will ever give it to her. Without an inborn love of natural beauty, no one will ever care enough about drawing to persevere ; with it, no one can fail to make progress, however slight. Beginners should, I think, never destroy their drawings ; they should be kept, not in conceit, but as a proof of progress. Every drawing, however, should be made with a definite purpose, and it is best—as a rule—for each one to draw what she most fancies ; the result will then probably not only be more satisfactory, but more original. But to begin sketch after sketch and study after study, and then give them up or throw them away half finished, is a form of self-indulgence most fatal to progress. It debilitates the intelligence and weakens the moral fibre, which alone conquers difficulties.

On the other hand, it is not uncommon for unfortunately conscientious persons to fall into the contrary error. They may perseveringly linger over unattractive studies, merely because they offer certain difficulties, on the ascetic principle of hair shirts and peas in our shoes. To these I would say : ' If you were pursuing a country path and turned back at the first stile, instead of climbing over it, you would never reach your destination. If, on the other hand, you decided that because climbing a stile is a disagreeable and tedious process, therefore it must be good for us, and you promptly climbed back again, you would delay your progress to no purpose. There is a distinction between overcoming obstacles

which obstruct our onward and upward path, and idly
creating difficulties for the fancied glory of conquering
them.'

Progress depends on a general brain power, and is not
so surely proportioned to effort as the sanguine and the
clever are apt to believe. It is unfortunately quite possible for amateurs to spend a great deal of time over
their drawings, to take a real interest in the pursuit, and
yet to achieve but small, very small, results. Such
failure is sometimes due to circumstances and to preventable causes. The most common of them is the
constant interruption to which all home work, and
especially women's work, is liable. The curious selfishness in this matter of even the best of mothers often
immensely surprises me. It is hard indeed to convince
parents and relations that women have any right to the
undisturbed use of any portion of their time. I think a
great deal of that desire, so commonly displayed now, for
girls to leave their homes and undertake some work, has
been brought about by this want of realisation of the
necessity of quiet, if work is to be done. These inter-
ruptions, so often quite needless, not only cause an
immense loss of time, but are actually a great hindrance
to improvement in art. It is always difficult, often
almost impossible, to take up work again in the same
spirit in which it was laid down. The threads are
broken, and cannot be joined together again, to say
nothing of the intense annoyance of finding the subject
moved, the colour-box upset, or the water spilt. The
power of working, in spite of such drawbacks, can be
cultivated, especially if it is possible to set up a table
either in the pupil's own bed-room, or if some disused
room can be handed over to her, where no one touches
her things but herself.

As a compromise to the undesirableness of leaving
home altogether, these difficulties may very well be met,
if one or two amateurs club together and hire a suitable

room elsewhere outside their own homes. It might also be possible to get the loan of a room in the house of a young married woman who is the mistress of her own time, where all materials remain undisturbed, and where the surroundings are not annoying or distracting. Unpapered walls, simply whitewashed, a plain deal table or two, a few pieces of cheap pottery, are to be procured at the cost of a very few shillings, a bunch of leaves or a handful of Poppies or Marigolds giving the touch of colour which is dear to the soul of the most incipient artist. Besides the advantage to the work of quiet and seclusion, it is to many women both a rest and a stimulus to go out to their work daily, as men do.

Another point which I would beg may be remembered is that water-colours are far more suitable to amateurs than oils. The use of oils encourages all those defects of slovenliness and carelessness, speed and showy display, to which amateurs are liable. A bad sketch or study in oils is far more distressing than a bad sketch in water-colours. The materials of water-colours are more manageable and convenient for those who have neither much space nor much time at their command— that is to say, for the majority of amateurs. Moreover, water-colour painting is our national art, and it perhaps can never be fully understood or appreciated save by those who have some experience of its great technical difficulties.

DAUGHTERS

School-girls—Ignorance of parents—The confidence of children must be gained—The way to do it—Drawbacks of nurseries and school-rooms—Over-education—Show-training—Delicate girls—A woman's vocation—Superficial teaching—Children's tempers—Modern girls —Herbert Spencer and education—J. P. Richter—Liberty and independence—Serious studies—What young girls should read—Parents and children—Friendships—Girls' allowances—Dress—Professions—Strong feelings—Management of house and family—Early rising—Life in society.

MUCH that I have said with regard to boys applies to girls too, but I would only recommend sending girls to school in very peculiar and exceptional circumstances. I used to think that, for town girls, the high-schools afforded the best method of education. I now think that the pupils there are worked much too hard. What is really wanted for women is a mental training, the creation of a habit of mind, rather than technical knowledge of any kind. Remember, such experience as I have of girls is entirely limited to the leisured classes—those who, by an unwritten law, are virtually brought up to amuse themselves first, and to marry afterwards. I know nothing of the wants and requirements of those girls who are aware, from the beginning, that they will actually have to earn their bread and decide on a walk in life, as a boy does. One merit of school is that if the father and mother have neglected the health of their children, as is too frequently the case, from idleness, ignorance, or prejudice, abnormal bad health is probably revealed by the school-life ; and if a boy cannot do as others do, some one has to discover the reason why. Hundreds of mothers will own how much healthier, for some cause or another, their boys are at school than they were at home. This limelight of criticism—which, I think, is thrown on the facts of the case at school—is, alas! never turned upon the unfortunate schoolroom girl. She is inclined to think that others suffer as much as she does ; or, at any rate, she would far rather endure almost anything in silence than make complaints which often cause the mother and the governess to accuse her of being fanciful, idle, or self-indulgent. It is a problem, never solved through a woman's life, when it is best to disregard her ailments or to attend to them.

One of the most startling things I know is the ignorance of parents as to what is going on in the lives and minds of their children. I am thankful to say that in all my long experience I have only known one or two really bad, indifferent, selfish mothers ; but even the kindest mothers, and those who devote most time and thought to the welfare of their children, are sometimes quite blind to the discomforts, the sorrows, and even the tragedies that are being endured in silence under their very eyes. I refer rather to the childhood of girls than of boys, for these last are almost always sent to school when quite young, and from that moment their independence and consequent outspokenness when at home are generally assured. But numbers of women have mentioned to me the troubles of their childhood, which never were suspected by their mothers, and which they themselves never dreamt of revealing till they were quite grown up, sometimes not till they were married and out of the home altogether. Every young mother says and thinks, ' This sort of thing shall never happen with my children ; ' but it does happen, again and again. The cause lies, not in the want of kindness, but in a want of intelligence—the intelligence to put one's self on the level of a child and to see its life from its point of view.

This faculty is so rarely displayed that it is safe to conclude it rarely exists. It is a gift of no mean order, for, however generous our intentions may be, it is an exceedingly difficult task to deal out justice. I do not deny that there is a tendency in most people to exaggerate the troubles of their childhood, which must be taken into account ; but how many a mother thinks that her darlings are all right, and so bright and happy, with every reason to be so, when, in fact, they are eating their little hearts out in misery and sorrow ! The capability for suffering in some children is quite extraordinary, and trivial things assume colossal proportions in their small lives.

When girls are brought up under teachers and governesses, as is generally the case in the houses of the wealthy, the difficulty is increased. To complain of these authorities to the still higher but more distant authority of a parent is a very doubtful means of redress, and, in case of failure, the risk of punishment or of an aggravation of the evil—real or imagined—which gave rise to the complaint, is too terrible to be faced. Almost all girls, under such circumstances, are afraid to speak the truth. In my own case I was not afraid of my mother, but this made the keeping of governesses very difficult. I had eight of them before I was fifteen, and I disliked all but one. I expect, though doubtless I was a ' horrid child,' that, as regards the governesses, I was pretty clear-judging. Of course, the governesses of to-day have a very different idea of their duties from what was usual fifty years ago. Special training is given to those who undertake to teach the young, and this is now recognised as an art in itself, independently of having knowledge and information to impart. Such a change has greatly helped to raise the vocation of a governess to a far more competent standard.

How to gain the confidence of children—that is the eternal problem. Broadly speaking, I believe no one ever helps human nature, except by assuming it to be higher and nobler than it is. It is humiliating to be deceived, but it is better to be so a thousand times than once to underrate a good quality or a good impulse, or to give up hope and trust. It is difficult to see and to be with our children enough, and the difficulty is not served even by the mother teaching the children their lessons herself. Anybody, I am inclined to believe, does this better than she can. No morning occupation or afternoon class together does away with the necessity for devoting to the children the all-important interval between five o'clock and bed-time, which it is hard for some mothers to give to them. In my opinion a wise mother should give up her friends rather than her children at that hour. If the father can be at home then, too, so much the better. At that time children are a little tired and want amusing. I think this is far better done by talking to them, and by playing the piano and singing to them, or by teaching them how to play by themselves some kind of semi-active game, than by obliging them to employ themselves quietly, or by reading to them. If they attend and listen, it is too tiring for them : and if they do not, it is a thorough waste of time. A great many children, if encouraged to speak openly, will tell you that they do not care about being read to, unless it is some child's story which they almost know by heart, and which is read to them over and over again, as the nurses do. Of course, I am now only speaking of children under eleven or twelve years old.

A great drawback, not only to the children but to the parents, in what is called upper-class life, is that the duties of that life necessitate the consigning of their children for a great part of the day to the care of others. If there were no nurseries and no schoolrooms, there would be no necessity for a ' children's hour ' at all, for the children would share life with their mother from the first, and she would derive her pleasure from taking care of them. A serious difficulty for the mother is that she has to compete with the devotion and constant attention of the nurses and governesses. It is this which often gives children the idea that it is only when with their mother that they are dull, neglected, and expected to occupy and amuse themselves ; and this is certainly an undesirable impression to produce at an age when impressions are strong and likely to be lasting. Every case must be judged individually, and a woman must put to herself how far it is necessary that she should separate her life from the life of her children. As a matter of fact, it ought to depend on what is her husband's social position, or on what is his idea of her duties to him. In the cases where it is most difficult for a woman to see much of her children—let us say, in the large houses of the rich in town or country—it is better that children and governess should be turned into the hosts, and that the parents and guests should go to them for tea, rather than the usual arrangement of the children being brought into the drawing-room.

In speaking to young mothers who are inclined to be over-anxious, and who begin worrying themselves over details of their children's education, I always try and remind them that no education really affects the character very much before about twelve years old, so long as attention is paid in every way to their health and to the kind of nurses who are about them. As one gets old, one remembers the numbers of children that were brought up in totally different ways ; and yet, roughly speaking, in spite of either spoiling or neglect, over- or under-educating, how few belonging to the same class are really much better or much worse than their fellows—in fact, what an ordinary level they attain ! What marked differences do exist are due much more to individuality of character than to the various trainings they have undergone. Even the most earnest mothers have sometimes to own that the children of parents who took no

pains at all turn out quite as well as their own.   I refer,
of course, to what is called intellectual education, and
not to the physical.   I once more come back to saying
that neglect of health and over-stimulating of the brain
before the age, say, of fifteen in excitable, clever children
are the only two things that really might work for evil
on the future.   No true opinion about the character of
a child can be arrived at till the age of sixteen or seventeen, though guesses more or less correct may be made
much earlier.   The education of children depends so
immensely on the gradual growth and development of
the mother herself, and on the influences through which
she passes.   Those mothers most admired in their devotion to their babies have generally turned out, according
to my observation, the least satisfactory, and the least
able to control and guide their children in later life.
This is due, of course, to temperament and to the woman
being one who is satisfied with the nursery, who never
looks forward, who ceases to cultivate herself after marriage, and who, above all, does not keep pace with the
generation which lies between herself and her children,
this generation being the only one that will interpret
her children to herself when they are grown up.   A
mother should be on her guard about changing her
methods because some one else's children seem more or
better instructed or prettier-mannered than her own.
To be actively influenced as regards your children by
the comments of others is, I think, a mistake.   Take all
the advice you can get all round, but never act upon it
till you have thoroughly digested it and seriously considered whether it agrees with your general plan or not.
Nothing is so easy as to train children like monkeys or
dancing dogs ; nothing so difficult as to make that sort
of show-training of the smallest use in the far more
important factor of character development.   Children
who are brought up naturally must often be naughty
and disagreeable in family meetings, which mortifies the

mother, but is only an experience gained to the child. What hurts us is not so much that those we love should say what they think, as that they think what they say.

I remember a boy who was once foolishly talked to by his mother for not being so clever or so industrious as the little A.'s, some neighbour's children. The boy instantly answered, ' But, mother, are you and father the least like Mr. and Mrs. A. ? ' There is a good deal in the answer; the first essential is to be ourselves, our best selves certainly, but no imitation of others, and never wishing to be so as regards our children. Even when we strive to be original, we often only end in being affected. Mr. Ruskin says : ' That virtue of originality that men strive after is not newness, as they vainly think (there is nothing new) ; it is only genuineness.' Every form of training has its merits and its defects, both in the present and the future.

On looking back myself, I can honestly say that what was least usual, least conventional, and most criticised by others is what I regret the least in the education of my own sons.

To continue what I have to say about little girls ; the moment they are what doctors call delicate—that is to say, have any constitutional or hereditary weakness—still more, if there is any organic disease—no sacrifice on the part of parents is, to my mind, too great, and no neglect of education is to be thought of compared to improving the child's state of health. Nothing is so likely to do that as high country air or sea air for a great part of the year. Girls may grow up healthy and strong, though they live in London nearly all the year round, but it is undoubtedly a risk which should never slip out of the mother's mind, especially if the remaining in London is associated with any selfish purposes of her own, either as regards pleasure or expense. In France the teaching of Rousseau still unconsciously influences society, and fashionable doctors insist on delicate children being sent right away into the country, to lead almost peasants' lives. This plan I never can feel is kind or even wise, though it ensures the advantages of no excitement, country air, and liberty to run in and out—so necessary an element in child-life. But it rather resembles turning thin-skinned stable-horses, with their tails cut, into a green field full of sunshine and flies. Delicately born and nurtured children must suffer from the rough life.

In England, on the contrary, I think we often sacrifice our girls' good to the selfish pleasure of keeping them with us, making the girls' education the excuse. Broadly speaking, it is far better for a woman to be strong, healthy, intelligent, observant, and, above all, adaptable to the changes and chances of this mortal life, than that she should be well educated, Intelligence is no doubt inborn, a gift that belongs to no class ; bad health may injure it, but no higher education will ever give it to those who are without it, nor will it ever make what I consider the ideal woman.

The longer I live, the more I believe that a woman's education, if she has not to learn some special trade, should be awakening and yet superficial, teaching her to stand alone and yet not destroying her adaptability for a woman's highest vocation, if she can get it—which is, of course, marriage and motherhood.

The word superficial, its dictionary synonym being shallow, is one that will, I fear, be a rock of offence to many ; and yet I know none better. Mr. Morley, in his lecture on Popular Culture, expresses what I mean when he says : ' What I should like to see would be an attempt to compress the whole history of England into a dozen or fifteen lectures—lectures, of course, accompanied by catechetical instruction. I am not so extravagant as to dream that a short general course of this kind would be enough to go over so many of the details as it is desirable for men to know ; but details in popular instruction, though not in the study of the writer or the University professor, are only important after you have imparted the largest general truths. It is the general truths that stir a life-like curiosity as to the particulars which they are the means of lighting up.' That is what I mean by superficial teaching, something which gives a desire in the child or the girl to learn. Instead of boring her to death with what teachers consider the roots and foundations of knowledge, and which no child can understand or appreciate, I would strive to arouse curiosity, and trust that she would go deeper herself when the desire for knowledge came.

Mr. Morley goes on to say : ' Another point is worth thinking of, besides the reduction of history for your purposes to a comprehensive body of rightly grouped generalities. Dr. Arnold says somewhere that he wishes the public might have a history of our present state of society traced backwards. It is the present that really interests us ; it is the present that we seek to understand and to explain. I do not in the least want to know what happened in the past, except as it enables me to see my way more clearly through what is happening to-day. I want to know what men thought and did in the thirteenth century, not out of any dilettante or idle antiquarian's curiosity, but because the thirteenth century is at the root of what men think and do in the nineteenth. Well, then, it cannot be a bad educational rule to start from what is most interesting, and to work from that outwards and backwards.'

I mourned a good deal in my own youth over the fact that I had been very badly educated, and this certainly stimulated me, at a period when time was wanting, to do what I could for myself. But on looking back over the last thirty-five years—and speaking again, of course, only from my own very limited experience—I should say that all the women who have done best in life among my married kinsfolk and acquaintances were those who were most superficially and casually educated. Two women are known to me who have filled the highest positions admirably, who have been crowns of glory to their husbands, and have been universally recognised as women of the noblest type by all who have come in contact with them in many parts of the world. As children they were by no means exceptionally clever, and their regular governess education ceased at the extremely early age of twelve. They were left, with occasional masters, to learn what they could and improve themselves ; but they had from their earliest years the great advantage of constantly moving about. Sometimes town, sometimes country, and often abroad, they were never in one place for six months at a time. Many parents are so afraid of making these breaks in the continuity of their girls' education, and—as is only human—the governesses and teachers are always against it. One of the disadvantages of classes and competitive education is that ambitious children themselves often object to their studies being broken into. But all the experience of moving about, the little hardships and privations that come even in our modern luxurious travelling, are an immense advantage and training to children,—revealing their individual characters to their mother as no home life ever can. The impressions gained through the eyes and ears are incomparably more lasting and real than any information learnt from books.

Bad temper in children is a thing that, in my opinion, ought always to be treated with the utmost kindness, gentleness, tenderness, and consideration. It is generally a matter of health and nerves, and often may be, in some mysterious way, inherited from the mother's irritability during her pregnancy, which is caused very frequently by a feeling of dislike at having a child at all. Surely, then, this demands our utmost tenderness. I think that, in a family, the children with good and even tempers ought to be talked to in a way to make them understand that, if they tease and annoy the child with the hot temper, they are quite as much to blame as the irritable ones themselves. The even-tempered child generally means the indifferent one, and this in itself is an irritation to one who is excitable and highly strung. Thwarting and contradicting only do harm ; love, tenderness, gentleness, and great attention to health may do good. In short, the true situation is revealed to us by the old Persian philosopher's prayer :—' O God ! be merciful to the wicked. To the good Thou hast already been sufficiently merciful in making them good.'

In my youth, and still more before my time, girls were brought up to think that marriage was their one and only chance in life, and that, if they did not marry quite young, they would never marry at all. Now they know much more about the difficulties and dangers of life, and pride themselves on not thinking about marriage. This seems to me a mistake ; they ought to think of it very seriously and from every point of view, so that they should be able and ready to seize on the practical solution when the difficulty arises. Marriage should not be a woman's only profession, but it should be her best and highest hope. Every girl should try and make herself worthy of it both in body and mind, and this attitude will not make a girl grow into a less sensible old maid if she has to be one. Galiani asked Madame d'Epinay, the writer of the famous ' Mémoires ' in the last century, and the friend of Rousseau, what were her views of woman's education. This is her reply :—
' Vous voulez savoir de moi ce qu'une femme doit étudier ? Sa langue, afin qu'elle puisse parler et écrire correctement. La poésie, si elle y a du penchant ; en tout elle doit cultiver toujours son imagination, car le vrai mérite des femmes et de leur société, consiste en ce qu'elles sont moins factices, moins gâtées, moins éloignées de la nature et par cela plus aimables ; en fait de morale elles doivent étudier beaucoup les hommes et jamais les femmes,

elles doivent connaître et étudier tous les ridicules des hommes et jamais ceux des femmes.'

In the days long ago, when my children were children, and as is apt to be the case when one is surrounded with a small growing-up family, half the population of the world seemed to me to be children, my thoughts were so centred on the subject that nothing else appeared to me of any great importance. At that time two books gave me much comfort, support, and instruction. One was ' Education : Intellectual, Moral, and Physical,' by Herbert Spencer. This book, now so much read and so widely known, requires no recommendation from any-one, but I do wish to say that every father and mother should read it—not once, but again and again. Some will disagree with one part and some with another, but I defy anybody to read it without a certain clearing of the head and opening of the mind, most essential to those who have the heavy responsibility of training the young. If there is one thing above all others that repeats its faults *ad nauseam* and is blindly conservative, it is the management of children in the nursery and schoolroom. Mr. Herbert Spencer's book has fortunately now reached a very cheap edition. It is a book created by the hand of genius, and not the result of personal experience. I humbly bow to it in grateful thanks for all the good I derived from its perusal.

The second book is called ' Levana, or The Doctrine of Education,' by Jean Paul Frederick Richter, and is only accessible to me through the translation into English. It is a book full of thought and wisdom, and it speaks of prosaic things in a poetic manner ; and though the opening chapters apply to both sexes, it refers rather to the training of daughters than of sons, as being the first and most important business of a mother. I can strongly recommend its perusal ; at the same time a good deal of it is, of course, out of date. It is written by a German, and entirely from a man's point of view.

The book is full of love and tenderness, and may perhaps be thought very high-flown and old-fashioned in these days. This does not matter ; it speaks of the undying facts of Nature, which will last as long as the world does. I cannot resist copying here one passage, which I believe will come home tenderly to every mother who is about to give away in marriage a loved young daughter :—

'Certainly a wisely and purely educated maiden is so poetic a flower of the dull world, that the sight of this glorious blossom hanging, some years after the honeymoon, with yellow faded leaves in unwatered beds, must grieve any man who beholds it with a poet's eye ; and who must, consequently, in sorrow over the common usefulness and servitude of the merely human life, over the difference between the virgin and the matron, utter the deadliest wishes ; yes, I say, he would rather send the virgin with her wreath of rosebuds, her tenderness, her ignorance of the sufferings of life, her dream-pictures of a holy Eden, into the graveyard of earth, which is God's field, than into the waste places of life. Yet do it not, O poet ! The virgin becomes a mother, and gives birth to the youth and the Eden which have fled from her ; and to the mother herself they return, and fairer than before : and so let it be as it is.'

We have of late been going through a transition stage on the question of giving liberty and independence to young women. The most enlightened mothers, during the last twenty years, in their anxiety to be in touch with the times, have perhaps given their girls too great liberty when too young, and when the girls have grown older, from fear perhaps of what people might say, they have made the fatal mistake of trying to tighten the reins. Let parents and even young husbands realise that liberty once given can never be withdrawn from individuals, any more than from nations, without quarrels and trouble. The liberty of women within certain limits must grow, and society will adapt itself to it. The good and the bad will go on as they have always done, uninfluenced by the swing of the pendulum or the fiats of fashion. One generation shows the shoulder and hides the arm, the other covers up the shoulder and displays the arm. In my mother's youth it was thought fast to valse, in my youth it was thought fast to sit out with a partner after dancing, and now girls valse and sit out and ride bicycles, and none of these things make or unmake good women.

I should say seventeen or eighteen was quite young enough for a girl to begin serious study, if she is inclined that way. In childhood attend to the grace and beauty of her body, let her know her own language well, teach her music (to discover if she has a taste for it, that can be developed) and foreign languages, for they cannot be learnt later, and are of great use to women in many positions in life. If she shows any taste for drawing, encourage it in all ways, giving her time in which to do it, but no serious lessons till she is much older. The drudgery of early teaching often destroys any taste the child may have. Pay great attention to handwriting; a good and cultivated handwriting is quite easy to acquire young, and is a continual advantage to a woman through life.

Another thing that mothers should teach their children, and of which they should ever remind their young men and women as they grow older, is the extreme importance of prompt note-answering. The habit of writing notes and letters, which is now going somewhat out of fashion, is certainly of great assistance in helping us to obey the golden rule never to turn a friend into an enemy by mere carelessness or idleness, for want of a little trouble or of the explanation which, if neglected, often changes the whole character of the situation into one that is hard and difficult, and even in some cases irreparable.

Some years ago I sympathised much and took great interest in the movement that tended towards the higher education of women. I still think that every door should be thrown open and every facility given, both as regards education and professional employment, to such women who have mind and strength for the competition. The great danger of over-educating young girls is that they are so much keener and work so much harder than boys ; and even if it does not injure their health, it very often unfits them for life, and makes them dissatisfied with their home and its surroundings.

The great objection to the superficial education I recommend and believe to be so advantageous to the prosperous, is that it may degenerate into idleness and frivolity in times of prosperity, and so prove an utter failure in times of adversity, and in the possibility of having to earn a livelihood later in life. I think most sensible young women of the present day feel the necessity of attaining a proficiency in some one direction, to which they could turn for help in the hour of need. Very often, however, the occupation that might best be turned to bread-winning is not the one to which girls are most addicted in their prosperity. In such a case, when money-making is not the object, they must make their own standard, and reach, if possible, a high order of proficiency ; for to take up any one thing, and then to do it badly, has a deteriorating effect upon the moral nature. The superficial beginning which, according to my theory, is conducive to largeness of mind, is a good preparation to later special training. The only other alternative, which is the worst of all, is if girls fold their hands and say they are not clever, and that they can do nothing. With patience and perseverance every girl can do something. Once a woman has made up her mind that she has to earn her living, no concentration of study for the one particular occupation she has in view can be too thorough or too severe. The essential requirement for bread-winning is that she should be able to do some one thing better than the generality of people with whom she is in competition.

Now we come to the eternal and ever-discussed question, what young girls should read. I have no hesitation in saying that, taking the question all round, the safest, wisest, most sensible way out of the difficulty, is to let girls read from childhood anything they like. Never make a child come and ask, never forbid this book or that ; the moment you do, you get into a sea of hopeless difficulties. Where a girl is pure-minded, nothing will hurt her ; where she is not, the forbidding of one book and allowing another raises a curiosity which will do far more harm than leaving it alone. All that is harmful in the Bible or Shakespeare is simply not understood. Why should it not be the same with other books ? No one ever dreams of what they do not know. Dreams often distort and twist our knowledge ; no dream ever instructs us in anything of which we are ignorant.

Without forbidding any one book or other, it would be wise for a mother to recommend her daughter not to read the current novels of the day, at the time they are being continually discussed in public, if they are of a nature which unfits her to join in the conversation. It is not that there is harm in having read the book, but there are some things which it is impossible for a girl to talk about. In Richter's ' Levana,' which I mention elsewhere, there are some excellent passages on this very subject. In this permission to read or not to read books, as in all else that seriously concerns the education of children, the all-important thing is that the father and mother should agree. Nothing has so bad an effect on children, and they are quick to learn it, as that father thinks one thing and mother another. A wife had far better allow a fault to pass than try to stop that which she knows her husband would allow ; and a husband had far better back the mother when he thinks her wrong than condemn her before her children. There is an old saying that widows' children turn out well. I do not think this means that women are more fitted to manage a family alone than men are, but men very rarely give the subject their consideration. There is nothing, when men really try, that they do not do better than women— from the highest in art and literature, to the humblest cooking and tailoring. I think the old saw merely means that one will and one law are better than a divided judgment. If a woman has strong views on education, let her begin by educating and persuading her husband. If she cannot do this, let her simply try and carry out his wishes and views, whatever they are.

Not an unusual trouble of family life is that the energetic, and those who are happy through employing themselves, no matter in what way, are apt to be a sore trial to the idle and to those who want to be amused and excited. Many of us know the disappointment of rushing into a room, anxious to confide something of great or no importance to a sympathetic human being, and finding presented towards us what can only be described as a busy back, and the chilled feeling which results from the doubt whether or not we have any right to disturb it.

Sometimes the parents are idle and the children industrious, which is perhaps the most common. The children must then not exact an interest in their work, which they are not likely to get. Schopenhauer says : ' Whoever seriously takes up and pursues an object that does not lead to material advantages must not count on the sympathy of his contemporaries.'

When parents are the energetic, hard-working ones, let them remember a passage in a letter of Madame de Staël's, whose biography is so interesting because she represents in a large sense what most women are in a smaller. She writes from England in 1813 :—' Il n'y a point de ressources dans mes enfants ; ils sont éteints, singulier effet de ma flamme.' So often children by their very natures are only contrasts to ourselves. What our children are born, they remain ; of that I am sure. By this I mean that there are certain qualities of character which we can no more change than we can alter the colour of the hair and eyes. What we can do is to help each one to make the best of what he or she actually is, still better said by an old saint, ' Do not try to be not what you are, but very well what you are ! '

How many years ago it is since John Stuart Mill wrote : ' When will education consist, not in repressing any mental faculty or power, from the uncontrolled action of which danger is apprehended, but in training up to its proper strength the corrective and antagonistic power ? ' This is only very old wisdom in other words, as it is Aristotle who says that true virtue is placed at an equal distance between the opposite vices.

This quoting the wisdom of others you perhaps will think very cheap philosophy. It is better, however, than trying, like Sydney Smith, to write a book of maxims, and failing to do so, as he himself says he never got further than the following : ' Towards the age of forty, women get tired of being virtuous and men of being honest.' I must, all the same, admit that there are many less true sayings than this one.

A tendency of the present day is towards a kind of hardness—at any rate, outwardly. It is not the fashion to be low-spirited, and for a woman to cry in public is thought a shame. I confess I think there is a certain danger in the cultivation of qualities in women that bring forth a sort of glittering brightness which gives out light, not heat, and therefore fails to warm. Perhaps this suppression is the very thing that helps to encourage one of the well-known complications of family life— namely, friendships. The difficulty follows us through life, as we all know how hard it often is to appreciate our friends' friends. This, however, is not of much importance, as the friends of our friends we can more or less avoid without discourtesy. But with the friends of our near relations the matter assumes considerable importance, and we absolutely owe it to them to treat their friends with extreme courtesy and kindness, however little may be our sympathy towards them, or however critically we may judge them.

Some people are born without what Mr. George Meredith so well describes as 'the gift of intimacy.' They would be reserved, even in love, the only key that ever unlocks such hearts. Friendships they have none, either with their own sex or with the other. No doubt life is simpler to such people ; to others it would be unbearably lonely. There are a few women who would have been very glad of friends, but whose loyalty to the disloyal around them forces them into loneliness and silence, for there is no friendship in the world without confidence.

Friendships are safety-valves, and the wisdom of safety-valves is easy to appreciate. All the same, these intimacies must be regulated and conducted upon the rules of civilised society. I love the young who wish to fight conventionalities and turn and boldly face Mrs. Grundy ; but I despise the old who do not help the young to see that they are only making useless martyrs of themselves in a cause which is, at the bottom, not noble and not great, but only a method of giving vent to their own selfishness and self-indulgence. Before you fight conventionality you must prove that conventionality is wrong, and this can never be done by the young. To deny friendships to natures that require them is to force on them what Mr. Morley calls ' the awful loneliness of life—a life full of acquaintances as a cake is full of currants, no two ever touching each other.' It is one of the great sorrow, of a high position that people cannot have intimates. Froude says somewhere : ' The great are expected to be universally gracious, and universal graciousness is perhaps only possible to the insincere or the commonplace, or to the supremely great and fortunate.'

We cannot give anyone our experience. This is a

common saying, and quite true from the point of view of the old. Nevertheless, if the young determine, through independence or pride, to work out their lives for themselves, and refuse to be helped, guided, or taught by the knowledge and experience of those who have gone before them—in the books of the dead and the speaking of the living—they throw themselves back in the race in a way that generally, to my knowledge, has resulted in failure. Even cases of marked talent and individuality must learn from others. In art and in music they must all work, at first, after the manner of someone else. Supposing, for instance, that Albert Dürer had lived in Venice, he would have been a Venetian painter, and not have worked on the lines of the old German painters. This would have been greatly to his advantage. It is true that circumstances do not make talent, but they immensely influence it; so nothing in the lives and training of the young who are no longer children, especially if they are precocious and clever, is unimportant.

On looking back, one of the disappointments of my life, when I recollect how the matter was discussed and written about in my girlhood, is the little progress that has been made in the laying-by and organising of fortunes for girls. I do not only mean leaving them a few thousand pounds at the death of both parents, but, as a matter of course, either giving them a sum of money, as the French do, when they marry, or giving them a sufficient allowance, according to the fortunes of the father, if they take to any employment and do not marry. The modern hack phrase, that children owe their parents nothing for bringing them into the world without their leave, is of course ridiculous; but I do think a right-minded father ought to realise that a woman who has not a penny she can call her own, is a kind of slave. The same thing applies to a husband if a wife goes to him with nothing. She cannot even give a present without asking him for the money. I think girls would be much happier if at twenty-one they were given allowances sufficient, not only for dress—which should begin, as with boys, much earlier—but to cover all expenses, except board and lodging : namely, journeys, theatres, doctors, dentists, amusements, masters, and so on. One girl would spend her allowance in one way and one in another, but she would get as much profit or pleasure to her individual self out of it as she could afford. If she were well, she would not want doctors and dentists ; if she were ill, she would not want amusements : and in either case she would be learning the value of money. We all know the discussions that go on in every family. In one case the mother wishes her daughter to have singing and piano lessons, though the daughter is indifferent ; the master is hired, and the money and time are more or less wasted. In another case the daughter is pining for drawing lessons, and the mother looks upon it as rather a waste of money. Both these cases would be adjusted if the deciding of their own education and the paying of the lessons rested with the grown-up daughters. This ought not to prevent mothers and daughters from discussing together what is the most desirable course to adopt ; it merely leaves the ultimate decision with the learner. In fact, I would extend these family discussions to all the important matters of life, and even call in some reliable friend or relation, whose opinion is valued by all parties, to help in the decision, on the lines of that powerful legal arrangement which, in French family life, is called *conseil de famille*. We get so many useful hints on family life by the reading of biographies that, to my mind, it is the most interesting of all literature for the middle-aged. In Darwin's ' Life ' I was immensely struck by an uncle interfering to overrule the decision of the good kind father, who had refused the offer that young Darwin should go for the scientific voyage on the ' Beagle.' The father instantly yielded to the opinion of his brother, and this perhaps decided the whole of Darwin's life.

When I say that it is wise to gather as many opinions as we can, it must always be with the idea of helping our own judgment, never as putting the responsibility on to others of any important decision, which ought to rest entirely with ourselves, and which, as in the case of Darwin's father, we may entirely alter ; but when we change, we equally accept the responsibility of any important decision quite independently of the adviser.

It stands to reason that when parents give their children money to spend according to their own wishes and tastes, they are acting a great deal more unselfishly than when they spend on their children, however lavishly, only to make them do what the parents consider desirable. This giving freedom to children means a good deal more self-sacrifice on the part of the parents, and, as the unselfishness of one person is very apt to produce the selfishness of another, it is a question for each parent to decide whether the sacrifice had better come from the old or from the young. It is an undeniable fact that the tastes of children are likely to be the reverse, rather than a repetition, of the tastes of their parents. In weighing these questions, however, you must always cast into the scale the importance of a true knowledge of the value of money, which nothing but practical experience can give.

Few things bring such ruin, in every sense of the word, to the happiness of married life as the extravagant wife—the wife who runs up bills, and who amidst tears and penitence and promises not to do the same again, immediately does so. Can anything as much as this, short of actual immorality, bring a respectable woman so nearly to the level of the unrespectable ?

Strong advocate as I am for marriage, I do agree with Miss Frances Power Cobbe, ' That for a woman to fail to make and keep a happy home is to be a greater failure, in a true sense, than to have failed to catch a husband.' I have noted somewhere the following sentence, and I think it as true as it is lofty in tone : ' There is only one real power in this world for man or woman, the power given by character. It carries far more weight than talent does without it. The woman who cultivates unswerving rectitude, firm energy, and persevering goodness, will become a centre and a factor in the lives of others, wherever her lot is cast. All round us we see such women forced by outside pressure into positions of comparative, if not positive, prominence, and they have no need to whine over the unalterable fact of sex.'

The better a girl or a woman is treated by a father or a husband in the matter of money, the more heavily does the duty remain with her to remember that, after all, the money is only conditionally hers, and that no woman has a right to eat a man's food, dress with his money, enjoy his luxuries to the full, and then not in every way try to please him ; and certainly she should never do systematically that which he distinctly disapproves. If she cannot persuade him, she must submit and do his will. No woman is really free who cannot keep herself ; and even if she earns her own livelihood, she has to submit to her employers.

One can hardly write a ' note ' on girls and avoid the great subject of dress. Certainly let the young dress in the fashion, in order to be attractive ; for there is no doubt that, even if the fashion is ugly, to be dressed in the fashion looks smart. When I was young I was scolded for trying always to get the last new pattern from Paris. I used appealingly to remark, ' I can't be graceful, let me be smart.' There are always certain women who can dress artistically and peculiarly, and who look well in whatever they put on ; but these are the exception, and their imitators—as is usual with imitators—are apt to adopt their faults rather than their merits. Exceptional dress, independently of the wearer, is rarely, I think, attractive. Women who have dropped out of the fashion themselves are apt to be a little tried, when their daughters grow up, by the dress of the day, and to think it rather exaggerated and ridiculous, just as the daughter would feel her mother's wedding-gown to be impossible and out-of-date. A mother can only give her daughter general training, and then leave her to dress as she likes, merely offering her the kindly criticism that would be given her by a friend or a sister ; for every woman looks best in that which she herself has chosen, and which is an indication of her own individuality. By this I do not deny that many a mother would dress her daughter much better than the girl would dress herself ; but the note of character would be wanting, which, in my opinion, makes dress in the long run the most becoming.

Even when they are children, little girls often surprise their parents by saying something unexpectedly different from what they have been taught. I know a father who, when walking with his small daughter in the streets of London, stopped before the window of a smart milliner's shop. When they had looked and admired for a little time, the father, perhaps rather priggishly, remarked : " After all, my dear, I like simplicity best.' The child answered : ' That's not at all like me, father ; I like splendour best.'

Deny it as we will, the real object of dress is to attract ; and for a woman to dress herself in crimson and purple, when she knows quite well that her husband or father prefers quiet colours, or even black, shows a neglect of the amenities of life that is stupid, if it is nothing worse.

From a higher point of view, there is nothing so important in dress as the accentuation of what are our physical characteristics. A fat girl in tight tailor-made clothes looks ridiculous. A girl with a tall slight figure, like a boy, looks well tight and neat, ready for the active

exercise she is fit for. The womanly woman looks best
in soft laces and ruffles and chiffons, be she fat or
thin.

Let middle-aged and old women, except when they
are widows, dress in the fashion slightly modified. They
are then neither conspicuous nor ridiculous. Is there
not wisdom in dressing rather in advance of your years
than behind it ? Many a dress lasts three or four years ;
so we ought, at turning-points in our lives, to remember
that this makes a difference. It has been said that the
lamp of life is not to be measured by the age of the vessel,
but by the supply of the light. Prettily expressed, I
admit, and there is something in it, but it is only a half-
truth, and the Baptismal Register is the best guide for us
personally. Nothing displeases the young so much as
to see the generation before them dressed too youthfully,
and nothing so accentuates the years that have passed
over a woman as the outward display of her having forgotten them herself. I remember once remarking to a
friend how well a tall slight woman dressed, and how it
suited and improved her. ' Yes,' said he, ' a thin, tall
woman is a peg for clothes ; but there is all the difference in the world, as the Frenchman said, between
une belle taille and *un beau corps.*' So there are consolations in all things, and many of the great passions
of the world have been for plain women—perhaps because they themselves are so much more grateful for
the affection given. Beauty added to other things is a
great power ; let no one despise it. It is often easier
for a beautiful woman to behave well than for her
plainer sisters. She has the ball at her feet, and she
knows it.

I have been asked whether an unmarried woman is
happier with a profession or without one. Without
hesitation of course I answer—' Yes, with a profession,'
especially if it is the outcome of any particular talent.
The real cause of the happiness which ensues is that it

gives her the same excuse and the same ease to her conscience for selfishness as a man has. It always works round to the same thing—how much can a woman evade her home duties in order to be able to indulge in any intellectual occupation which takes up her mind, to the detriment of the ordinary, petty drudgeries such as practically absorb most women's lives? The great difficulty for a woman who is head of a house, or even for a daughter who helps much in the management of a house, allowing herself the pleasure of any intellectual employment—be it writing, or art, or music, or even reading conducted as a study—is that the very meaning of work is absorption. Women are by their natures impressionable and too apt to become engrossed in anything they are doing, to the neglect of the claims of others. It is not exactly the time that it takes from the husband and children, but the thoughts of a woman are not quickly brought back to the level of her ceaseless duties. I heard once of the wife of an Ambassador, who was devoted to drawing, having arranged for a dinner for royalties, &c., planning the details with her servants in her usual careful way. The day arrived, she had time on her hands, the weather was lovely; she took her sketching things and went out. She became so absorbed in her drawing and the beauty of the evening that the royal guests, the husband, and the dinner became absolutely effaced from the tablet of her memory. She arrived home at half-past nine, to find her husband agonised, her guests expectant and a little angry, all believing she must have come to some injury. This little anecdote exactly illustrates what I mean, and describes the struggle that goes on, more or less, in many women's lives. Of course the same thing occurs, to a great degree, with busy men, whose brains are often as much occupied, to the exclusion of other things, in the work that interests them. But since, as a rule, they have more power of arranging their lives to suit their tastes, their absorption affects less the happiness or convenience of others, and they often have a practical wife who helps them out of their difficulties. No doubt there are instances of both men and women who have the power of combining, in the highest sense, both work and play. A pathetic little touch in a woman's biography is of how Mrs. Browning wrote ' Aurora Leigh ' as an invalid in Paris. She was constantly interrupted by friends and visitors, and used quietly to tuck the little bits of paper under the pillow of her sofa, to resume her imaginative work when again alone. The complications of life were lessened for her by the fact that she inhabited a sick-room. I think the women who will do most for the cause of their sex in the future are those who cease to fight for an equality with men, which is practically an impossibility, and will strive, from their youth up, to keep a just balance between duty, pleasure, and intellectual pursuits ; sometimes asking the help of others to decide when the two last must give way to the first. I am terribly tempted to scratch out this last sentence—it sounds so odiously priggish ; and yet, of course, we all know there is a good deal of truth in it.

If a woman has been ever so successful in a profession, it is my experience that she gives it up after marriage. Every man always says, at the time of engagement, that he would not for the world interfere with her work ; but it always ends in the work being given up, if the house is to be properly kept. Imagine, if there were sickness or any other kind of domestic disaster in the house, the man would never dream of giving up his work, whatever it might be. But think of a woman, head of any such household, sitting down under the circumstances to write a poem, or to paint a picture, or going out to her modelling studio ? The woman's profession must go to the wall, unless it is under the very exceptional circumstances when the woman is the bread-winner, or even partially so, and when disaster may increase the necessity for her earnings.

Perhaps many Englishwomen would deny what I really believe to be the truth—namely, that passion is the great moving power of life, the root of all that is highest and noblest in us, the developer of all that is artistic, intellectual, affectionate, and even religious in ourselves. Some people may accuse me of inconsistency in saying this. Of that I should be proud, for can anything ever approach the inconsistency of life—especially, perhaps, the life of women? Women—Englishwomen, at all events—imagine that there is but one danger in having strong feeling, and that, if that is sufficiently suppressed in the direction which is natural and ordinary, it ceases to cause any alarm at all. I do not agree with this. It is a platitude to talk of the dual nature which we all have within us. The contrast between these two natures is much more marked, and causes a fiercer struggle, in passionate natures than in cold ones.

Women as well as men have a twin within them, often concealed, which represents all that is strongest and most lovable in their natures. They generally have something which they like doing better than anything else in the world, and which for that reason is very apt to interfere with their duty, however innocent or even meritorious it may be in itself, whether it takes the form of writing, art, politics, philanthropy, or the practice of religion. If a married woman throws all this power, so often described as suppressed steam, into any employment that makes her daily duties tiresome and hateful to her, she is yielding to a form of self-indulgence which more or less feeds her vanity and robs her home and her children of that which is the most vivifying portion of herself and of the one most likely to call forth from them both admiration and esteem.

This to many will be a hard saying, as it means leaving the higher employment of women to those who are most free from natural duties ; that is, generally, to the unmarried, who for that very reason are in some ways the least understanding of our sex.

Mothers and fathers should never lose sight of the fact, as their daughters grow up, that confidence is only likely to begin when given first by parents to children, from the old to the young. Sympathy is not the consequence of confidences, but the magnet that attracts them ; so by confiding in our children, we may fail to get their sympathy, but we are always able to give them ours.

I think that mothers might remind their sons and daughters, especially when they are grown up, how very much the old like receiving the attention of the young, and seeing that the young have no fear of them ; for I do not doubt that, if young people really believed this, they would probably pay these attentions more often, with both advantage and interest to themselves. There is a great deal to be got out of the experience and memories of those much older than ourselves, if we can only make them realise how much we wish both to hear and to learn.

In the management of house and children, as in a larger rule, let us remember that liberalism is a frame of mind which has for its root the simple morality of doing unto others as you would they should do unto you.

It is a very doubtful question whether, in the houses of the fairly wealthy, the daughters can be of very much help to the mother, unless she herself finds that she has more than she likes to do, and apportions certain departments—such as housekeeping, card-leaving, writing notes, or gardening, &c.—to one or other of the daughters. The vague expectation in a mother that her daughter ought to help her, often results in a good deal of ordering about, a waste of time on the daughter's part, and that state of things generally which ends in friction. If a daughter is unusually unselfish, and constantly thinking how she can please and serve her mother, the result is that the daughter becomes a mere drudge, while the mother but half appreciates the sacrifice she has made of her life.

We often discover in families the ideal woman of family life. She is always willing to immolate herself on the altar of duty and unselfishness, unconscious of this at the time, because to serve others is her pleasure, and consequently for the moment the development of her own nature. That woman, especially if she has intelligence as well, fills a want in the world that everyone acknowledges and admires. But, unless the situation is carefully watched, she herself may discover too late that she has let her youth go by in the suppression of herself, and, without intending it, has ruined her own life. The one thing that is of vital importance is that the young should never be sacrificed to the old or the healthy to the unhealthy. Even if the mother and daughter work well together, there is hardly enough to occupy the time of two women, and divided rule never is satisfactory. It is a common view that housekeeping is rather an inferior employment for women, and only done well by the commonplace, who are devoted to it. I do not think this, though I quite admit that housekeeping is often very tiresome—or, rather, I would say wearisome —and every woman pines to get away from it now and then. Every head of a house—be she wife, mother, or daughter—has to do it, and no woman worth her salt likes to do a thing and do it badly. If it is badly done, it is a humiliation ; when it is well done, it becomes a pride : and the approval of those we love is always a joy. Men differ, of course, very much in their appreciation of cooking and other housekeeping matters. When the man cares, though he scold, or sigh and look miserable when things go wrong, it is more stimulating to the woman than when he appears indifferent ; but all men and most women appreciate a well-kept house, though I ave heard there are some women who make such grievance over their duties that the man almost wishes they were left alone.

One of the most useful gifts in life is to be able to organise, command, and instruct others ; to use, in fact, the materials under your hand, instead of doing everything yourself. Servants certainly do not respect those who do their work for them, and the irresponsibility of the situation only makes them careless and indifferent. On the other hand, it should be thoroughly realised that no one can depute to others the control of their expenditure without greatly increasing it.

In cooking, in dressmaking, in gardening, it is, so to speak, the scientific and æsthetic part which really ought to be done by the mistress of the house. She has time to study the books and newspapers ; and if she really knows her work she will find no difficulty in teaching it.

Every generation is known to complain that servants have become useless and bad. I see no difference during my life-time ; in fact, I should say that the proportion of good servants had increased, rather than the contrary. Of course, their customs and ways have changed with telegrams, posts, and railways, as have the habits of everybody else ; and if any housekeeper has moments of depression, as we all have when things go cross, and thinks the world is going to the dogs, may I recommend a little study of eighteenth-century literature—above all, Boswell's ' Life of Johnson.'

The spread of education is often brought forward as a reason for the deterioration of servants. I must put in a protest against this. I never will believe it ! On the contrary, Mill's definition of education will always remain true to me : ' The best employment of all the means which can be made use of for rendering the human mind, to the greatest possible degree, the cause of human happiness.'

It is essential, for the well-regulating of a house the orders to servants should be given early in the n, ing. Everything except flower-arranging ought to got through in an hour. When people complain tha housekeeping takes so long, it is either that they are ignorant and undecided, or that they are out of health, and come down very late in the morning, and things get out of order from being left to the servants for several days in the week.

I fear many young people will probably think me priggish and disagreeable if I say that, be a woman ever so delicate, it is far better for her to get up early and see to her work, even if she finds it necessary to take a rest at twelve or three. I am a great believer in early rising, partly because it implies a generally healthy life, and means that there are no large late dinners or late going to bed ; for it is impossible to burn the candle at both ends. I think most women would work best in the morning ; but I quite admit that, owing to the faults of family life, time is seldom entirely her own, except in the privacy of her room, either at night or in the very early morning.

Some years ago I was asked by a rich woman who had come to London with a view to entertaining, how I did it. She had come prepared to make a regular London list of unknown swells, and was rather surprised when I answered : ' I never send out formal invitations, and I never ask anyone who is not more or less a per-sonal friend of my own, or someone brought at the request of one of these friends, this last being a distinct element of success.' If two people are really happy in a room, it sheds a glow of brightness all around them. This, to my mind, applies to all private and unofficial entertaining which is done for pleasure—one's own and that of others—rather than duty. All entertaining, to be good, should be a collection of people who meet because they either really know each other or would like to do so. The moment people are brought together for any reason connected with duty, the party, unless it is very large, is sure to go badly and to be dull. The dinners we all dread are those where the host and hostess ask people to meet each other because they have duties of various kinds to pay off. The deadly dulness of all garden parties in the country is a marked example of the extraordinary flatness that results from turning society into a social duty, and having to ask a whole neighbourhood at once, which is in no sense true hospitality. Duty and charity are excellent things, but they cannot be turned into agreeable social gatherings.

I think it often surprises people, and especially men, that middle-aged women, even those who have no daughters, are so energetic and indefatigable in their efforts to go into society in a way they rather avoided than courted when they were younger. Society is always only too glad to shunt the middle-aged, and the middle-aged themselves so often feel it to be only a treadmill. I am sure the secret is to be found, consciously or unconsciously, in the love of power. It gives people the opportunities to help, not only their own children, if they have any, but other people in whom they may happen to be interested, who are often benefited by an opportune word in high places. This is what transforms the treadmill and the burden and the labour into something so worth while that it almost becomes a pleasure.

In entertaining at home, our object should be rather to help those who want help, and who may unexpectedly rise into positions of power and trust, than always to be making up to those who are already in high places, and who are full of suspicion with regard to the civilities that are paid to them. To practise the wisdom of life, without standing on the stilts of higher morality, is rather a virtue than a vice in the middle-aged. It is as old as Æsop, who bids us not to despise making up to the mice ; for though you yourself may be very much a lion, the day may come when you will need the services of a mouse. We all know La Fontaine's summing-up of the old story :—' Il faut, autant qu'on peut, obliger tout le monde. On a souvent besoin d'un plus petit que soi.'

One of the unexpected consolations to a woman who is leaving her youth behind her, is that she can take broader and more lenient views of the moral faults indulged in by her friends and acquaintances. It is a revelation that comes sooner or later to every woman how much is excused and sanctioned by society which in her youth would have seemed to her impossible. The middle-aged woman may often say to herself, half in fun, ' After all, a little remorse is better than a vast amount of regret. At any rate,' she adds, ' I will not police society. I might crush the weak, and I should do no harm to the strong.' Is it not true and even beautiful that ' tout comprendre c'est tout pardonner ' ? Middle-age is essentially the time of a lowered moral standard. This is the attitude of mind, let us say, between forty and fifty—a little sooner or a little later, according to the temperament. Then comes another phase, which is in no sense an hypocritical one. As the young around us grow into men and women, with the temptations and trials that life must always bring, we recall our own youth, and a feeling of responsibility, almost of awe, comes over us. Anyone who has gone through the ages would know what I mean. To forgive and excuse the mistakes and faults of life is a very different thing from helping the young out of the strait way. It has been truly said that it is all very well to sneer at commonplace morality in the abstract ; but the moment it is a question of any young people who are dear to us, we cannot help desiring it for them, though we may have laughed at it for ourselves. Then the young think the old uncharitable, narrow-minded,

and unkind ; but they are not so. One of the saddest
things in life is the isolation of the old. They can partly
understand the young, but the young never can understand them, for are they not far away along a road the
young have never seen ?

> Strange, is it not, that of the myriads who
> Before us passed the door of darkness through,
> Not one returns to tell us of the road,
> Which, to discover, we must travel too ?
>
> *Omar Khayyam.*

APPENDIX

JAPANESE ART OF ARRANGING CUT FLOWERS.*

IT is now some years since Mr. J. Conder's excellent book, 'The Flowers of Japan and the Art of Floral Arrangement,' was first published. But the principles laid down in it have so little penetrated the art of cut-flower arrangements in England that it may be assumed either that the book is still very little known or that its teaching has been set down as unsuited to English flowers and flower-vases. The book is not published in England, but almost any bookseller will get it from Japan ; the cost is 2l. 2s. The coloured plates, to which chiefly this high price is due, do not materially contribute to the expounding of the theory, and, although full of character and beauty in themselves, could be omitted without loss to the main object of the book. A smaller and much cheaper edition of the work could then be produced and published in England.†

* From the *Garden* of October 6, 1894.
† Mr. Conder has lately published three articles on the same subject in the October, December '96, and January '97 numbers of the *Studio*—that unusually artistic magazine which is to be had monthly for one shilling. Mr. Conder's articles are beautifully illustrated with numerous plates of Japanese designs, reproduced from photographs ; and in the text he sums up many of the most interesting points contained in his book. He does not suggest that the art of which he writes could be applied to the arrangement of cut flowers in England, but it is to be hoped that these articles—which are, unfortunately, already out of

In the meanwhile, however, it is my object to spread its teaching and to show how, with but slight modifications and relaxation from the stricter Japanese rules, this artistic science may be adapted to English flowers and English drawing-rooms. It has a strong claim to being adopted by all lovers of the beautiful and the practical combined because, first, these decorations have a quite unique beauty and refinement ; secondly, cut flowers and shrubs live long in water when supported by a flower-holder in the Japanese way, to be described presently ; thirdly, only very few flowers or branches are required—a great advantage to those who have but small gardens, to people living in towns, where flowers are expensive, and for the seasons of the year when flowers are scarce. Also an extremely decorative effect can be produced without making the room airless from the scent of many flowers. Fourthly, the infinite variety of design it is possible to produce with but few branches on the Japanese principle as compared to the English may be likened to the number of changes that can be rung on a few bells when a given system is followed, whereas the different bells rung simultaneously produce only one, and that a discordant, sound.

Roughly speaking, the Japanese art of cut-flower decorations may be classified into three fundamental principles :—

1. Not alone the flowers and leaves, but also the stems or branches should be considered as part of the design —in fact, it is the most important part.

2. The branches are not allowed to lean against the edge of the vase, as in the English manner, but must be firmly supported either by a wooden fixer fitted into the neck of the vase, or by coils of iron if open basin-shaped or flat-bottomed vessels are used, this

print—may be republished in book form. The great beauty of the illustrations would do more to spread the practice of the art amongst English people than any written theory upon it.—C. L., *March* 1897.

giving to the stems the appearance of growth and self-support.

3. Only such flowers and trees as are easily obtainable should be used. Rarity is not considered a merit, and foreign or out-of-the-way plants are only permitted to be used by those who have a thorough knowledge of the nature of their growth, characteristics, &c. The flowers used should be in season, and the design of the decoration suited to its position in the room—*i.e.* if under a picture, on a shelf, in the centre of an alcove, &c.—as well as adapted to the vase which holds it.

Although one of my objects is to show how much the English method may be improved without too great a subservience to the strictest laws of the Japanese art, yet it would be difficult to make myself understood by the uninitiated without first giving an outline of that science, which was originally, it is supposed, a religious rite, and which to-day is still a much-reverenced art in Japan. For this purpose I shall quote freely from Mr. Conder's book, as it would be impossible to improve upon his lucid and concise treatment of the subject. The following are selected as the most important rules to be observed :—

The surface of the water in which the flowers are placed is technically considered to be the soil from which the floral growth springs, and the designer must here convey the impression of stability and strength.

The *springing*, or point of origin of the floral group, is of great importance, and the firm and skilful fixing of the stems or branches in the vessel which holds them is one of the most difficult parts of the manipulation. Ordinarily, the stems are held in position by small cylindrical pieces of wood, fitting tightly across the neck of the flower vase, and having a slit, wider above than below, for threading them through. The wedge-shaped form, wider towards the top, which is given to the slit allows slightly different inclinations to be imparted to the several branches. The fastener should be fixed about half an inch below the surface of the water, and should not be visible from the front of the vessel. Some schools affect a rustic simplicity in their appliances, and employ a naturally forked twig to hold the flowers in position. For arrangements in neckless vases, such as sand-bowls or shallow tubs, other sorts of fasteners are necessary. One kind consists of a sheet of copper perforated with holes of different sizes, to receive the extremities of the different stems. Another fastener is made of rings or different sections of bamboo of varying diameters attached to a wooden board, the stems finding lodgment in the sockets thus formed, and being further held in position by pebbles being placed over them.

The direction of the stems at starting need not be strictly vertical ; but, if curved, the curves should be strong ones.

The artist studiously avoids an equal-sided or symmetrical arrangement, but obtains a balance of a more subtle kind.

The triple arrangement may be taken as the original model of all arrangements. The *Principal* is the central and longest line of the design, and is made to form a double curve, with the upper and lower extremities nearly vertical and in a continuous line, the general shape being that of an archer's bow. The *Secondary* line should be about half, and the *Tertiary* line about one quarter of the length of the *Principal*, supposing all to be straightened out ; and these two lines are arranged on different sides of the *Principal* in graceful double curves of varied character. As a general rule, the *Secondary* has a more vertical and the *Tertiary* a more lateral tendency, the former being on the outside of the arched bow formed by the *Principal*, and the latter making a counterpoise on its hollow side. By changing the direction and giving a different character to the curves of these three lines, a great variety of design is produced.

There is another style of design applied to a large class of flower arrangements, in which the *Principal* line of the composition has a horizontal, or almost horizontal, direction; the intention of such compositions being to suggest floral growth on the edges of cliffs or banks, when used in hanging vessels or vases placed on raised shelves.

The different lines have been spoken of as if existing in one vertical plane parallel to the spectator; but actually these lines have also directions of varying degrees forward or backward. In other words, the extreme points of these lines would require a solid and not a plane figure for their enclosure.

The various directions imparted to plants and branches of trees on the above principles are obtained first by a careful selection of suitable material, then by twisting, bending, building together and fixing at the base, and lastly by means of cutting and clipping off defective or superfluous parts.

Flower arrangements are made sometimes with one species of tree or plant alone, and sometimes with a combination of two or more species. The use of many different kinds of flowers in one composition is opposed to the principles of the purer styles.

In arranging two or more species in one composition, variety must be sought by combining trees and plants. In a three-line composition the branches of a tree should never be 'supported' on both sides by a plant; nor should a plant be placed in the centre with a tree arrangement on either side. The two branches of the same kind must of necessity be used, but they should adjoin, not sandwich, the remaining one. For example, a composition with Irises (plant) in the centre and branches of Azalea (tree) and Camellia (tree) on either side would be defective. A correct composition would be one with a Plum branch (tree) in the centre, with a Pine branch (tree) on one side and Bamboo stem (plant) on the other.

In cases of variety being obtained by land and water plants, this rule is sometimes violated.

The manipulation of different plants and tree-cuttings with the object of preserving their vitality needs special study. In some cases merely sharply cutting the extremity is sufficient to preserve the succulence ; but with other material the charring of the end, or dipping in hot water to soften it, is common. The Bamboo is particularly difficult to preserve. The inner divisions are generally removed, and the inside of the tube filled with spiced water or other stimulants. The object of these methods is to get the water to rise in the stem, so that the vitality of the bouquet may be preserved for days. Other means are resorted to in order to prevent the advanced blossoms falling off or dropping. In the case of some large and heavy flowers, invisible Bamboo spikes are employed to keep them erect. Salt is also applied at the base of certain blossoms, to keep the connection moist, and thus defer the shedding which often takes place owing to dryness.

The flower-vases are made of wood, porcelain, pottery, bronze, brass, iron, and basket-work, with wooden, earthenware, or tin receptacles inside for holding the water. They vary as much in form as in material, the most common standing vessels being broad and flat, or long-necked, opening out to a broad flat surface at the mouth ; tall, narrow vases are also used. With the ordinary tall vase, whether of wide or narrow mouth, the height of the flowers is generally fixed as one and a half times that of the vase. In the case of broad, shallow receptacles, the height of the floral composition is made about one and a half times the breadth of the vessel. Vases for hooking on to walls and for suspending from a shelf or ceiling are also frequently used.

Having thus briefly quoted from the main principles of this Japanese art as given by Mr. Conder, I shall now make a few homely suggestions as to how they could be applied by any of us in England.

The following practical directions may be found useful to those who wish to try this system of flower arrangement at once with as little trouble and as little expense as possible :—

Go round your house and collect all the china, earthenware, and metal vessels that can be spared—even a kettle, if nothing else can be found, would do. Earthenware dog-troughs are specially adapted to water decorations ; three-legged witch's cauldrons and common salt-jars also do very well ; an ordinary earthenware flower-pot, with the hole at the bottom corked up, would lend itself to wedging purposes ; and every house contains some ornamental pottery, bronze, brass, or silver vessels of a suitable kind. Glass cannot be used, as the pressure of the wedge would crack it ; and for the same reason it is inadvisable to try to fix a wedge in fine or valuable china.

From all these select those of a most suitable shape—*i.e.* either broad and flat for water decorations ; or narrow-necked with a wide mouth ; or a tall, narrow-necked shape, suitable for supporting only one branch without a wedge. If the vessel be small, and made only of thin pottery or china, it should be weighted by placing stones or something heavy inside to balance the weight of the flower erection ; without this precaution a tall arrangement might overbalance the whole thing. If the vessel be heavy in itself—of bronze, brass, silver, or other metals, or if of earthenware, sufficiently large to become heavy when filled with water—then this additional weighting is not necessary.

Your next step should be to procure some narrow wood—fire-lighting wood, or laths of any kind. Measure the width of the vase at the place where the wedge is to be fixed ; this should be slightly below the surface, so as to be concealed when the vase is filled with water.

Cut two pieces of wood to the required length, and shape them at the end to fit the sides of the vase ; then scoop out the inner side of each piece of wood, so as to form an oval-shaped opening when they are placed together, slightly narrower below than at the top surface, so as to allow the stalks a freer play of direction, at the same time holding them firm. Then cut out a small notch at each angle of the wood, at a distance of about half an inch from the ends ; place the two pieces together, and tie them firmly with string at both ends in the rut of the notches. The string should first be soaked, wound round two or three times, and firmly knotted ; it will then remain quite secure. Wire is even better adapted to the purpose than string.

A yet simpler way is, instead of scooping out an oval-shaped opening, to insert a small extra piece of wood at each end between the two woods that form the wedge, and, by thus keeping them apart, make an opening large enough for the width of the stems.

When the wedge is made, soak it in water for a few seconds to make the wood swell ; then fix it firmly in the neck of the vase.

Yet another fastener, and perhaps the most adaptable of any, consists simply of a spiral coil made of sheet-lead cut into ribbons. This can be bent about to suit the various sizes of the stems. The weight of the leaden coil will balance flowers and branches of considerable height, and it can always be additionally weighted with stones if necessary. This fastener may be used in almost every shaped vase, of no matter what material ; for there is no danger, as in the case of the fitting wooden fasteners, that it will crack glass or fine china. Any plumber will supply the strips of sheet-lead, which should be about 2 ft. long, $\frac{5}{8}$ in. wide, and $\frac{1}{8}$ in. thick, though the sizes vary, of course, according to the vase. It is quite easy to bend these strips into a spiral coil.

These are simple ways of making flower-holders at

home with the most ordinary materials ; but, of course, with more trouble a great variety of fasteners can be made.

The next thing to be done is to get a branch of Bamboo or other thin stick, not too brittle, and cut it up into pieces of about an inch long, so as to have a heap of different thicknesses. Before proceeding to cut or buy your flowers, you must decide in what part of the room to place the decorations, so as to have an idea of what would be suitable as to colour, size, and form. If for the corner of a shelf or mantelpiece, the arrangement might be high on one side of the vase, with a long streamer pendent on the other. If for a table under a picture, it might tend upwards, and the *Tertiary* line form almost a right angle—in complement, as it were, to the shape of the frame when placed to one side underneath it. For any purpose special kinds of flowers are required, as it would be contrary to the fundamental laws of the art to try and make a stiff or upward-growing plant hang downwards, or to try and erect a flower with a limp stem. One place, too, requires a tall, narrow decoration ; another a wide or more solemn one. When you have the destined situation of the decoration in your mind, go out and choose flowers and shrubs accordingly, bearing in mind as you pick them the directions the stems will have to take. It is as well always to have a basin of water ready in which to place the flowers immediately after picking them, as in the process of selection, fixing in the wedge, &c.—especially until you are practised in the art—the flowers are apt to wither and the vigour in the curves of the stems to get limp, so that it is difficult to carry out any design. The best plan is to place the vase, before filling it, where it will eventually be required to stand, so as to be sure and procure the suitable effect. It is advisable not to put water in the vessel until the composition is completed, as it sometimes tips over in the process of fixing the stems in the wedge.

Before beginning the bouquet, make up your mind, in a general way, what branches and flowers to use and how to dispose them. Then first place the principal ones, fixing each firmly in turn with the bits of Bamboo if not large enough to fill the space, or by pruning the bottom of the stems if too thick, so as exactly to fit the wedge. All tree-branches and shrubs should have the bark peeled off the part which is under water, as this allows a freer entrance to the moisture, and so enables the plant to last fresh for a much longer time. When you have finished the arrangement, stand at a little distance, and remove all leaves, shoots, or flowers which interfere with the clearness and beauty of line from various points of view. Then fill the vase with water—slightly tepid is best, especially if the flowers are at all faded. If the wedge is still visible above or through the water, cover it over with a little Moss or other very light leafage or, in the case of a water-plant decoration, with some small water weed.

There is hardly a flower, shrub, or tree which is not, at one stage of growth or other, adaptable to this style of arrangement, but some of the most obviously suited are here mentioned by way of suggestion. All fruit blossoms, wild or cultivated : Blackthorn, May, Dog Rose, Bramble, Willow (more especially in bud, known as ' palm '), Maple, Oak, Rhododendron, Azalea, Laburnum, Wistaria, Tree Pæony, Syringa, Berberis, Laurustinus, Holly, and almost all kinds of Pine trees ; Irises, Narcissi, Bulrushes, Marsh Marigolds, Water Lilies, Honeysuckle, Clematis, Chrysanthemums, &c.

I have dwelt almost entirely upon the technical side of the art, this being the indispensable means to the end in view. But the goal is one untouched by theory, unmolested by hard-and-fast rules. The wonderful beauty of proportion and balance, the choiceness of selection, the effect of growth and vitality, of dignity and grace, with which the whole of this art is penetrated, are not to be expressed in any doctrinal terms. The tender solicitude which it exacts for the habits and characteristics, tastes and welfare of each plant, endows the least thing utilised by this art with almost a personality. The relative connection of one plant with another —the tall, aspiring *Principal ;* the *Secondary*, which seems inclined to follow its lead, yet hesitates half-way with questioning doubt ; the *Tertiary* below, in squat contentment—these admit of endless variety of interpretation. To the Japanese every flower has its meaning and associations, as well as every combination of flowers. The force of contrast is ever present in their designs ; the opposite sexes are supposed to be represented, strength and weakness, sternness and tenderness, &c. Without learning the grammar of their complicated flower-language, might we not nevertheless increase our artistic pleasure in flower arrangements by trying to give them a suitableness and a meaning which they have hitherto lacked ? The old, long established English fashion of massing together in a vase may still hold its own for certain kinds of flowers ; but, so strong is the fascination of the Japanese principle, that, once it is adopted, it will probably assert its authority even amongst a bunch of Primroses or Violets.

CONSTANCE LYTTON.

THE END.

Lightning Source UK Ltd.
Milton Keynes UK
UKHW012127250620
365566UK00003B/510